Clarence A. Lindau(?)
Illinois. 11/6/23

INTERNATIONAL GOVERNMENT

INTERNATIONAL GOVERNMENT

TWO REPORTS BY

L. S. WOOLF
PREPARED FOR THE FABIAN
RESEARCH DEPARTMENT

WITH AN INTRODUCTION BY
BERNARD SHAW

TOGETHER WITH A PROJECT BY A
FABIAN COMMITTEE FOR A SUPERNATIONAL
AUTHORITY THAT WILL PREVENT WAR

BRENTANO'S
NEW YORK
1916

JX1975
.W62

Copyright, 1916, by Brentano's

CONTENTS

INTRODUCTION. By Bernard Shaw ix

PART I

AN INTERNATIONAL AUTHORITY AND THE PREVENTION OF WAR

CHAPTER
- I. INTRODUCTION 3
- II. THE CAUSES OF WARS 8
- III. INTERNATIONAL LAW 11
- IV. TREATIES 15
- V. CONFERENCES, CONGRESSES, AND THE CONCERT OF EUROPE 24
- VI. ARBITRATION AND JUDICIAL TRIBUNALS . . 64
- VII. AN INTERNATIONAL AUTHORITY . . . 98
- VIII. CONCLUSIONS 124

PART II

INTERNATIONAL GOVERNMENT

- I. INTERNATIONAL GOVERNMENT, INTERNATIONAL AGREEMENT, AND INTERNATIONAL DISAGREEMENT 139
- II. INTERNATIONAL ORGANS AND ORGANISMS . 153
- III. THE INTERNATIONALIZATION OF ADMINISTRATION 179
  - (*a*) Communications
  - (*b*) Public Health and Epidemic Diseases
  - (*c*) Industry and Commerce
  - (*d*) Morals and Crime

CHAPTER	PAGE
IV. COSMOPOLITAN LAW-MAKING	266

    (a) International Maritime Legislation and the Unification of Maritime Law
    (b) International Labor Legislation
    (c) Other Examples

V. INTERNATIONAL SOCIETY AND INTERNATIONAL STANDARDS 311

VI. THE INTERNATIONALIZATION OF COMMERCE, INDUSTRY, AND LABOR. 327

VII. SOME CONCLUSIONS 344

PART III

ARTICLES SUGGESTED FOR ADOPTION BY AN INTERNATIONAL CONFERENCE AT THE TERMINATION OF THE PRESENT WAR

(By The International Agreements Committee of the Fabian Research Department)

I. INTRODUCTION 371

II. THE ARTICLES OF THE TREATY . . . 376
    (a) The Establishment of a Supernational Authority
    (b) The Constituent States
    (c) Covenant Against Aggression
    (d) Covenant Against War Except as a Final Resource
    (e) The International Council
    (f) Different Sittings of the Council

	(g) Membership of the Council and Voting	
	(h) Legislation Subject to Ratification	
	(i) Legislation on Matters of Secondary Importance by Overwhelming Majorities	
II.	THE ARTICLES OF THE TREATY (*continued*)	
	(j) Facultative Enforcement by Overwhelming Majority of Legislation Carried by Overwhelming Majorities even if of Primary Importance, and Not Ratified by a Small Minority of the Minor States	
	(k) Non-Justiciable Issues	
	(l) The International Secretariat	
	(m) The International High Court	
	(n) The Judges of the Court	
	(o) The Court Open Only to State Governments	
	(p) Justiciable Issues	
	(q) Immediate Publicity for all Treaties, Existing and Future	
	(r) Undertaking to Submit all Justiciable Questions to the International High Court	
	(s) Provision for Abrogation of Obsolete Treaties	
	(t) Provision for Cases in which International Law is Vague, Uncertain, or Incomplete	
	(u) Enforcement of the Decrees of the Court	
III.	APPENDIX—A SELECT BIBLIOGRAPHY	411

INTRODUCTION

By Bernard Shaw

THE present war has produced many catchwords, among them, A War to End War, An Inconclusive Peace, The Destruction of Militarism, The Establishment of the Rights of Nationalities on an Unassailable Basis, Free Negotiation by Free Peoples, and This Must Never Occur Again. Most of these shibboleths proclaim their own thoughtlessness. War can do many things, but it cannot end war. No peace can be a conclusive peace: it is beyond the wit of man to draw a treaty of peace which will make it impossible for war to recur between Britain and either her present enemies or her present allies. The destruction of militarism cannot be attained by a military triumph: war is the creator, the sustainer, and the reason-for-existence of militarism. The rights of Nationalities, far from being placed on an unassailable basis by war, are at present wiped out by it: the Englishman is forced to fight as a pressed man for Russia, though his father was slain by the Russians at Inkerman, and for France, though his grandfather fell at Waterloo charging shoulder to shoulder with Blücher's Prussians. The German is compelled by the Prussian, whom he loathes, to die for Turkey and for the Crescent as against Anglo-Saxon Christendom. Every one of the belligerents is holding down some conquered race or nation. The establishment of the rights of nationalities on an unassailable basis would cause the instant dissolution, first of the British Empire, then of the Austrian, with political earthquakes in the French Republic, the Italian Kingdom, and the Russian Empire, leaving Germany, on the whole, the strongest of the survivors. This is so obvious that the phrase can mean nothing but the rescue of Belgium from dependence on the Central Empires, and its restoration to a state of complete political dependence on France and Britain. Free negotiation by free peoples is impossible because there are no free peoples engaged in the present war: nobody pretends that the German people or the Russian people are free; and if we take the belligerent Republics and limited monarchies of the west as comparatively free, yet we find that the one department in which they do not even make a pretense of democracy is diplomacy, which is as autocratic in London as in St. Petersburgh or Berlin.

Thus we see that none of the catchwords except the last can possibly mean what they say; and when they are cheered each time they reappear in the Prime Minister's stock peroration, it is evident that he himself offers them as no more than oratorical orchestration to the patriotic sentiment of the assembly. They can be taken literally only by ignorant and simple persons to whom a

European war is simply a football match conducted with cannons.

The only catchword, then, that has anything in it is, This Must Never Occur Again. But it quite certainly will occur again if nothing is done to prevent it. Crude people recommend the destruction of Germany as a preventive. In Germany the same sort of people recommend the destruction of England. Among the neutrals they say, "By all means let these two quarrelsome and arrogant Powers destroy one another like the Kilkenny cats and leave the world in peace." But even if such a solution were physically or morally possible, which everyone who is not a cretinous Yahoo knows perfectly well it is not, in what way would the recurrence of war, or even the continuance of the present war in a fight over the spoils, be prevented by it? Cato's formula for the ending of the Punic wars was, Annihilate Carthage. Carthage was annihilated; but its annihilation brought no peace to Rome. The Irish are a contentious and troublesome people; and the proverbial receipt for peace in Ireland is to sink the island for ten minutes into the Atlantic. Let us suppose that Ireland is duly sunk, with England and Prussia moored to it, not for ten minutes, but for ever. The white and yellow races will still confront one another across the Pacific. Italy, France and Spain will still have to divide the heritage of the Moors. Sweden will still watch Russia with her hand on her sword-hilt; and Russia will still burn to protect the Balkans, to wrest Con-

stantinople from the followers of "the accursed
Mahound," to cling to Poland like a big brother,
and to pick up more of the White Man's Burden
in Asia than the other Powers may think healthy
for her, or than India, for instance, may be disposed to cast on any shoulders but her own. Of
South America I say nothing except that it does
not look convincing as a Temple of Perpetual
Peace. At all events, the notion that the most
completely decisive victory either by the Allies
or the Central Empires, pushed to the most
ruthless extremities by the victors with a view
to the eternal disablement of the vanquished,
would guarantee the peace of the world for five
years, or even for five minutes, is on the face of it
mere moonshine. The world would remain full
of explosive material, and be so heavily demoralized
into the bargain that it would be less than ever
capable of keeping lighted matches away from the
powder magazine.

Besides, the reduction to absurdity of military
wars by stalemate, or by increasing the cost of
victory beyond any possible advantage, direct or
contingent, to be hoped from it, would still leave
tariff wars possible, and even encourage them by
guaranteeing them against military reprisals. At
present a clamorous section of the British public
is demanding a perpetual tariff war against Germany, peace or no peace. They openly and reck-
lessly class tariffs with hostilities and insist on
their destructive and malicious character. They
are naïvely unaware of the fact that if protective

duties really bear this construction we are at war with our ally France at this moment; for France has locked the door of her vast dominion in the north of Africa against our manufactures, and it has never been suggested that our alliance should unlock it, either during the war or after it. The modern empire state is not an Arnold von Winkelried, opening the way for all the world to rush in at his heels: on the contrary, the modern Arnold, the moment he is through, turns swiftly and bars the entry against all competitors. The wise man looks for the cause of war not in Nietzsche's gospel of the Will to Power, or Lord Roberts's far blunter gospel of the British Will to Conquer, but in the custom house. The formal conquest of a territory may loom large as a sentimental grievance; but, as the case of Alsace-Lorraine shows, it does not produce war. But the appropriation of a market is another matter: a very small economic grievance will rapidly become the nucleus of an enormous mass of martial and patriotic emotion. There is no prospect of the end of this war being the end of international market-cornering and tariff blockades; and as long as war remains physically possible, such operations will produce it as fatally in the future as in the past.

Again, take the Balance of Power aimed at by our diplomatists. As long as each State works for its own hand, as at present, every diplomatist is necessarily engaged in a constant struggle to upset the balance of power in his own favor. He pretends to aim at nothing beyond preserving it; but he exposes all the rest as aiming at hegemony, at command of the sea, and so forth. Each nation feels that supremacy is absolutely necessary to its security, and that it, and it alone, can be trusted not to abuse it. War intensifies this feeling, and the present war is no exception: it began as a pure Balance of Power war; and it will not only stimulate to the highest degree those passions of fear and jealousy which are the motive force of the equilibrist diplomacy, but will throw political power into the hands of those who are entirely governed by them. The Napoleonic wars threw Europe into the hands of Metternich and Castlereagh, who had no other desire than to stereotype the conditions which had produced the war and to stifle the new moral world in its cradle. In the Franco-Prussian war of 1870–71, even so thorough-paced a Junker as Bismarck went under because he was not reactionary enough for the victorious military party, and Alsace-Lorraine was annexed in spite of him. And if the present war should end in a decisive victory for either side, that victory will be used and abused to the uttermost in spite of the Bismarcks, to say nothing of the moderate men and Pacifists, so vainly urging a friendly settlement whilst the combatants go steadily on fighting for the strongest position at the finish, and most certainly not fighting for it with any intention of foregoing an inch of it when it is gained.

Let us therefore not deceive ourselves with

good-natured dreams. Unless and until Europe is provided with a new organ for supernational action, provided with an effective police, all talk of making an end of war is mere waste of breath. There is only one alternative to government by police, and that is government by massacre. We, like the Ottoman Turks, have found that to be true in our own affairs. The Turks, in the Balkans and in Armenia, and we, in the Indian hills and in Africa and Australia, have found that where our police stops, its place must be taken by raids of soldiers, killing, burning and destroying indiscriminately until enough is judged to have been done to keep the district in awe for some years to come. The fact that we call such expeditions massacres when the Turks resort to them, and punitive expeditions or brigandage commissions when we resort to them, does not change their essential character; and the protests of the few humanitarians who know what the official formulas which occasionally leak out in the press really mean, are quite unavailing; for though the reign of terror is necessarily cruel, anarchy is apt to be crueller still, and the reign of terror is thus forced on us as the best practicable alternative to the reign of law. Our habit of looking the other way and talking busily about the weather on such occasions is not, as we imagine, civilization; it is only our attempt to hide from ourselves the fact that civilization means law, and that where law stops, the most civilized people in the world have to act like Timour the Tartar and Ivan the Terrible, or like the highly respectable and civilized French ladies and gentlemen who, during the French Revolutionary wars, had to connive at the September massacres by pretending that nothing particular was happening when the regular tribunals could not cope with the public danger. In the territories of the United States, pioneered by men quite as civilized by teaching and tradition as their cousins in London and Brighton, the revolver and the bowie knife reigned where the sheriff and the vigilance committee fell short. And the sixteen-inch gun and the submarine torpedo reign in Europe at present solely because there is no supernational sheriff or vigilance committee to adjust the disputes of nations.

As this well-established conclusion of political science is not very recondite, there is no lack at present of schemes and proposals for the establishment of some sort of supernational court. American projectors have been specially active, and one of them has actually applied to influential persons throughout the world for powers of attorney to enable him to represent them at what may be described roughly as a Hague Conference of the Human Race. Besides these more definite schemes, there is a vast mass of opinion which can be compared only to that of the elder Weller in Pickwick. It will be remembered by good Dickensians that when the case of Bardell *v.* Pickwick was entered, Mr. Weller recommended Mr. Pickwick to plead an *alibi;* and when Mr. Pickwick lost his case, his humble counsellor uttered the famous lamentation, "Why wornt there an alleybi?" Substitute the word Arbitration for Alibi, and you have the state of mind of ninety-nine Pacifists out of every hundred now living. They know that a war between England and the United States over the *Alabama* was averted by arbitration, and they have ever since regarded arbitration as a simple and sufficient alternative to war. Since 1899 they have attached a peculiar sanctity to the soil of The Hague, owing to the establishment there of the Hague Conference as a permanent arbitrating body. But it is just this limitation of the Hague Conference to arbitration, and to quite unauthoritative attempts to codify and establish such rules of the ring as war admits of, that makes it practically negligible as a pacific agency.

The present volume will, it is hoped, help to clear away this benevolent vagueness and to explain what is needed as an alternative to war. From it our preachers of arbitration will learn what arbitration really is; and they must set off their disappointment in finding how little it can do against their surprise and satisfaction in learning how much it has already done; for there have been many more arbitrations than the public have heard of, and several of them may fairly claim to have averted war. But no arbitration court can supply the need for a Supernational Legislature, a Supernational Tribunal, and a Supernational Board of Conciliation; and the members of these bodies must not be private philanthropists on a holiday, qualified in the first instance by their ability to pay the expenses of a trip to Holland, but responsible representatives of the actual Governments of the constituent States. No question can be entertained of any further representative character on their part: the essential and indispensable qualification must be ability to, as the phrase goes, "deliver the goods." Sages and saints, plebiscitary or volunteer representatives of the heart of the people, will not serve the purpose: only the plenipotentiary who has the effective Government of his State behind him, and whose Aye or No may be depended on as the Aye and No of that Government, will be of any use.

How it may all be done if there is the will to do it is suggested in the following pages. It is the peculiar business of The Fabian Society to supply progressive aspirations with practical methods. The process adopted in the present case has been, first, to refer the question to the Fabian Research Department. As practically nobody knew more than bits and scraps of what had actually been done in the way of International Organization, the Department had to begin by finding an investigator and skilled writer with the necessary qualifications and devotion for the task of preparing a report and suggesting conclusions. A certain endowment was also needed, not to remunerate the investigator on the usual professional basis, but to prevent its bare expenses from falling too heavily on a single worker. The endowment was provided by a timely donation from Mr. Joseph

Rowntree, who, as often happens, is not a member of the Society, but appreciates its manner of doing useful jobs in the building up of social tissue; and the man was found in Mr. L. S. Woolf, who turned cheerfully from *belles lettres* to the production of the present volume on terms which would certainly have been rejected with emphasis by a dock laborer.

The report, both in installments as it was produced, and when it was completely drafted, was subjected to keen discussion in the Research Department, where experts in this kind of work are six a penny. It was then published as a supplement to *The New Statesman*, and thus offered for general public discussion. Later on, at a summer meeting on the shore of Lake Derwentwater, it was submitted to a conference at which the members of a group which had been working independently on the subject under the presidency of Lord Bryce were present, with such other non-Fabian experts as could be secured; and a point was there reached at which it was apparent that the sounding of the report by skilled discussion and criticism had been carried to exhaustion. It is now published as being as good as the Fabian Society can at present make it. Nothing but actual experience can determine the limits of its practicability; but it at least plans the experiment as carefully as possible.

The main difficulty will be to make our party politicians aware that any such piece of work has been done in England. It has occurred repeatedly within the experience of the Fabian Society that Ministers, finding themselves under electoral pressure to introduce some reform which is only known to them as a platform phrase, have proceeded in complete ignorance of the work that has been put into the proposal by English thinkers and political scientists, and, after a carefully advertised trip to some country where something of the kind is supposed to be in operation (usually Germany), have come back and introduced a Bill containing every possible blunder that sciolism can make after five minutes' contemplation of a half-understood subject, and have actually passed it into law, only to be forced to pass an amending Act after a year of easily avoidable wreckage. It is a striking illustration of the want of touch between the intellectual life of the country and the House of Commons, that Cabinet Ministers always assume that political science, as distinguished from the arts of electioneering and managing the House, does not exist in England. German bureaucrats and Swiss and Italian professors are readily credited with political scholarship; but their works are not read; and it is consequently not noticed that they quote English sociologists with respect, and often build on their foundations. The British statesman sails along quite convinced that, except for an occasional university professor's text-book, which is assumed to be unpractical and useless, England has produced nothing but a few agnostic essays, Ruff's Guide to the Turf, The Hundred Best Investments, and special articles in the newspapers on Tariff Reform to serve as party kites to test how the electoral wind is blowing, or to set it blowing in a desired direction.

It is a pity; for much excellent work is done; and it is not cheerful for the Fabian Society, which has organized a considerable share of it, to be obliged in common honesty to warn workers that not only will they get no pence for their labors, but that nobody with any executive authority will take the smallest notice of it.

Still, the vocation of the Fabian Society is to chart all the channels into which the ship of State is being irresistibly driven by social evolution. The certainty that the ship will be piloted by a person calling himself a Practical Statesman, fanatically devoted to the method of Trial and Error, and finding all the rocks, both the hidden and the obvious ones, by the simple method of steering the ship crash on to them, and then getting her off as best he can, would not justify the Fabians in leaving the channel uncharted. They are, after all, no worse treated than those English chemists and metallurgists who have seen their discoveries appreciated and exploited in Germany and elsewhere whilst receiving nothing at home but a good-natured contempt as faddists. They do not complain of their own particular share of the general neglect; but they take the opportunity to point out that a supernational political constitution can no more be built without science than an airship or an ironclad, and that a governing class which is still repeating that "The Republic has no need of chemists," and exempting hunt servants from military duty whilst driving scientific workers contemptuously into the trenches by way of "giving them something real to do," must not be surprised if it finds itself outwitted by States which take skilled advice instead of relying on the theory that country gentlemen are, as a class, inspired.

More than this it is not prudent to say, for a total neglect of science may be better than the sudden conversion to it of gentlemen who conceive it as a means of discovering miraculous cures for diseases, especially distemper in foxhounds. Fortunately there is little opportunity in political science for the elixir of life and the philosopher's stone. There will be neither quackery nor science about the Congress which will patch up the present war when it has reached the end of its tether. It will be a repetition of the Congress of Vienna: that is, a crowd of diplomatists will gather round the booty, and try to secure as much as they can as best they can for their respective States. Few if any of them will have ulterior views; and most of them will regard those who look for an end of war as an institution as vulgar ideologues. Nevertheless, the reaction against the monstrous slaughter and destruction of the war, and the heavy financial burden it will leave, may be too much for diplomatic routine; and it may also happen that the only acceptable terms of peace may be impracticable without new supernational machinery of a much more definite and permanent kind than the old Concert of Europe which it was so hard to keep in tune, and which was so dismal a failure as regards the prevention of war. In such an event the following pages may prove useful, embodying as they do many months of research and discussion of at least as trustworthy a quality as the British Foreign Office, on a comparison of its publications with those of the Fabian Society, can reasonably be expected to achieve.

G. B. S.

PART I

AN INTERNATIONAL AUTHORITY AND THE PREVENTION OF WAR

By L. S. Woolf

"Now Europe balanced, neither side prevails,
For nothing's left in either of the scales."—Swift.

CHAPTER I

INTRODUCTION

"ON the conclusion of the war the working classes of all the industrial countries must unite to . . . establish some international authority to settle points of difference among nations by compulsory conciliation and arbitration." "It would clearly be desirable, if possible, that they (the terms of peace) should include provisions obliging Germany, along with the rest of Europe, to submit to some form of international organization designed to prevent future war."

These quotations are from the resolutions of a Socialist Conference and from the pages of a well-known paper, but they are typical of the hopes and desires which one meets continually upon the lips or pens of a large number of more or less intelligent persons of all classes and of every variety of political belief. A certain vagueness permeates the expression of these hopes and desires, and the outward and visible sign of this vagueness is the invariable use of the phrase "*some sort* of international authority" or "*some form* of international organization." The object of this enquiry is to give data which may, if possible, enable people to transform the vague "some sort of" into a more definite object of their hopes.

The problem is not a new one. It has for many centuries exercised the minds of those people who, because they were civilized, have at all times been contemptuously called theorists and Utopians by plain men, their contemporaries; but periodically, when the world is swept by the cataclysm called war, plain men, amazed to find that they are not civilized, have themselves raised a cry for the instant solution of the problem. One cannot, however, avoid some doubt whether the most opportune moment for solving it is the hurried and temporary reaction which comes to men when they see what a very barbarous and inefficient method of arranging international affairs they have adopted in the arbitrament of arms. The question is, indeed, generously complicated. In its broadest aspect the problem is to develop a whole system of international relationship in which public war shall be as impossible between civilized States as is private war in civilized States: in its narrower aspect the problem which the world has still to solve is the development of a machinery capable of settling international differences and disputes.

It is possible to say without begging the question that in the last 100 years a system of international relationship has been very rapidly developing with rudimentary organs for regulating the society of nations without warfare. If we are really to transform that "*some sort of international organization*" into a definite international organization which will commend itself to the disillusioned judgment of statesmen and other "practical" men, we must build not a Utopia upon the air or clouds of our own imaginations, but a duller and heavier structure placed logically upon the foundations of the existing system. I, therefore, propose to analyze the most important parts of the existing system, in order to see in what respects it has, during the last century, succeeded and failed in preventing war.

Before proceeding to this task it will be advisable to answer a preliminary objection which in the present temper of the world is bound to occur to one's mind at various points of the enquiry. Systems and machinery, it is said, are not the way to prevent war, which will only cease when men cease to desire it: Europe, relapsed to-day into barbarism, shows that men will never cease to desire it: we must face the fact that International Law and Treaties and Arbitration will never prevent these periodical shatterings of our civilization: one week in August, 1914, was sufficient to sweep away the whole elaborate progress of a century. One meets this train of reasoning continually at the present time. It is woven out of pessimism and two fallacies. The first fallacy is the historically false view which men invariably take of the present. It is almost impossible not to believe that each to-day is the end of the world. Our own short era seems invariably to be in the history of the world a culmination either of progress or dissolution. But in history there are really no culminations and no cataclysms; there is only a feeble dribble of progress, sagging first to one side and then to the other, but always dribbling a little in one direction. Thus the French Revolution was for everyone in it the end or the beginning of the world. The aristocrat dragged through the streets of Paris to the guillotine saw himself perishing in a holocaust of all Law, Order, Beauty, and Good Manners; the men who dragged him saw only the sudden birth of Justice and absolute Liberty. Both were wrong, just as both would have been wrong if they had suddenly found themselves transported some thirty years on into the Paris of the second decade of the nineteenth century, for the aristocrat would have seen the culmination of his hopes and the Red of his despair. In each case it was only a little sag in the progress of history, first to this side and then to that, though the main stream was dribbling slowly in the direction of Liberty, Equality, Fraternity. So with this war. Its tremendous importance to us produces in us a delusion that in the history of the world it is tremendously important. But it is neither the beginning nor the end of anything; it is just a little sagging to one side, to violence and stupidity and barbarism, and in ten or fifteen or twenty years' time there will be a sagging to the other side, to what we dimly recognize as progress and civilization.

The other fallacy is of the same nature as that dreary assertion that you cannot make men good by Act of Parliament. In one sense the assertion is a truism, and in another it is simply false. It is true that human society is so simple that if a majority of men want to fight, no International

Law, no treaties or tribunals will prevent them; on the other hand, society is so complex that though the majority of men and women do not want to fight, if there are no laws and rules of conduct, and no pacific methods of settling disputes, they will find themselves at one another's throats before they are aware of or desire it.

CHAPTER II

THE CAUSES OF WARS

BEFORE proceeding to our analysis it is necessary to say something about the causes of war. War is only one method of *attempting* to settle differences and disputes which arise between nations. The causes of war are those differences and disputes, and if we could substitute other methods of settlement which men would willingly adopt, we should have taken a long step towards preventing war. The differences and disputes arise themselves from the various relations in which nations stand to one another. Now, disputes which arise from one kind of relation may be capable of a settlement by some method which would be incapable of settling disputes arising from another kind of relation. I propose, therefore, to group roughly the different relations in which nations stand to one another and the kinds of disputes which arise from them and have tended to produce wars, and I do this in order that in the course of the enquiry, when I examine the different methods of settling disputes, I may refer to the classes of disputes which have tended to war. The following is a rough classification:

1. *Disputes arising from legal or quasi-legal relationship*—e. g., (a) as to interpretation of treaties;

(*b*) as to contractual rights and duties; (*c*) as to definitions of boundaries; (*d*) as to delicts.

2. *Disputes arising from economic relationship, trade, and finance.*

3. *Disputes arising from administrative or political relationship*—e. g., as to questions of territory, subject races, expansion, nationality, supremacy and predominant influence.

4. *Disputes arising from what may be called social relationship*—e. g., as to questions of honor.

This classification is probably not exhaustive, but it does, I think, draw attention to important distinctions in the origin within the society of nations of those differences which have led to wars. All the wars of the last century can, I believe, be traced to one or more differences arising from these four types of relationship distinguished above. Thus, let us take two of the recent wars in which Great Powers have been involved—the Spanish-American and the Russo-Japanese. The real causes of the first war were two: The United States and Spain had to settle differences which had arisen between them owing to economic and political relations in Cuba and as to the quasi-legal responsibility of Spain for a particular event, the destruction of the *Maine*. It is arguable and has been argued that the economic and political differences could and would have been settled by diplomatic means if the second difference had not arisen. Spain herself proposed that the quasi-legal difference should be settled by arbitration.

The United States refused, and the only remaining method of attempting a settlement was resorted to—namely, force of arms.

The Russo-Japanese war arose from three causes. There was, first, the dispute which arose from the legal relationship of Russia, Japan, and China established by the treaty of 1902. But this dispute was complicated by differences arising from the political and administrative relationship of Russia and Japan in "the spheres of influence" claimed by them in Manchuria and Korea. Thirdly, questions of international trade arose out of the concessions to a Russian speculator in Korea.

CHAPTER III

INTERNATIONAL LAW

IN treating of the system of international relationship and the different pieces of international machinery for ordering the society of nations, the first question to be considered is the general rules which regulate the conduct of nations to one another in their various relations. International Law is the body of such rules. I do not propose to touch such academic questions as whether International Law is or is not law, or even the question what it really is, but no practical enquiry is possible into the means of pacifically settling international differences without a clear understanding of the part which International Law has played, and will play, in the matter.

It would be an easy and a human thing to say, what you may hear said repeatedly to-day in any intellectual company of human beings, that International Law has been proved not to exist. As a matter of fact, the whole history of the nineteenth century and of this war shows that International Law does exist, and is of supreme importance. The cry that it does not exist is merely the cry of shallow despair at finding that it does not exist precisely in the form that we desire. The fact that the rules of International Law are broken, and that those rules have not been able to prevent certain wars, does not prove that the rules do not exist, or that they have not been, and will not be, the most potent instruments in keeping the peace. People still do commit murders, and a man occasionally spits into the drawing-room fire, but it would be a false deduction that therefore the law against murder is useless, or that the social rule which regulates the conduct of gentlemen in drawing-rooms does not help people to repress a natural desire to expectorate. The mere fact that every belligerent is discussing questions of International Law more or less acrimoniously with neutrals, and is violently accusing its belligerent opponents of breaking International Law, shows that whatever we mean by the words, "International Law" has a very practical effect upon international relations.

It is clear that unless there are certain general rules generally observed regulating the conduct of nations to one another, and forming the constitution of the society of nations, a peaceful solution of international differences will always be doubtful. In the growth of those rules during the nineteenth century certain points deserve attention. In the first place, it is only since the Congress of Vienna that there has been any real attempt consciously to *make* these rules in the sense in which law is now *made* in States. Within a State the laws are not merely customs and rules generally observed and admitted, but they are also "made" by legislative and judicial organs. Ever since the time of

Grotius there have been many customs and rules in the society of nations observed and admitted by the nations, but at the beginning of the nineteenth century there were not even rudimentary organs, legislative or judicial, which could lay these rules down as law. In the nineteenth century there has been a rapid development in two directions.

In the first place, nations have attempted to substitute agreements or treaties for general rules. Treaties clearly do not, as a rule, *make* International Law; they are like contracts or agreements between individuals. Owing to the want of any law-making organ, nations have tried to regulate their relations to one another by an enormous number of such separate agreements. The efficacy of this system will be discussed when I deal with treaties. In the second place, for the first time in history, during the nineteenth century attempts were made on a considerable scale to make International law in conferences and congresses. The success of these attempts will be considered when I come to deal with conferences and congresses; here it is sufficient to note that these nineteenth-century assemblies are undoubtedly the first signs of the growth of an International Legislative organ.

It is unnecessary for our immediate purpose to examine more closely into International Law, but it is advisable to state shortly a few facts about it which really require no detailed proof, but have great bearing upon our enquiry. A large number of its rules are quite definitely admitted, are acted upon every day, and really do help to regulate pacifically international society. On the other hand, much of it is vague and uncertain. This is due largely to two facts: there is no recognized international organ for making International Law, and no judicial organ for interpreting it. The consequences are two: whenever new circumstances arise which require a new rule of conduct for nations, the nations concerned have to set about making the new rule by bargaining and negotiation. If they cannot agree, either it remains uncertain what the law is, or the question has to be settled by war. Secondly, when there is already a rule, but nations disagree as to its interpretation, they again have to attempt by bargaining and negotiation to come to some agreement as to how it shall be interpreted. And, again, if they cannot agree, the only method left is to cut the knot by war.

CHAPTER IV

TREATIES

UNDER treaties I include, of course, all international instruments of agreement—*i. e.*, conventions, declarations, etc. Very few people realize the enormous number of such instruments in existence. If you open at random a collection like the great Recueil Général de Traités of Martens, you find that in one series, which is not absolutely exhaustive, there have been collected between 800 and 900 treaties concluded in the ten years 1874–1883. These instruments deal with questions which arise from all the four types of relationship given above. Far the greater number of these agreements are scrupulously carried out. In a sense they form the substitute for statute law in the society of nations. The whole body of Anglo-French treaties, for instance, plays the part of statute law regulating the relations of England and France.

But the history of treaties brings one face to face at once with what is at the root of the problem of preventing war. The difficulties which have beset nations have been how to obtain guarantees for the carrying out of treaties, and at the same time how to make it possible to alter treaties in accordance with altering circumstances. What is required in every kind of society in which things grow and decay is an arrangement which maintains the existing order of things, and yet allows for upsetting it in an orderly manner.

Now, as long as a treaty remains *merely* an agreement between two or more isolated sovereign States, it is clear that nothing can be included in the treaty which can ensure compliance with it. When many of the nations of Europe agreed to the Treaty of London of 1867 to constitute Luxemburg a neutral State, they tried to make the fulfilment of that treaty more certain by guaranteeing the neutrality. "Ce principe (neutrality)," they affirmed, "est et demeure placé sous la sanction de la garantie collective des Puissances signataires." That is to say, they first agreed to respect the neutrality of Luxemburg, and then agreed to guarantee collectively, not the neutrality of Luxemburg, but their agreement to respect it. Suppose the Powers had merely agreed to constitute Luxemburg a neutral State, and to respect its neutrality; then, if a Power desires to violate the neutrality, in the last resource the only thing that that Power will have to consider is: "Will any other signatory Power regard my breach of this agreement as a *casus belli?*" But things are in exactly the same state when the neutrality is placed under the collective guarantee of the signatory Powers. There is no "sanction" and no "guarantee," except the agreement of isolated sovereign States. The insertion of the words "sanction" and "garantie collective" only makes the form of the agreement a little more solemn than if they were left out. There is nothing inside the treaty, and nothing outside the States themselves, no collective power or organization or machinery or guarantee which makes it one jot more certain that the treaty will be fulfilled or the conditions established by the treaty maintained.

The whole intention of treaties is to maintain an existing order of things, to establish a stable society of nations. They seek to embody and perpetuate the *status quo* in ink and paper. Each is an isolated promise, and the value of a promise depends upon the good faith of the promisor and his ability to make good his word. The ordinary way of making these international agreements is by the casual bargaining of diplomacy, not on the face of it a very good way of arriving at arrangements designed to be eternal. When one considers these facts, one wonders, not that some treaties are broken, but that such an enormous number are fulfilled. Diplomatists themselves occasionally recognize the thinness of the thread upon which they have hung international relations. Thus, at the Conference of London in 1871, the Powers solemnly declared that "it is an essential principle of the law of nations that no Power can liberate itself from the engagement of a treaty, or modify the stipulations thereof, unless with the consent of the contracting Powers by means of an amicable settlement." And yet a leading writer on International Law, in a recent work, comes to the correct but astonishing conclusion that "the standard value" of this declaration "has become doubtful again," because, when Russia in 1886 suddenly notified her withdrawal from Article 59 of the Treaty of Berlin of 1878, the signatory Powers tacitly consented with the exception of Great Britain, who protested.

The truth is, of course, that an agreement, arrived at by bargaining and compromise, designed to be eternal, and containing no provisions for varying or modifying it, is the worst method of maintaining the order of things established by such agreements, because the sole way of modifying them will often be to break them. It is only in a world in which nothing ever changed that they would succeed, and there they would be unnecessary. Nations themselves are always developing, and their economic, political, and administrative relations often change fundamentally. It is absolutely imperative, therefore, on occasions that a nation should demand an alteration in the *status quo*. It can only effect this by the bargaining of diplomacy, and any other nation whose interest it is to maintain the *status quo* can bring the first up against the brick wall of treaties which profess to bind nations for all time. The only method left of bargaining oneself out of such an agreement is to threaten to break it, and therefore to appeal to arms.

The repudiation of treaties by Russia many years ago caused Mill to propose that nations should bind themselves only for a definite term of years. In certain cases this is clearly the only reasonable course, and has, in fact, been done, especially in commercial treaties. No business man would enter into a business agreement which bound him for ever, and in treaties regulating the commercial and financial relationships of nations the expediency of including a time limit has been acknowledged. Thus the final act of the Conference of Berlin, 1884, by articles 1–5 laid it down that the commerce of all nations should enjoy complete freedom within the Congo area, but it was stipulated that the *franchise d'entrée* should be for only 20 years, after which the matter might be reconsidered by each Power. But in many cases, particularly where the larger political and administrative relations of nations are involved, there are obvious disadvantages in the time limit. People who have just settled a difficult and dangerous international question do not look forward with complacency to the whole matter being raised again, probably in its original form, at a definite and possibly inconvenient moment some years afterwards. Indeed, the time limit for the commercial agreement in 1884 was not accepted at the Berlin Conference without demur by some nations for precisely these reasons. It is well known that the period just before the "falling in" of a commercial treaty between nations is often a period of acute tension, and it has been pointed out as significant that the present war occurred during such a time of tension between Russia and Germany.

It is worthy of remark that the great treaties which were designed to introduce a millennium of peace have been precisely those which turned out to be the most dangerous threateners of war. Vienna and Berlin have always formed fruitful themes for the wise cynics who like to dwell upon international bad faith and the absurdity of regulating the future of Europe by treaties which are only made to be broken. But the Congress of Vienna and the Berlin Congress did not lay up trouble for Europe because there is any absurdity in founding the society of European nations upon a written constitution, nor merely because many of the details of the constitutions framed in 1815 and 1878 were arrived at, we now see, upon wrong principles. The really important thing to realize about these treaties is that they came into being before the world was ready for them. To be successful, treaties of this kind would require a highly organized society of nations. Such treaties are legal documents, fixing in more or less precise language the constitution of Europe and the rights and duties of nations. But even constitution makers and law makers are human, and are therefore liable not only to err, but to be ambiguous: so that legal documents of that kind would be certain actually to promote discord in any society unless two conditions were fulfilled. The first condition is that the society should be so organized that there is a well-established and easy method of modifying the legal constitution; the second is that there should be a well-established and easy method of interpreting the legal document when a difference as to its meaning arises between individuals in the society. Now, both these conditions are unfulfilled in the society of nations, and it is clear that while this is so any elaborate attempt to found a stable constitution by means of legal bonds will do as much to promote as to prevent war.

It remains to make one further remark about all treaties, which follows naturally from the preceding paragraph. The real value of treaties is in the future. The great point of them lies in the fact that they create a legal bond between nations. They create rights and duties which are clearly *capable* of being the subjects of judicial decisions. They tend to transform political and administrative relations of States into legal relations, and so they change the nature of the disputes and differences that arise from those relations. Political and administrative differences are often of a nature which would make it extremely difficult, if not impossible, even to state a case to a court for decision upon questions either of facts or law. But once the political and administrative relations have been defined, however vaguely, and rendered legal by the words of a treaty, any "incident" that may occur afterwards can easily be adjudicated upon by a court, for the question will usually reduce itself to the ordinary judicial question: "Given these facts and this contract, what are the rights and duties of the parties in the present circumstances under the contract?" This can best be shown by taking an actual example, the Anglo-French Agreement of 1904. Prior to 1904 the political and administrative relations of France and Britain in Egypt and Morocco, but particularly in Egypt, were of a kind which not only created friction between the two nations, but were peculiarly dangerous because it would have been difficult to know how to begin to settle any dispute arising out of them. The political relations and the reciprocal rights and duties of the two nations in Egypt were of so vague and ill-defined a nature that it might have been impossible to agree upon what basis to refer any particular question to a court of arbitration or other judicial body. It cannot be said that the Agreement of 1904 defines the relations in any but the broadest and, indeed, the vaguest terms, but the important point is that it does define them in such a way as to create legal rights and duties. France has bound herself not to "obstruct the action of Great Britain in that country (Egypt) by asking that a limit of time be fixed for the British occupation or in any other manner." The consequence is that any question of French or British action in Egypt is now peculiarly suitable to be the subject of a judicial decision in the form: "Is this act in conformity with the legal rights and duties created by the Agreement?"

But the importance of these facts is obscured at the present moment by the inchoate organization of the Society of Nations. To transform vague political relations into definite legal obligations is of value only if there is an established judicial system to which questions falling within the scope of those obligations can be easily and almost automatically referred. But there is at present really no such system, and it is normally as difficult to settle that a particular dispute shall be referred, say, to arbitration, as to settle the whole dispute by negotiation. This is not the place in which I propose to discuss international judicial organs, nor do I wish to prejudge the question of compulsory arbitration as the panacea of war, but one can say this with certainty, that if war is ever to become an impossibility or even an improbability in the society of nations, there must be in that society a regular, easily working, recognized system of obtaining in *some* kinds of international disputes a judicial decision. When that time comes the enormous value of treaties will become apparent in ensuring that when disputes arise they usually are of such a kind that they can be referred to a judicial tribunal for decision. Treaties perform in international society the part of anæsthetics in surgery; they get the patient into a condition which makes it possible to operate; but, unfortunately, up to the present, the means and instruments for operating have been wanting. It is no good giving gas to a man with toothache unless you have a dentist with his nippers on the premises; and it is no good dosing international society with law in treaties unless you have a judge handy to decide the legal disputes.

CHAPTER V

CONFERENCES, CONGRESSES, AND THE CONCERT OF EUROPE

IT HAS become apparent from the previous chapters that in international society three things at least are wanted if disputes and differences are to be amicably settled. First it is necessary that the general rules or laws regulating the relations of States should be laid down with authority and precision; second, the society of nations should be founded upon a stable constitution; thirdly, it should be possible to make new rules and alter the constitution without great difficulty or violent upheavals. In the society of which the units are individual men and women, these functions are usually performed by what we call legislatures; and it is remarkable that in the society of which the units are nations the first real attempts to provide for these functions have been made in the nineteenth century by international organs bearing a strong resemblance to rudimentary legislatures. From the pacifist's point of view the nineteenth century should be remembered as much for its Conferences, its Congresses, and its Concert of Europe as for the growth of arbitration.

It should first be observed that in States legislation consists roughly of two kinds. There is, first, the body of general rules which merely regulate the conduct of individuals to one another—*e. g.*, nearly all criminal laws, laws of contract, sale, etc.; in the second place, there is the "law of the land," which defines the constitution and structure, administrative and political, of society within the State—*e. g.*, the Act of Union of 1707 and the Home Rule Act. The power of initiating and altering both kinds of law is, as a rule, vested in the same legislative organ. Now, in the nineteenth century, for the first time, a tentative, sometimes conscious and sometimes unconscious, movement has shown itself towards two similar kinds of legislation for international society by means of representatives of nations meeting together much in the same way as representatives meet in legislative assemblies of States. I propose now to examine what has been done by these meetings and concerts, and in that examination it will appear, I think, that remarkable progress has been made towards the possibility of a peaceful organization of international society. But it is necessary at the outset to insist upon the importance for anyone in search of "some international authority" or "some form of international organization," of distinguishing between these two kinds of legislation. It is only by neglecting to distinguish them that enthusiasts have been led to believe that war can be abolished by some system of universal compulsory arbitration. Neither kind of legislation could possibly find a substitute in any judicial process. The Conferences which led to the founding of a sovereign

State in Greece, and the conference which constituted Luxemburg a neutral State, did as much to prevent war as the *Alabama* arbitration. The work of those conferences could no more be done by a judicial tribunal than the question of Home Rule for Ireland could possibly have been decided in a court of law. Nor is it easy to conceive of any working form of society in which, say, a court of law had not only to interpret but also to make an Act like the Sale of Goods Act.

I propose first to examine briefly what exactly has been effected by these Conferences, Congresses, etc., and then to enquire more closely into the way they work, their possibilities and limitations. I shall, as far as possible, deal separately with their achievements in making general rules regulating the conduct of nations and in laying down a constitution and arranging the political relations of nations. First, as to the general rules: at the Congress of Vienna, for the first time in history, an international law of this kind was made by the nations of Europe in general assembly. The declaration in the Final Act as to the freedom of navigation on rivers lays down a general principle of international action in exactly the same way as a law of trespass or right of way would prescribe within a State a general principle of individual action. It is remarkable, too, that the navigation declaration was not only the first example of deliberate international legislation, but it led to the creation of the first international Executive in the Danube Commission.

It cannot be said that the Congress of Vienna was followed by any very rich crop of this kind of legislation during the next century. The full harvest consists only of some half-hearted declarations at that Congress with regard to the abolition of the slave trade, some remarkable provisions regarding freedom of commerce and acquisition of territory in Africa at the Congo Conference of 1884, laws of war made by the Declarations of Paris and St. Petersburg and the Geneva Convention, and finally the achievements of the Hague Conferences. This is not a very brilliant record, and for our present purposes only two remarks are necessary upon it. In the first place, it does show that it is possible to call together representatives of nations who will make international laws affecting vital interests of nations. The Congo Conference dealt with the economic and political relations of States, with those fundamental questions of trade and expansion, territory and subject races which, stimulating at once the passions of cupidity and patriotism, are in the present stage of the world peculiarly liable to lead to violent actions. It is true that the Conference only made rules for a part of Africa, and that those rules did nothing to relieve the subsequent tragedy of that unhappy country. But it is none the less true that the object, not altogether unsuccessful, of the Powers represented—and they included all the great colonizing and acquisitive Powers—was to lay down general principles of international conduct in one of the least-exploited parts of the world, so that the dangers of friction and rivalry from its exploitation might be reduced to a minimum. As Bismarck said in his introductory address, the fundamental idea of the programme of invitation was to facilitate access to Central Africa for all commercial nations, and to prescribe formalities which nations should be bound to observe in future occupations of territory on the coast of Africa. No one who reads the Final Act of the Conference can doubt that if its provisions were extended to all the "colonies," and "suzerainties," and "spheres of influence" of civilized Powers in uncivilized parts of the earth, one at least of the greatest menaces to the peace of Europe would be abolished. With free access to the flags of all nations, with complete liberty of commerce, with no concession of commercial monopolies and privileges, we should hear less of Far Eastern Questions, of the Partition of China, of Persia and Bagdad and Morocco.

The second point with regard to international legislation of this kind is that it has concerned itself far too much with war and far too little with peace. Perhaps this is because Conferences and Congresses are usually summoned by Kings and Emperors and attended by diplomatists, two classes of persons who by tradition are perpetually thinking and talking of war. At any rate, before the Hague Conference, international legislation in Conferences had taken as its most important subject the Laws of War, and again, at The Hague Conferences, if one excepts arbitration, the only question really discussed and the only results arrived at concerned the conduct of nations during war. There is no doubt that in this way International Law and Conferences have not been given a fair chance. What should we think of a State in which there were no laws to prevent riot and murder and violence, and no police to enforce the law, but yet there were very detailed and complicated laws governing the conduct of persons engaged in riots, murder, and violence? To appeal to force is to appeal to the opposite of law; and it is natural that nations should be far more ready to break the rules of International Law during war than during peace. The Laws of War should be not the first, but the last, to be made in the Society of Nations. If Conferences and Congresses were called for the purpose of making rules of conduct during peace in matters which continually cause and will cause friction between nations, the popular contempt for International Law would prove to be undeserved, and more good would be done by one such conference than by all the rules ever devised for helping men to kill one another humanely. Take the question of the rights and treatment of nationals of one country in the territory of another. This is a question which has and will again endanger the peace of the world. Nations have tried to settle it piecemeal by treaties. The Law has therefore varied from time to time and from territory to territory, and a fluctuating law of this kind is itself a danger. If the representatives of nations could arrive at agreement in the complicated Final Acts of the

Hague Conferences, it is absurd to believe that they could not settle satisfactorily at a conference what is after all a comparatively simple question.

If the achievements of Conferences in the making of general rules of international conduct are disappointing, one can look back with more satisfaction to their efforts to settle the larger political relations of States and the constitution of national society. This is possibly not the ordinary view, even of historians, but if one be content to view the past soberly and without impatience, it is, I think, the true one. The fact is that it was only at the end of the Napoleonic wars that emperors and statesmen began to think and to talk of "some form of international organization" instead of war and offensive alliances as a practical method of constructing international society. One cannot altogether neglect in an enquiry of this kind the hopes, the theories, the intrigues that were trumpeted to the world or whispered in audiences at Vienna and Aix-la-Chapelle and Troppau and Laibach and Verona. The hopes and intrigues of the Congresses and of the Holy Alliance went the way of all hopes and intrigues: a tiny portion of them succeeded and an enormous part of them failed; but none the less there was born of them a new and a practical system of regulating the affairs of Europe.

The begetter, or, at any rate, the foster-father, of that system was unfortunately the unstable mind of the Emperor Alexander. He began with a vague idea of a kind of concert of Europe, which should preserve the "public peace, the tranquility of States, the inviolability of possessions, and the faith of treaties." The great Congress of Vienna was undoubtedly conceived as, in a sense, a Parliament of Nations settling the Constitution of Europe. From this conception again grew the idea, actually embodied in the Second Peace of Paris of 1815, that questions affecting "the peace and prosperity of the nations" should be brought before and decided at similar meetings to be held at fixed intervals, and the Congresses of Aix-la-Chapelle, Troppau, Laibach, and Verona were, in fact, called with that object.

The immediate result of these Congresses, of the "European System," and of the Holy Alliance was failure, and it is really important to understand the causes of that failure. In the first place, the idea of the new system was continually vacillating. At one moment the nations were to form "a general association having for foundation the compact of Vienna and the Treaty of Paris," a kind of European Confederation with an immutable constitution and a legislative assembly meeting at fixed intervals. At another time and more frequently Europe was considered as under the hegemony of the four great Powers, bound by alliance to preserve the *status quo*, and to act together in international politics. Now, here we have no academic, but a living question, and a vital difference. "Some sort of" confederation is at the opposite pole of international systems from "some sort of" hegemony. An hegemony of powerful and allied States must be prepared to impose its will upon Europe or the world. Peace will depend upon two things—the maintenance of overwhelming power in the great nations, and the continuance of their agreement. One has only to state this truism to see that such an hegemony must be an unstable international system. National power is itself a shifting, fluctuating thing; at any particular moment it can be tested only by war, and it exists, therefore, for the most part, only in the fallible imagination and estimation of men. Nor is the mere hope that three or four powerful sovereign States will continue to find themselves in agreement a good foundation upon which to build international society. The congresses very soon showed this. They ceased to be in any sense rudimentary legislative organs, and became merely the meetings of diplomatists negotiating to maintain the agreement and alliance of a few powerful States. They collapsed at the first real difference of opinion.

But the visionaries of 1915 can learn another lesson from the faded and broken visions of 1815. The congresses failed because their authors refused to face and answer a fundamental question as to the constitution of international society. If there is to be any kind of legislative organ, what are the questions which that organ is to be competent to deal with? Alexander and his Continental allies proposed to discuss at the congresses, not only the relations of States to one another, but the internal affairs of nations. Castlereagh first, and Canning later, very soon showed that they would have nothing to do with such a system. At Troppau, Castlereagh refused to agree to a protocol which would "lead to a species of general government in Europe, with a superintending Directory, destructive of all correct notions of internal sovereign authority." In 1823 Canning wrote: "Our engagements have reference wholly to the state of territorial possessions settled at the Peace; to the state of affairs between nation and nation, not . . . to the affairs of any nation within itself." And in the same year, when he saw the visions of 1815 and the European system and the Holy Alliance crumbling at the Congress of Verona, he congratulated himself and Sir Charles Bagot that "things are getting back to a wholesome state again. Every nation for itself, and God for us all."

This question over which Canning and his Continental allies fell out has got to be faced to-day. If the society of nations is to be constructed upon the model of the society of individual human beings—that is to say, if certain questions in which national desires, beliefs, and interests clash, are to be submitted for discussion and decision to assemblies of national representatives—then it is absolutely essential to agree first upon what such assemblies can and what they cannot discuss and decide. At first sight, Canning may seem to many, with the sound British instinct of common sense, to have drawn the right distinction. "The state of affairs between nation and nation," the relations of nations to one another, are the domain of an international legislature, whatever particular form it may take; "the affairs of any nation within itself" are the exclusive concern of the nation itself. It is true that in a large number of cases this common-sense distinction would probably solve the problem satisfactorily. There is no difficulty in seeing that the differences and disputes which arise out of the economic relations and out of many of the political and administrative relations of States concern the "state of affairs between nation and nation." To have the commercial relations of European States in Asia and Africa submitted to some kind of permanent deliberative conference, to have the commercial and political relations of European States in such countries as Persia and Morocco settled in open debate rather than by the secret weaving of intrigue and the silent pressure of armaments, is not only a desirable dream of the future, but is also a scheme which practical men might actually put into operation to-morrow. But as soon as one comes to questions of nationality the case is entirely different. It is often extremely difficult to decide oneself whether such questions are international or national, and therefore—and this is the important point—there will often be in practice a fundamental difference of opinion as to whether a particular question should be decided internationally or nationally.

Let us take actual examples. Everyone would admit that the position of Bosnia and Herzegovina in the society of European nations is an international question; in fact, as long ago as 1876, at the Conference of Constantinople, a rudimentary international legislature, to which the six Great Powers sent representatives, discussed and decided upon the nature of the administrative system to be applied to those countries. If ever "some international authority" is to "settle points of difference among nations" by means of deliberative or legislative conferences, then undoubtedly the differences about Bosnia and Herzegovina should be submitted to such a conference. The question is one of nationality and administration. There are within a certain area persons of various nationalities. Is that area to be under the administrative system of that country or of this country, or are its inhabitants to be left to work out their own system? At first sight it might seem that the fact that two or more nations are differing over what should be done makes the question international, but a moment's consideration will show that this does not go to the root of the difficulty.

The difficulty is this—if Bosnia and Herzegovina are to be the subjects of international legislation, then logically the whole Home Rule question in Ireland and Ulster and the position of India within the British Empire are international and not domestic questions. The point is that at every particular moment there is a *status quo*, at every particular moment the people living in any area are under a certain administrative system. The differences, which lead to war over nationality and administrative systems, arise because some people desire to change and some desire to maintain the *status quo* within a given area. In every case there always is, and always will be, one party who can and will rest on the *status quo* and insist that the whole dispute is one which concerns only the internal affairs of the nation. The Turk could in the past plead as logically that the Bosnian was a domestic question to be settled between him and the inhabitants as the Englishman can now plead that Home Rule must be settled in the House of Commons. It is impossible to say exactly when the Balkans became, and when Ireland will become, an international question. The truth is that we are dealing here with the fundamental constitution of the society of nations. It is necessary that that constitution should be firmly established, but the surest way of making wars inevitable is to try to establish it immutably and eternally. The position of nationalities as opposed to nations within the society may at any moment make it imperative to change the constitution. Any change, or movement for change, in the constitution is extremely likely to lead to international differences; but, because the constitution is based upon nations and not nationalities, it is always possible under present circumstances to argue that these questions of nationality and administration are not international.

I cannot pretend to offer a solution of this problem. All I can do is to try to show how and why it exists, and to suggest certain conclusions. It seems to me so important that I propose to restate it. Any form of international organization in which conferences or any other kind of deliberative and legislative organ are to decide on questions which at present are very likely to lead to war is useless, unless there is agreement as to what questions are to be so decided and machinery for submitting them automatically for decision. To say that such an organ is only to deal with international questions is to shirk the difficulty. Owing to our existing conception of "States," "nations," and "nationality," there will always be a wide divergence of opinion whether a question involving nationality is, or when it becomes, international. Thus, if Russia comes into the international organization, the position of the Finns within that Empire is, for the moment, we may allow, a matter to be decided between Finns and Russians. But it is not difficult to conceive of events happening which would lead insensibly to a Finnish question, and a war between, say, Sweden and Russia over it. The difficulty is to say at what point Russia is to admit that the Finnish question is no longer purely domestic, but concerns Sweden. The essence of the situation is that Sweden, who wishes to change the *status quo*, will at once affirm, and Russia, who wishes to maintain the *status quo*, will deny, that the question is international.

The simplest way out of the difficulty is, of course, to say that the position of nationalities within States is always a right subject for international legislation. But we are discussing the matter from a practical standpoint, and we have to ask ourselves whether there is, this side of the year of our Lord 2000, the slightest possibility of the British Empire and Russia entering an international system in which the future position of Indians, Irishmen, and Finns in the respective Empires is to be decided at some sort of international conference. The possibility seems to be remote, and that undoubtedly means that the possibility of any pacific settlement of differences involving nationality is also remote. It means that at the end of the war we shall again try to establish international society in Europe with an immutable constitution. For a few brief weeks or months the position of Poles, Italians, Serbs, even Finns and Irishmen, under that constitution may be a subject of international discussion; but, once Europe has been settled in this way, there is to be no international method or machinery for revising the constitution. Four million Finns and Swedes are to be permanently handed over to the generosity and liberality of some 83,000,000 Russians, just as 4,000,000 pure-bred Irishmen are to be permanently handed over to the 40,000,000 mixed population which inhabits the rest of the British Isles. National questions will remain domestic until and unless they have become so acute that war has broken out and is, therefore, according to the popular philosophy of history and war, "inevitable."

We shall have again to return to this and similar

problems, and I therefore, for the present, will only make the following remarks upon it. In the first place, the difficulty is largely due to our extraordinarily crude conceptions of "States" and "nations." Practically everyone, from Foreign Secretaries to public-house politicians, is obsessed by the mysterious sovereignty of sovereign Powers. The ordinary view is that the action of a nation is to be determined solely by its own ideals and desires. In a sense, therefore, any international question is not international, but domestic, and a sovereign Power always has to consider only two things—what it desires and whether it is strong enough to enforce its desire. But the whole of an international organization and authority implies an agreement that each nation is willing that its action will be, in part, determined by what other nations desire. Any kind of conference which is to *decide* things involves the submission of one nation to the expressed will of other nations. Perhaps the main thing is that we should see that we do not cease to be a nation, or, at any rate, a nation with "national honor," because we make that submission.

Secondly, one may doubt whether a certain degree of unanimity as to the internal organization of States is not an absolutely necessary antecedent to any highly developed international organization. The Russian view, for instance, of the rights of nationalities within the State is so different from the British that neither of us could with equanimity allow the other a voice in the decision of a national question nearly affecting our own State. It would seem, then, that the first work of an international conference should be to lay down some general principle of action in this matter, and such apparently is the idea underlying many of the published and unpublished proposals which one hears at the present time for settling the terms of peace. Thus the Union of Democratic Control urges the adoption of the principle that "no province shall be transferred from one Government to another without the consent by plebiscite, or otherwise, of the population of such province." The adoption of this principle as part of the international constitution would indisputably be a great step forward, but one may point out that really to ensure a permanent peace it would be at least necessary to add: "Nor shall any province be compelled to remain under any Government against the consent of the population of such province." Whether the Russian Government or Unionist and Home Rule politicians of this country would be prepared to adopt such a principle is a matter of personal opinion, but if adopted it would undoubtedly revolutionize the current conceptions of "nations" and "patriotism."

All this may appear to be a digression from our main purpose, which is to examine the achievements of Congresses and Conferences; but, in fact, it is not. One of the first questions which occupied statesmen after the Congress of Vienna, and was actually settled by a series of conferences, was concerned precisely with these problems, and the method by which it was solved is extremely illuminating. In 1815 the position of the Greek nation in the Turkish Empire and international society was, according to the accepted view of international law and history, a domestic question to be settled between Greek and Turk. But the real result of the congresses was that a vague feeling persisted that the affairs of any nation which threatened the peace of Europe were the concern of all other nations. States were still regarded in theory and profession as isolated units whose actions within certain physical boundaries could not be the subject even of notice by any man or thing outside them; but in practice it began to be admitted that the nations of Europe formed a real society, the constitution of which might be established and altered by methods other than warfare.

As a matter of fact, the Greek revolt of 1821 involved a serious danger to the peace of Europe. There sprang into existence at this time the bogey of international politics, which persisted all through the nineteenth century—the isolated interference of Russia with Turkey. And yet by 1824 Russia was already proposing collective intervention and a Conference of Powers. Turkey logically protested that the question was a domestic one to be settled between herself and the Greeks, and even Greece refused to accept the decision of a conference. Now, there were really two ways of settling the question. First, each Power, including Turkey, might be treated as an isolated sovereign Power. In that case Turkey had to settle with the Greeks by herself, though, of course, any other Power might make any demand of her which she thought she could enforce by arms. In the second case, the European Powers might say to Turkey: "You form part of the society of nations. Your internal affairs are already endangering peace. We and you will now send representatives to a conference, and that conference will decide for us and for you how these affairs are to be settled."

In fact, the Powers adopted neither method, but tried to combine them. Two States—Austria and Prussia—stood outside, and refused to have anything to do with the matter. Russia, France, and Great Britain, by the treaty of 1827, under cover of the specious term "mediation," professed to deal with Turkey as a sovereign Power. Actually they formed themselves into a kind of legislative committee, and at a series of conferences, held off and on for ten years, settled the affairs of Greeks and Turks, and compelled both parties to accept that settlement. They transformed a Turkish province into an independent kingdom, they selected and gave it a king, and defined its boundaries. Incidentally, they invented a new term in international law, and pacifically destroyed the Turkish fleet at Navarino. These two facts alone prove, however, that the international conferences which settled the question of Greek independence were the central point of a new, if rudimentary, international system. When the three Powers blockaded the Greek coast in 1827, in order to enforce these decisions of their conferences, for the first time in history we hear of a pacific blockade, and even when they destroyed her fleet they denied that they were at war with Turkey. The fact is that, though they never said so, they unconsciously regarded their conferences as a kind of committee upon which had devolved the legislative power of a larger European organ. A blockade and a naval action between isolated sovereign Powers involves war, whether some of them call themselves mediators or anything else. But if the decisions of an international conference are binding upon the nations of Europe, then a blockade, or even a naval massacre, to enforce those decisions, undertaken in the name of Europe, can reasonably be called pacific.*

It is also noteworthy that all through the nineteenth century the right of, first, the three Powers,

* Text books on International Law treat the action of the three Powers as an example of collective intervention. Such labelling of things in technical terms is useful, but it has the disadvantage of making one think that having attached the label one has explained everything. The important point is, not that the three Powers intervened, but why and how they intervened. As regards pacific blockade, there is a difference of opinion among international lawyers. The orthodox view now is that such blockades are not acts of war if they can be classified as "interventions" or "reprisals." The layman, however, will be inclined to agree with writers like Mr. Baty (*vide International Law*, Chapter VI), and consider "pacific blockades" of this nature acts of war in everything but name. But it is clear that the distinction drawn in the text is a real one. There is a real difference between a nation enforcing its own will by violence and one enforcing the will of an international authority by violence. It is the difference between a hooligan and a policeman. My point is that the three Powers were half conscious of acting as a European police, and were right in protesting that they were not at war with Turkey.

and later a larger group of Powers, was recognized to "arrange" the affairs of Greece. At every point this right was exercised through international conferences. In 1857 a commission of representatives of the three Powers met at Athens to enquire into the Greek financial situation. In 1862, when King Otho was deposed and the National Assembly offered the throne to Prince William of Denmark, a conference again met and confirmed the choice. In 1863 a conference of the three Powers and Prussia and Austria "confirmed" the cession of the Ionian Islands. In 1878 the Congress of Berlin dealt with the rectification of the Greek-Turkish boundary. When Greece and Turkey failed to agree upon the new boundary, the Powers held another conference at Berlin in 1880, and decided by a majority of votes—an almost unique mode of procedure at an international conference—upon the line of frontier. Though Turkey objected and Greece mobilized, the Powers refused to allow war, and in the following year military officers specially delegated by them handed over the new line mile by mile to the Greek nation.* Finally, it is interesting to note that in 1885 five of the great Powers undertook another pacific blockade of the Greek coasts in order to prevent Greece from going to war with Turkey.

It would, of course, be absurd to exaggerate the importance of these facts, though it would be equally absurd to underestimate it. Europe did

---
* *Vide the European Concert and the Eastern Question*, by T. E. Holland, pp. 4-69.

not invent a new and perfect system of international government to settle the Greek question. The Powers themselves were at great pains to prove by the use of such terms as "mandate"* from the Greek nation and "mediation" that they were making no innovations. But when one looks beneath the verbiage of protocols and treaties, one sees clearly that there was the spirit of a new system of international society. The relations of Greece and Turkey were being continually regulated by quasi-legislative international conferences. Russia and England were certainly at no time very well disposed to one another or disinterested parties, yet they were throughout able by means of these conferences to come to a reasonable agreement. Though the Powers were not able completely to prevent bloodshed, they contrived again and again to compel Greece and Turkey to accept international decisions without resorting to violence, and they undoubtedly settled reasonably and justly a number of difficult questions which, if they had not intervened, would have led to incessant massacre and fighting. Finally, it must be remarked that, although the conferences formed, in fact, a rudimentary kind of international legislative organ, they had this peculiarity—that usually the interested parties, Greece and Turkey, had no representative at them.

It is perhaps advisable to point out that the representatives of the Powers were almost always

---

* *Vide Protocol of Conference of London,* 1863.

eager to insist that they had no kind of international authority. The Powers were always "mediating" between two sovereign States; they were only making "suggestions" which those States had full liberty to accept or reject. The proceedings of the Conference of Paris of 1869 are full of interest from this point of view. Turkey had presented an ultimatum to Greece regarding the help afforded by her to Cretan insurgents, etc. Greece refused to comply, and Turkey threatened the Greek coasts. The Powers intervened under the *vœu pacifique* in the XXIII Protocol of the Congress of Paris. At the first meeting the Greek representative withdrew because he was refused equality of representation with the Turkish representative. The representatives agreed that the Conference was not a commission of enquiry into the facts, because such a manner of procedure would be contrary to the independence of the two parties, for it would imply a real intervention in their internal administration. The Conference, it was said, has not to make decisions of a nature to interfere with the liberty of action of the two Powers to which it offers its good offices; it can legitimately only examine facts, say what it thinks is right, and present the basis of a reconciliation. It is not a "tribunal chargé de rendre un arret," but "un Conseil international dont les appreciations ne sauraient engager les parties que par la liberté même qu'elles leur laissent et l'absence complete de toute autre sanction que celle qu'implique necessairement, dans l'ordre moral, une telle manifestation de l'opinion publique et en quelque sorte de la conscience Européenne." What the Conference actually did was to lay down in a declaration the principles of international law which it considered that Greece was bound to observe. This declaration was forwarded to Athens with an expression of the conviction of the Conference that Turkey would not proceed to carry out the measures threatened in the ultimatum if Greece notified the Conference that she deferred to the opinion expressed by it. The Greek Government replied that it adhered to the principles of international jurisprudence contained in the declaration, and had decided to act in accordance with them.

I have dealt with the affairs of Greece and Turkey at some length because they show very clearly the elements of the whole problem, and because they are also the first example of an attempt to regulate the relations of States and the constitution of international society by a series of international conferences. The fact is that for the whole of a particular area in Europe and in European politics a new system and theory of inter-State relationship grew up in the nineteenth century. That system involved "a negation of the right of any one Power and an assertion of the right of the Powers collectively, to regulate the solution of the Eastern question."* The development of the system was gradual, and only

---

* Holland, *The European Concert*, p. 221.

occasionally penetrated the consciousness of the diplomatists and statesmen who invented it. Diplomatists are naturally so conservative that, even if once a century they are compelled to take a step forward, they spend a great deal of time and ingenuity in assuring themselves and the world that they have really been standing still. When one turns from the Greek to the Balkan question, one can see clearly what a big step had been taken.

The events of the years 1876–1878 deserve detailed mention. The insurrection in Bosnia-Herzegovina had been supported by armed action on the part of Montenegro and Servia against Turkey. In 1876 the six Great Powers came forward as "mediators." It was a curious form of mediation. They held an international conference at Constantinople from December 11th to December 22nd. They discussed two questions: (1) The conditions to be offered to Turkey on the one side and Montenegro and Servia on the other; (2) the nature of the administrative system to be applied to Bosnia-Herzegovina and to Bulgaria, and the guarantees for securing execution. The Conference decided these questions, and actually agreed to send into the Balkan Peninsula an international police force composed of from 3,000 to 6,000 Belgian soldiers as a "material guarantee." They then held another conference from December 23, 1876, to January 20, 1877, to which Turkey was admitted, and at which the proposals of the Powers were communicated to her. Turkey rejected the proposals. Now, if the Powers had been merely mediators, there was an end of the whole matter; but what the Powers really felt themselves to be doing was shown by the action of Russia. She sent a circular note to the Powers asking them what measures they proposed to take in order *to enforce the decisions of Europe;* and, when no measures were taken, she went to war with Turkey. Moreover, when after the war she attempted to make her own terms with Turkey by the Treaty of San Stefano, the other Powers intervened and insisted upon a European settlement at the international Congress of Berlin.

Now, at first sight, one might be tempted to say that these facts simply give an example of the failure of an international conference to regulate affairs without war; but such a view would, I think, be superficial. Clearly the Conference of Constantinople regarded itself as an international legislative organ, and was prepared to go to the lengths of creating an international executive and an international armed force in order to ensure that its decisions should be carried out. Turkey was being treated, not as an isolated sovereign State, but as a member of a system of European States, bound to carry out the will of those States as expressed in an international Conference. When she refused to carry it out, Russia logically asked what steps were to be taken to compel her to abide by the decision of Europe. If the Powers had had the courage of their convictions, they would have said to Turkey what was, in fact, the truth: "We are treating you, not as an 'isolated'

State, nor yet as a dependent State, but as one of a group of European States. The condition of your affairs is such that you are endangering the peace of Europe. We—that is, Europe—have decided that you must take these steps to put your house in order, and we are now going to use every means in our power to see that you do so." If the Powers had said this and acted upon it, there cannot be the slightest doubt that there would have been no war between Russia and Turkey, and the Conference of 1876 would have achieved pacifically exactly what the Congress of 1878 achieved after warfare. The point is that, in so far as Europe treated the Conferences as international legislative organs, they succeeded; in so far as it treated them as Councils of Conciliation and Mediation, they failed. In everything they proposed to do, and in their negotiations with one another, the Powers acted not as mediators, but legislators; it was only at the final point when they had to consider *how* they proposed to do what they proposed to do, that they turned round and said: "Oh, but we are only mediators!"

If one looks at the events of 1876 to 1878, not as isolated facts, but as a chain of complicated relations, one is forced to recognize the efficacy of international conferences when treated as legislating organs. In a sense, one may rightly regard Russia merely as applying force in the war of 1877 to compel Turkey to carry out the decisions of Europe, because if one looks at the results that is really what she did. And it emphasizes the point, which I wish to make, that Russia herself, as is shown by the Treaty of San Stefano, probably did not intend to do so. She was playing for her own hand, but the international system was too strong for her, and at Berlin she was compelled to tear up the Treaty of San Stefano and herself bow to the decisions of Europe. And it must be remembered that the real danger of the Eastern question has never been that some Power will go to war with Turkey, but that diplomatic or armed interference by some Power with one of the diseased or atrophied extremities of the Turkish Empire will set the rest of Europe fighting one another. That danger existed in 1876–1878 no less than it did in 1914; it was avoided solely by the acceptance by the great Powers of a system of international conferences, involving "a negation of the right of any one Power, and an assertion of the right of the Powers collectively, to regulate the solution of the Eastern question."

Both examples of this system which I have dealt with concerned the Turkish Empire. But the system of conferences and the principle underlying it have been extended to other parts of the field of international relationship. I propose briefly to refer here to only two cases in order to show that in these two dangerous and important cases this same principle was insisted upon, the principle involving a negation of the right of any one Power, and an assertion of the right of the Powers collectively, to settle an international question.

The first is that of Luxemburg in 1867. A grave international situation arose from the proposal to sell Luxemburg to France, for the Duchy is obviously one of those small territorial bones of contention lying between two great Powers. France and Holland, as two sovereign States, had under the ordinary view of the international system and international law every right to settle the question of the sale of Luxemburg between them. The result of such a settlement would almost certainly have been war between Prussia and France. The Powers intervened and asserted their right to settle the question collectively. This right was asserted by the outward and visible sign of the international conference of London, to which Austria, Belgium, France, Great Britain, Italy, the Netherlands, Prussia, and Russia sent representatives, and at which the neutrality of Luxemburg was declared and received the "collective guarantee" of the Powers.

The second case is still more interesting, because the principle was definitely enunciated, and the facts themselves are of very recent date. I am in no way concerned here with the rights and wrongs of the Morocco question as between France and Germany. It is just as easy to use a good principle for bad ends as to use a bad principle for good ends. We are dealing here, not with the ends of either Germany or France, or with the ultimate objects of their diplomatic policy and intrigues, but simply with the principles involved in the history of this international problem.

Now, there is no doubt that the principle insisted upon by Germany in the events which led up to the Conference of Algeciras was that the regulation of the question of Morocco belonged, not to any one Power, but to the Powers collectively. The danger of the Morocco question for the peace of Europe was that France and Germany would act as isolated sovereign Powers towards Morocco. The essence of the French case was that France could, and would, so act; the essence of the German case was that the Powers should act collectively. That was why Germany in 1905 was demanding, and France resisting, an international conference. France gave way, and the principle of international regulation was first recognized by the calling of the Conference, and, secondly, by its decisions embodied in the Final Act.

I have now dealt with what has actually been effected by international conferences in four important cases. There have been other conferences to settle other cases, but enough has been said to show their efficacy, and I now propose to pass on to the more detailed criticism of their machinery. It is, however, worth while to point out first, that there is only one instance in the nineteenth century of a conference called in order to settle a question which threatened to endanger peace failing to prevent war. That instance is the conference or conferences preceding the Russo-Turkish War, and, as I have shown, in that case the failure was more apparent than real.

I have throughout treated conferences as rudimentary International Legislatures, and I have done so because I conceive a legislature as an organ in which representatives of various interests attempt by discussion to arrive at decisions which are in some way and degree binding upon the persons or communities represented. International conferences have been only rudimentary legislatures, because they have never completely, though they have partially and practically, fulfilled these conditions. The main question for us is whether it is practicable and desirable to develop these conferences until they completely fulfill the conditions of a legislature. It is in order to help us in deciding this question that I propose to examine more closely into the actual machinery of previous conferences.

The first point to be noticed is at first sight a minor one, but is really of some importance. When a conference has met several times and published its protocols and its Final Act, and we read that it has settled an international question, we are inclined to imagine that the question has been settled by discussion round a table at the conference. Now, sometimes our imagination has some resemblance to the facts. Thus at the Conference of Constantinople the details of the administrative system to be applied to Bosnia, Herzegovina, and Bulgaria were discussed at length; there was real difference of opinion, and the question was settled by discussion and suggestion. But very often the question or dispute is not settled at the conference at all; the settlement has taken place by negotiation before the conference meets. Thus the Conference of London of 1867 did not settle the Luxemburg question by discussion. The settlement had taken place before the Conference met, by the Powers accepting as a basis of negotiation the neutrality of Luxemburg under a collective guarantee. The Conference really only drew up the treaty to give effect to that settlement.*

Now, there has always been a strong tendency among diplomatists to narrow the functions of conferences merely to the arrangement of the details of settlements already arrived at by negotiation. But it is important to remark that any narrowing in this direction prevents their development into legislative organs capable of settling disputes in which diplomacy has failed. It is the free discussion of representatives face to face that in a large number of cases would by itself ensure agreement. The first thing, and the minimum, to aim at is that questions involving real disagreement, which diplomacy has not settled or which cannot be referred to a judicial tribunal, shall be of right and necessity referred to the free discussion of representatives in conference. It follows from this that it is absolutely essential that the question of whether or not a particular ques-

---

* Perhaps it is hardly necessary to point out that this does not invalidate what was said above regarding the Conference. The Powers did settle the question by accepting the principle that the regulation of the Luxemburg affair could only be undertaken by the Powers collectively. The International Conference was the outward and visible sign of such acceptance.

tion is to be referred to a conference must never be allowed to be the subject of negotiation, otherwise the free discussion by representatives becomes itself only a pawn in the diplomatic game, and the conference is either used as a threat with which to extort a concession, or as a committee of diplomatic gentlemen called together to reduce an agreement to writing and ambiguity.

The second point is the one which goes to the root of the question of whether it is possible to set up an international authority with a real international legislature. The fundamental difference between a legislating and an advisory, conciliating, mediating or reporting body is that the former can come to a *decision binding on its members*, and the latter cannot. And the difference practically resolves itself into the question of whether there is voting and whether a minority is bound by the vote of the majority. Now, prior to the Hague Conferences, there was practically never any voting at these international assemblies. The conference had to be unanimous or nothing. It was held, and is still held, that for a sovereign State to agree to be bound on any question by the decision of an international assembly would be to abandon its sovereignty. "Le premier principe de toute Conference," said the President of the second Hague Conference, "est celui de l'unanimité: ce n'est point une vaine forme, mais la base de toute entente politique." That is why it is the rarest thing in the world to find any provision for arriving at a decision by voting, or for ascertaining the opinion of a majority in any diplomatic arrangements or proceedings.* And the result is, of course, an extraordinary difficulty of arriving at any decision at all.

It is advisable once more to distinguish the function of a conference that is making general rules or laws from that of one that is attempting to settle some particular question within the society of nations. First, as to the general rules or laws: The experience of the Hague Conferences is most instructive. Here we have two conscious attempts at full-blown international legislation. In 1899 the representatives of twenty-six, and in 1907 the representatives of forty-four, States met together and tried to make international law. The fundamental question as to how far the Conference could make laws binding upon the States represented was never faced, and the result was disastrous to the procedure and to the utility of the Conference. Each State was given one vote, but for any use that it was to them they might just as well have been given five hundred or none. In practice, unanimity was required before anything of importance was enunciated as the de-

---

* It is worthy of note that where it is absolutely imperative to arrive at a decision, diplomatists have in rare cases been forced to adopt a system of voting—*e. g.*, where an agreement has been arrived at which requires further details to be agreed to in order to give effect to it. The question of the Turkish Greek boundary has been noted above. Another instance is the Act of the Algeciras Conference, Article 76 of which provides that "in all cases dealt with by the present Declaration in which the intervention of the Diplomatic Body is required, decisions shall be taken by a majority of votes, except in respect of Articles 64, 70 and 75."

cision of the Conference.* The actual legislation appeared as Conventions, Declarations, etc., annexed to the Final Act. The Final Act merely presented these Conventions, etc., for acceptance or non-acceptance by the Plenipotentiaries; and, even if signed by the Plenipotentiaries a Convenvention was not binding upon a State unless it was subsequently ratified.

The result showed that international legislation is impossible if every law and every detail of each law has to be unanimously accepted by the thirty or forty States represented in the Legislature. To expect such unanimity is ridiculous, and the Conference of 1907 spent four months in a hopeless attempt to attain it. There is no doubt that international legislation by conferences will remain sterile unless sovereign States can agree that to some extent the will of a majority is binding upon a minority. That this is not a theoretical or Utopian question is shown by the official report of Great Britain's representative, Sir Edward Fry, at the Second Conference. "The machinery," he wrote, "proved in a high degree dilatory and confusing," and one of the few questions which he specifies as demanding solution "before another meeting of the Conference can prove satisfactory"

---

* The Conference formed itself into committees to consider the various subjects—*e. g.*, the Laws and Customs of War on Land, the Pacific Settlement of International Disputes, etc. The committees prepared and recommended the Conventions to the Conference. The committees acted on the principle that "unanimity was requisite before a Convention could be recommended for acceptance."

is "the rights of a majority over a minority in the absence of unanimity." *

The importance of this question cannot be exaggerated. The chief defects of international law are its uncertainty, intangibility, and vagueness, and it is the existence of these defects which stands in the way of the settlement of international disputes by the decisions of judicial tribunals. If a tribunal is to apply the law to particular cases there must be a law to apply, and, it seems to follow, a body capable of laying down what the law shall be. But no body modelled on the form of the Hague Conferences will ever be capable of laying down what international laws shall be.

This question, like most of those raised in this chapter, will have to be considered again and more fully when I come to deal with the co-ordination of international machinery and the possible forms of an international authority. But the same problem occurs in a slightly different form with regard to conferences called to deal with some particular difference or dispute which has arisen between nations. It is possible to conceive of such a Conference acting in three different ways. It might first act as a true legislature—that is to say, it would give a decision as to what ought to be done, and every State would send its representative on the understanding that the matter would be regulated by the collective decision. As I have shown above, Conferences have approximated in

---

* Miscellaneous, No. 1 (1908), (Cd. 3857), p. 20.

practice to this form, though they have never fully attained it. The reason is that States will not agree to send a representative to any Conference at which the decision of the majority would bind a minority, and it is difficult to see how a decision can be ensured without the rights of a majority over a minority being defined or admitted. Secondly, a Conference may be constituted merely as an examining and reporting body. The Conference of Paris of 1869, referred to above, which intervened between Greece and Turkey, was professedly a body of this sort. It endeavored to come to no decision binding upon anyone, nor in the strict sense of the word did it mediate between the two Powers. It merely examined the facts and gave a public pronouncement as to what it considered the disputing Powers ought to do. It specifically stated that it considered that in making the pronouncement it was merely manifesting the public opinion of Europe upon the dispute. The same difficulty, though obviously to a less degree, occurs with this kind of Conference. If the use of them were extended—for instance, if every dispute between nations which diplomacy failed to settle, and which was not referred to a judicial tribunal, had at least to be referred to a conference for examination and report—there can be no doubt that provision would have to be made for cases in which there was a difference of opinion in the Conference itself. Thirdly, a Conference can act merely as a kind of Council of Conciliation between two disputing nations. This was the capacity in which the Conferences professed to act with regard to the Turks and Greeks. They professed not to decide what should be done, not merely to examine and report, but rather to act as mediators, to suggest methods of compromise which might reconcile the interests of the two parties. There is no doubt that mediation of all kinds has been, and will be again, extremely useful in preventing war, but it is important to notice that the whole intention and therefore procedure of a Conference acting in this way must be different from one acting either as a legislating or examining and reporting body. The main object of a mediating Conference will be to find some compromise which will be accepted by, and acceptable to, both parties; it is, in fact, an extended and elaborated form of ordinary diplomatic negotiation. It need not necessarily come to any *decision* at all, but might perform its task merely by suggesting different methods of settlement. In this kind of Conference, therefore, the difficulty of obtaining unanimity and the question of majorities and minorities need never arise.

I now propose to leave the question of Conferences and Legislatures in order to examine that of arbitration and judicial tribunals, but before doing so it will be useful to summarize the conclusions which I have ventured to draw from the facts discussed in this chapter:

(1) A new system of international relationship began to appear in the last century. The pivot of the system was the making of international laws

and the regulation of certain international affairs at international Conferences of national representatives. The important part of the system was the expressed or unexpressed acceptance of the principle that such affairs could only be settled by the collective decision of the Powers.

(2) The functions of these international Conferences may be of three different kinds, which, in practice, have not been clearly recognized and distinguished. Their function may be:

(*a*) To come to a decision binding upon the States represented—*i. e.*, to legislate; or

(*b*) To examine facts and express an opinion or issue a report; or

(*c*) To act as a Council of Conciliation or Mediation between two or more disputing States.

3. The efficacy of Conferences in preventing war and in settling international questions has been remarkable. It has, however, been limited by the fact that the submission of any question to a Conference has always been a subject for negotiation, and therefore only a move in the diplomatic game. The first step towards the peaceful regulation of international affairs would be to remove this question of submission altogether from the sphere of negotiation and diplomacy, and to define the cases in which a Conference must be called or could be demanded.

4. Little progress in the making of international laws by Conferences can be expected unless the rights of an international majority to bind a minority—if only of an exceptionally overwhelming

majority, in specific cases—are admitted and defined.

5. The development of Conferences into full international legislative bodies depends principally upon the possiblity of:

(*a*) Agreement as to what are international questions which are to be submitted for collective decision to Conferences.

(*b*) Agreement as to the rights of an international majority to bind a minority.

CHAPTER VI

ARBITRATION AND JUDICIAL TRIBUNALS

ARBITRATION has received so much attention and prominence in discussions as to the possible means of preventing war, that anyone who tries to say anything original on the subject is in danger of writing a great deal too much or a great deal too little about it. In this chapter I shall therefore limit myself to the discussion of a definite question—namely, a consideration of the achievements and working of actual arbitration and other tribunals—with a view to forming an opinion as to the possibility of settling international differences and disputes by the decision of a tribunal, and as to the proper place of arbitration or a judiciary "in some international authority."

The arbitrationists and anti-arbitrationists in their quarrels appear again and again to neglect a vital distinction which has more than once been pointed out. There are two distinct forms of judicial tribunals to which the term International Court of Arbitration can be, and has been, applied, and the whole purpose of each, and therefore their efficacy, are absolutely different. Discussion of arbitration is useless until this difference is clearly grasped and unless it is kept securely and perpetually before one's mind.

Every judicial tribunal is a court composed of one or more persons to whom a difference or dispute is referred for a decision. It is the basis upon which the judge or arbitrator is required to come to a decision that marks the broad line of distinction between the two forms of tribunal. In the first form—and it is the one upon which, at least in theory, the judiciaries of States are constituted—the judge or arbitrator has merely to base his decision upon law; he has to find what the facts are, interpret the law, and declare the legal rights and the legal obligations of the parties. In the second form, the judge or arbitrator is not concerned with law at all; he is expected to examine the facts, and then, as an open-minded and reasonable human being, to decide what would be a fair settlement of the dispute.

It is clear that, if we are going to refer international disputes to arbitration or judicial tribunals, we must first make up our minds which form of tribunal we want. Our whole conception of the Society of Nations and of international relationship will differ according as we adopt the first or the second form. In the first case our aim and hope will be that the relations of States will be regulated by general rules or laws, and that when disputes arise a judicial tribunal will decide them strictly according to the general rules or laws. But in the second case our idea can be best expressed thus: "Here we have a number of disputes arising between nations which negotiation cannot settle. Certain persons must be selected by

States as likely to be reasonable and open-minded, and such disputes will be referred to their decision, which will represent a fair and reasonable settlement or compromise."

Clearly to keep this distinction before one's mind is of immense practical importance, particularly in discussing the question of universal obligatory arbitration as a substitute for war. For the many people who believe that war might be prevented by an agreement to refer to arbitration all disputes which cannot be settled by negotiation must face the fact that in a large number of cases it is the second kind of tribunal to which they would have to be referred. International Law is so fragmentary and incomplete that it does not touch at all a number of very important international relationships, and a dispute arising from such relationships could not at present be decided according to law. Take the dispute between Russia and Austria at the beginning of this war, or between Spain and the United States at the beginning of the Spanish-American war. No human being could possibly decide either case by determining the legal rights and obligations of the parties, because the rights and obligations actually defined by International Law were so few and so unimportant.

The first question, then, which one has to put to oneself is how far it is reasonable and practicable to expect nations to accept the decisions of this second kind of tribunal in disputes in which negotiation has failed. And it is a very remarkable fact that nations very rarely have accepted them.

The argument from the past is all against this kind of arbitration. If one examines in detail the numerous collected cases in which nations have referred disputes to judicial tribunals, one finds that in nearly every case the tribunal had to decide either a question of fact, or a question of law, or both. So much so is this the case that frequently, when no international law has existed on the subject in dispute, it was only after negotiation had settled what the law should be that the dispute could be referred to arbitration. This is true of the most famous of all arbitrations—the *Alabama* case. This case is usually cited as a triumph for the principle of arbitration, because here arbitration settled a dispute which kept two great nations for many months trembling on the edge of war; and, in a sense, it was a triumph, but only in the sense that it proved the efficacy of arbitration in disputes in which the question had been reduced to one of legal rights and obligations. The real difference between Great Britain and the United States was as to what the legal duties of a neutral Government in time of war *ought* to be. It was a case in which there was no international law on the subject, and if this real difference had been referred to a judicial tribunal we should have a notable example of success for the second form of arbitration. But, as a matter of fact, this question was never referred to arbitration, and it was only *after* it had been settled that arbitration was considered possible. The Treaty of Washington, which constituted the Tribunal of Arbitration, laid down in Article 6 three rules by which the arbitrators were to govern their decision. These three rules define the obligations of a neutral Government, the very subject of the dispute between the two countries, so that, as has been pointed out, the Treaty of Washington "practically reduced the arbitral tribunal of Geneva to a board for the assessment of damages."

The same conclusion is even more forcibly impressed upon one by a detailed examination of arbitrations in the mass. Sir Frederick Pollock has made a rough analysis of the 200 arbitrations (in round numbers) which took place between 1815 and 1900, and his classification is as follows:

	Per Cent.
Claims arising out of warlike operations and for alleged illegal operations or denial of justice	40
Questions of title and boundaries	30
Pecuniary claims of citizens in miscellaneous civil matters	20
Construction of treaties other than boundaries	10

This bare classification would show by itself the narrow field in which arbitration has, in fact, been resorted to; and it is a field narrowed, not by those exclusions, honor and vital interest, upon which so much controversy has been lavished, but by a single characteristic. It is essentially a legal field. These international tribunals have been called upon to decide questions which are precisely of the same nature as those which in States are decided in courts of law — questions of fact, of pecuniary claims principally to compensation for loss or injury based upon law or legal documents, of the interpretation of treaties and other legal documents, of title to property.*

The fact, however, that in the past nations have been willing to accept arbitration only in legal questions—by which I mean cases in which a legal right or obligation could be defined, or a fact demonstrated, or a legal document interpreted—does not, of course, prove, though it makes it probable, that nations will not accept it in non-legal cases in the future. We are still left with the problem whether general obligatory arbitration is practicable and reasonable. I believe that there is good reason for concluding that it is neither. It is not altogether safe to argue from the society of individuals to the society of States, but in this case a comparison is useful. Differences between individuals within States which used to be settled by private war are now, it is argued, settled by judicial decisions; therefore the same process can, and must be, substituted for war in international differences. But

---

* An analysis of the later references to the Hague Tribunal will give the same results. Up to 1913 twelve cases had been decided; of these, six were pecuniary claims, two turned solely upon the interpretation of treaties, in two the Court had to find on the facts whether there had been a breach of rules of international law, and in one the question was as to boundaries. The criticism is often made that only unimportant cases are referred to arbitration, and that nations will never consent to it in cases involving honor and vital interests. The statement is incorrect, and based upon misapprehension. The *Alabama* case, the Venezuelan Boundary question, the Alaskan Fur Seal difficulty, the Alaskan Boundary question all involved either national honor or vital interests, as Sir Thomas Barclay has pointed out. It is not that nations will not refer important questions to arbitration, but that they will not so refer questions which cannot be put in a *legal* form. They are willing to submit disputes to a judge who only has to pronounce on facts and interpret the law, but not to an arbitrator who has to make the law as well as interpret it.

a moment's reflection shows that the premise in this argument is untrue. It is only a strictly limited and clearly defined number of differences between individuals within States that are settled by judicial decisions—those, namely, to which the existing rules of law can be applied. Differences as to what the law ought to be are no less dangerous to peace than disputes as to the interpretation of the law; but no one would suggest that in modern States the work of legislation could satisfactorily be entrusted to impartial arbitrators.

Moreover, there are actually within States certain questions almost exactly analogous to some international questions which have in the past been particularly liable to lead to war. Those differences which arise within States as to the relations, political and administrative, of groups of individuals to one another are of the same type as the international differences arising from the political and administrative relations of the groups of individuals which we call nations. Such differences are never within States referred to judicial tribunals. No sane man would suggest that the Home Rule question could find a satisfactory solution in a court of arbitration. And the reason is obvious—the interested parties could not possibly feel that it was rational to expect that the settlement would be just, and therefore to accept it. Experience has shown that one can find persons sufficiently unbiased to determine more often truly than untruly whether a thing has or has not happened, and usually to apply justly and correctly

an existing law to admitted or ascertained facts.
But it is absolutely impossible to believe that one
or more distinguished gentlemen chosen at random,
even if they were really open-minded and unbiased, would necessarily arrive at a reasonable and
right decision on the Home Rule question. The
application of arbitration to such questions could
only be justified by the acceptance of chance as the
final arbiter in political affairs; and in that case
it would be more sensible to simplify the procedure
by spinning a coin or by drawing one of the rival
solutions out of a hat.

It follows, that general arbitration treaties which
would bind nations to refer to arbitration all disputes in which negotiation has failed are useless and
dangerous. Sooner or later there will occur under
one of these treaties a case in which arbitration is
essentially not a reasonable method of deciding the
issue, and then either the treaty will be broken or
the decision will not be accepted.* But to say this is
in no sense to belittle the importance of arbitration.
It will have its place, possibly a supremely important place, in the pacific regulation of international society, but it is not a panacea; and, having
recognized this fact, the wise man will pass on to the
consideration of a further practical question—the
possibility of defining those differences and dis-

---

* There are, of course, in existence such treaties—*e. g*., the Convention
of 1905, between Italy and Denmark, and the Convention of 1907, between
the five Central American States, but they have not yet stood the test
of time. The ordinary treaties, of which so many have been concluded
since the first Hague Conference, by excepting questions of honor and
vital interest, really make arbitration optional in all cases.

putes which it would be practicable and reasonable for nations to bind themselves always to refer to a judicial tribunal.

This question has, of course, received considerable attention, not only theoretically, but practically, at the Hague Conference, and in successful and unsuccessful attempts to negotiate arbitration treaties. But the failure of the Committee at the second Conference shows that up to the present no solution has been found. This result can, I think, be shown to be due to the fact that diplomatists, into whose hands these things are surrendered, have persistently approached the question from two wrong angles. In the first place, they have invented the legend that the importance of certain disputes makes them unsuitable for judicial settlement. The statement is made either that people will not, or that they cannot, accept arbitration in cases affecting vital interests or honor. The facts prove that this statement is quite untrue. The importance of the question has nothing to do with the willingness to accept arbitration. The past has shown that nations can, and will, accept judicial decisions in questions affecting honor and vital interests provided that: (1) A rational and suitable judicial procedure exists; and (2) the question can be put to the tribunal in a legal form. This is proved by the arbitrations already referred to in the footnote on page 69, and still more so by the Dogger Bank Commission of Inquiry. There will never be a case in which national honor is more dangerously and vitally affected than it was in the Dogger Bank incident. The danger lay in the fact that the honor of the Russian Fleet was in question when Lord Lansdowne demanded apology, compensation, and the punishment of offending officers. War, as usual in such cases, "appeared to be inevitable." But it so happened that five years before there had been invented at the first Hague Conference a Procedure by International Commission of Inquiry which enabled this Dogger Bank question to be put to a tribunal in a judicial form. The diplomatists who invented that Procedure were, of course, careful to see that the Convention recommended its adoption only "in the differences of an international nature *involving neither honor nor vital interests*," and yet the very first time it was used "honor" was most acutely involved. The Convention had laid it down that Commissions were "to facilitate a solution of these differences by elucidating the facts," and the Dogger Bank Commission was directed "to make inquiry and draw up a report . . . particularly upon the question of where the responsibility lies and upon the degree of blame." A difference involving honor was therefore reduced to the common legal and judicial questions of fact, and of the degree of responsibility and blame attaching to different persons for the results of certain actions. And so the inevitable war was avoided.*

* A Commission of Inquiry is technically not arbitration. As Mr. Higgins points out in his book, "The Hague Peace Conferences," the terms of reference to the Dogger Bank Commission were wider than those con-

The truth is that diplomatists have, almost certainly with deliberation, produced a vicious circle by this exclusion of differences involving honor and vital interests. Professedly they are going to make arbitration obligatory in cases to which it applies by defining those cases to which it does not apply. But as each country is the judge whether any particular case does involve honor or vital interests, arbitration becomes in every case optional and not obligatory.

In the second place, at the last Hague Conference a genuine attempt was made in another way to define those differences which it would be practicable and reasonable for nations always to refer to a judicial tribunal. The attempt was unsuccessful, because, instead of covering them by a general definition, based upon the real distinction pointed out above, the diplomatists tried to enumerate the particular differences to which arbitration was applicable. It is true that in one case, the recovery of contract debts, in a roundabout way they did succeed in introducing the principle of obligatory

---

templated in Article 14 of the Convention of 1899. The Convention limited the report of the International Committee to "a statement of facts." The Dogger Bank Commission not only made a statement of the facts in dispute—namely, that no Japanese torpedo boats were present, but delivered judgment as to responsibility and blame—namely (1) that the firing was unjustifiable; (2) that the Commander of the Fleet was responsible; and (3) that the facts were "not of a nature to cast any discredit on the humanity" of Russian officers. It is important to remember that the Commission was composed of five naval officers and two jurists (the latter being assessors without votes); it was therefore an International Court-martial or Court composed of experts. "It is doubtful," writes Sir Frederick Pollock, "whether a formal tribunal of jurists and diplomatists could have handled this delicate affair so well, if at all."

arbitration, and this, it should be noticed, is obviously a "legal" case. But in Committee there were weeks of futile discussion over the subjects proposed by Great Britain. A large majority in the Conference were in favor of making arbitration obligatory in differences concerning the interpretation and application of treaties relative to seven subjects, but even if practical effect had been given to this willingness, it is doubtful whether the cause of peace would have been materially advanced. One imagines that there must have been someone at the Conference possessed of a cultivated sense of irony and cynicism to choose as subjects for obligatory arbitration the interests of indigent sick persons, of the working classes, of dead sailors, of writers and artists. We shall be too near the millennium to need any but a Celestial Authority when the Foreign Offices of the world think sufficiently about the interests of such persons for the Third Secretary of an Embassy even to remember that they exist. Meanwhile it is hardly necessary to take steps to prevent our rulers mobilizing fleets and armies on their behalf. If the interests had been those of capitalists and financiers, syndicates, and concessionnaires, our conclusion might have been different, but the diplomatists at The Hague were silent as regards such persons.

The fact is that diplomatists have attempted by this method to include for arbitration only disputes of no importance, just as by the former they have attempted to exclude all disputes of importance. The one thing that they have never attempted is a general definition of those disputes which could be referred to a judicial tribunal in a legal form—those disputes, in fact, which alone it is reasonable for a nation to bind itself to refer to arbitration. A casual reading of the proceedings of the Hague Conference of 1907 might lead anyone to conclude that this statement is incorrect or exaggerated, but a careful study of those tortuous and tedious labyrinths will prove that it is strictly correct. It is true that the diplomatists and jurists distinguished *questions juridiques* from *questions politiques*, that they meant roughly by *questions juridiques* what I have called legal questions, and that they frequently assumed and asserted the principle that *questions juridiques* were suitable for obligatory arbitration. But their whole vision was distorted by their obsession regarding questions of vital interest and honor. They never seemed quite certain whether they should not identify such questions with their *questions politiques;* but, obviously, if you do make this identification, you mean by *questions juridiques* not questions which are concerned with legal rights and obligations, but simply questions which do not affect vital interest and honor. The result of this fog of diplomacy is very clear in the discussion of the Anglo-American proposal. This proposal starts by declaring that the contracting States agree to submit to arbitration differences *d'ordre juridique* which do not affect vital interests, independence, or honor. It then goes on to enumerate certain differences, *d'ordre juridique,* which States will agree to submit to arbitration without this reserve. Now, clearly, if the differences enumerated are merely examples of legal questions which could not affect honor or vital interests, the enumeration adds nothing to the first clause. Accordingly, the Conference appeared to start by trying to make a list of those legal questions which should be referred to arbitration, even if they did affect honor or vital interests. And yet the diplomatists when they sat down to make the list seemed only to consider as possible of inclusion those questions which could not affect honor or vital interests. The confusion became inextricably confounded, and it is amusing to read, after days and days of discussion, that one diplomatist at length remarked that any question may affect the honor and vital interests of a nation, and another pointed out that you can never tell when a *question juridique* is going to become a *question politique.*

One must repeat, that to make arbitration obligatory is impossible if you try to distinguish questions which do and do not affect honor or vital interest. The distinction is based neither upon fact nor reason. Even a dead sailor or a live artist *may* affect a nation's honor or conceivably even its vital interests. Once this is realized the problem is not really a difficult one. The past has shown that nations will accept arbitration in questions which are simply *d'ordre juridique*—that is to say, where differences can be reduced either to questions of fact or of the rights and obligations of the parties under admitted or ascertained rules of law. Nations went to war over boundary disputes before the nineteenth century, and settled them by arbitration during the nineteenth century, not because such disputes suddenly ceased to affect vital interests, but because it was suddenly realized that boundary disputes can always be reduced to a mixed question of fact and law.

The only way of approaching this problem is to keep before one's mind the analogy of judicial tribunals in States and the analysis of those international differences which have been referred to arbitration. Anyone who does this will, I believe, come to the conclusion that it is possible to define those disputes which could be put to a judicial tribunal in a legal form, and that they actually fall under the following general heads:

1. *Questions of fact.*

This is a most important class and one which clearly can always be settled judicially. Many disputes can be reduced to a question of facts—*i.e.*, both sides admit that if such and such a thing happened, then certain rights and obligations exist; but one side asserts and the other denies that the thing happened. The Dogger Bank Inquiry referred to in detail above is the best example of such a case.

2. *Questions of title to territory and of boundaries.*

These questions are now practically always settled judicially. They are always mixed questions of law and facts of the kind which the civil courts of every nation under the sun are continually deciding. They fall into two clearly marked divisions:

(1) Where the divisional line between two States is admitted or has been agreed upon and a dispute arises as to the actual position of the line at some particular place. These cases are very common and are really settled merely by interpreting agreements or treaties. To take an instance at random, the Costa Rican-Nicaraguan Boundary Dispute was referred to arbitration in 1886. One of the chief points that the arbitrator had to determine was what the Treaty of 1858, which fixed the boundaries, meant by "the centre of Salinas Bay."

(2) Where the divisional line has not been admitted or defined in an agreement or treaty, and the dispute is as to the title to particular pieces of territory. These cases invariably involve questions of interpretation of documents, or of facts, or both. The claims are based upon possession, occupation, usucaption, or prescription, and upon international documents alleged to grant rights over the territory. The Court has merely to interpret such documents and to find whether the fact of possession, occupation, etc., has been proved. To take, again, an example at random: In the Argentine-Paraguayan Boundary dispute, referred to arbitration in 1876, Paraguay claimed title to a piece of territory—

    (i) On first occupation;
    (ii) On uninterrupted possession;

(iii) On a royal decree of 1783;
(iv) On usucaption and prescription.

The Argentine Republic tried unsuccessfully to rebut these claims.

3. *Questions as to the interpretation and application of treaties or International Law, of claims founded on treaties or International Law, or alleged breach of treaties or International Law.*

These are cases in which one side claims a right and another denies an obligation under an existing treaty or International Law. As regards treaties, anyone who thinks that nations ought to be bound by treaties must admit that the best way of settling disputes as to the rights and obligations created by particular treaties is to refer them to a judiciary. Many people, however, who would agree to this would hesitate over International Law. It is often said that it is impossible to ask an International Court to administer International Law, because the Law is based on custom and does not exist. But if law based on custom cannot be interpreted by courts of law, practically every court in Great Britain would have to be shut up to-morrow. Many international laws exist and are ascertainable, and the courts of this country and of the United States have frequently had to take cognizance of them. Many international disputes are concerned simply with the rights and obligations under, or the interpretation of, such laws. For example, the dispute referred to in the last chapter, between Greece and Turkey, settled by the Conference of Paris of 1869, was a case in point. The Conference drew the attention of Greece, as it said, to a "rule of conduct common to all Governments." "The principles of International Law," it was pointed out, "oblige . . . all nations not to allow bands to be recruited on their territory, or ships to arm in her ports, to attack a neighboring State." Clearly the rights and obligations of two States under this law can in any particular case be decided by a judicial tribunal, and they must be so decided if the society of nations is ever going to be governed by general rules of conduct.

4. *Questions as to the responsibility or blame attaching to national agents or representatives for the results of acts of such agents or representatives.*

The Dogger Bank Inquiry alone is sufficient to show that such questions are always capable of being put to a judicial tribunal in a legal form. Another example of importance was the Casa Blanca dispute between France and Germany, which was referred to the Hague Tribunal in 1908.

5. *Questions as to certain kinds of pecuniary claims.*

There are certain definable kinds of international claims which are exactly of the same kind as those which are adjudicated in every civil court. First, there are *claims for pecuniary damages when the principle of indemnity is recognized by the parties.* At the Hague Conference such claims figured on the Anglo-American list of questions upon which arbitration was to be obligatory, and thirty-one States voted for the proposal and only eight against it. Secondly, there are *questions as to the recovery of contract debts claimed from the Government of one country by the Government of another country as being due to its nationals.* Arbitration is in fact already obligatory for differences as to the recovery of such debts.

These five classes are all strictly judicial questions; that is to say, that if they were referred to a tribunal, the court would be required to decide either (1) whether alleged facts were proved to exist or to have existed; or (2) whether certain rights and obligations resulted under particular circumstances from certain contractual documents or general rules of international conduct; or (3) the exact sum of money due from one party to another under a contract or as an indemnity. If, then, nations are to be bound by the contracts into which they enter and by general rules of conduct in the form of law, then it seems both practicable and reasonable that they should bind themselves to submit these five classes of questions to arbitration.

But in the present state of affairs there would be more likelihood of nations actually doing so if an additional safeguard to national interests could be introduced. International Law, it must be admitted, even where it exists, is extremely unsatisfactory and confused on many points. It is doubtful, therefore, whether any nation would be well-advised to bind itself *absolutely* to refer all disputes to a tribunal which would be compelled to decide every issue strictly in accordance with the existing law. Moreover, we come back once more here to the problem of the *status quo*. A judicial tribunal of this sort must by its nature recognize and uphold the existing constitution of the society of nations based upon treaties. It would be essentially that conservative element which we showed to be necessary in every society and which maintains the existing order of things. Nor must we forget that it so happens that it is always our particular interest as a nation to preserve the existing order of things. In the international system Great Britain is naturally in the position which the rich capitalist employer holds in the industrial system. She has usually nothing to gain by a change and therefore thinks that she must lose by it. She is always conservative and therefore in favor of arbitration and a rigid adherence to existing treaties. But that ought not to blind us to the fact that it may be in the interests of other nations and of the world generally that changes should take place, and that, if an arrangement which maintains the existing order of things is essential, an arrangement which makes it possible to upset it in an orderly manner is no less essential.

At the present moment there are only two methods by which the existing order of things can be upset—negotiation and war. It is only obtuseness and lack of imagination on our part if we do not see that no nation, whose interests are not in preserving the *status quo*, will give up the power of going to war and will bind itself absolutely to arbitration unless some other possible method of varying the *status quo* is assured to it. The fact that Germany opposed and Britain supported obligatory arbitration at the Hague Conference does not prove the wickedness of Germany and the pureness of Britain, any more than the refusal of the wage earners to accept the employers' proposals—namely, to give up their weapon, the strike, and bind themselves to arbitrate—proves a moral superiority of the employing over the employed class.

I suggest that, although nations whose interests are not, as ours, bound up with the existing order of things will not accept obligatory arbitration alone, they might agree to refer all "legal" questions falling under the five heads defined above either to a judicial tribunal or to a true international legislative conference. My proposal is that nations shall bind themselves to refer all legal questions, not settled by negotiation, to a judicial tribunal, but that in every case either party to a dispute shall have the right to demand that the question shall be submitted to an international Conference of representatives before it is referred to the judicial tribunal. A nation refusing to accept immediate and direct arbitration would be required to state:

(*a*) Whether it demanded that the Conference should consider and pronounce a decision on the whole question in dispute. If it did so demand, then it would be bound to abide by the decision of the majority of the Conference, and the question would not be remitted to a judiciary; or

(b) Whether it demanded merely that the Conference should consider and decide by a majority vote the rules of law and the international rights and obligations of which the judicial tribunal should take cognizance in deciding the matter in dispute. It is necessary to guard against misunderstanding, and, at the risk of repetition, to insist upon the following points in this suggestion:

(1) It is not a proposal that nations should consent to be bound in all cases either by the decision of a judicial tribunal or by that of a legislating Conference. It proposes that nations should do so *only* in legal cases—i. e., in disputes which can be decided by a consideration of existing law and existing legal rights and obligations.

(2) There is no doubt that in the large majority of such disputes the case would be remitted direct by both parties to a judicial tribunal.

(3) But in a minority of such cases, owing to the unsatisfactory condition of international legislation and the other causes discussed above, it is unreasonable to expect nations to allow the dispute to be settled by a tribunal which can only strictly interpret and apply the law. My proposal would permit a nation in such cases to bring the dispute before an international Conference, which would take into consideration not only what was strictly legal, but what was equitable. Thus the objecting

State might ask the Conference either to lay down the principles of law suitable for the particular circumstances and upon which the tribunal should base its judgment, or to declare how far under the particular circumstances a strict application of the letter of treaties would be equitable. In either of these cases the tribunal would then decide the dispute upon the principles laid down by the Conference. But, further, it would be competent to either nation to demand that the Conference should not only define the principles, but should give a decision in accordance with equity upon the whole dispute, and in this case the two nations would be bound to abide by that decision.

(4) The last point to be noticed is that provision would have to be made for cases in which the question whether the difference was one which fell under one of the five heads given above, and must therefore be referred to a tribunal, was itself in dispute. This, of course, is an example of a question as to the competency or jurisdiction of a court, which continually arises wherever there is a judiciary. Municipal courts frequently have to decide questions as to their own competency, and there seems no reason why an International Court should not be given the power to do the same.

I have now said all that I have to say upon the definite question which I put to myself for discussion at the beginning of this chapter. The answer suggested is that there is a class of international differences and disputes which have now been defined, and which could always be settled by the decision of a judicial tribunal, and that therefore the proper function of arbitration or a judiciary in "some international authority" is exclusively to decide such disputes. There is now a question which does not strictly fall within the limits set for this chapter, but which can hardly be entirely ignored in a discussion of arbitration and international tribunals—namely, the constitution of an International Court.

This problem has achieved great prominence because it was discussed at great length at the Hague Conference, where diplomatists made long and abortive attempts to set up a permanent International Court. The importance of the question has, I believe, been in this way exaggerated; but before proceeding to discuss it, it is advisable to state shortly the facts of which people are not always fully aware. Judicial tribunals to which international disputes have been referred have been constituted in many different ways, being called commissions, commissions of inquiry, or courts of arbitration. They have been composed either of the head of a sovereign State or of one or more distinguished persons, frequently publicists and jurists or, as in the Dogger Bank Commission, of technical experts. The method of choosing the commissioners or arbitrators has always been a matter for negotiation and agreement, and has often been one of considerable difficulty. The first Hague Conference instituted what is called in the convention "the Permanent Court of Arbitration." This tribunal is not strictly a permanent court at all, but a permanent list of arbitrators, appointed by the signatory Powers, from which in any particular case arbitrators and an umpire can be selected to form a court upon rules laid down in the convention. The persons appointed by the signatory Powers are to be persons "of known competency in questions of International Law."

It will be seen that hitherto it has always been necessary to constitute an International Court anew for each particular international dispute. The second Hague Conference attempted, without success, to institute a permanent international judiciary side by side with the existing "Permanent Court of Arbitration." They proposed to call this tribunal "The Judicial Arbitration Court," and they were able to agree so far as to draft a convention regulating its constitution. It was to be a permanent tribunal in the sense that it was to be a court composed of judges, appointed for twelve years, sitting in regular and continuous sessions. But when the Conference came to consider the way in which the judges should be appointed they failed to reach any agreement, and the "Judicial Arbitration Court" exists only in a draft convention. The failure was due almost entirely to the insistence of the smaller States upon their absolute equality as sovereign States with the Great Powers. If a large number of States each appoints a judge, and each judge actually sits for the same length of time, one of two things must happen. Either the court which actually tries cases must be composed of so large a number of judges that it will be impossibly unwieldy, or the duty of trying cases must be taken by the judges in rotation, and in this case each judge will be called upon only at very long intervals to take his part in the administration of International Law. It is hardly to be wondered at if the Great Powers hesitate to constitute a permanent international judiciary, of which the actual court might more often than not consist of judges appointed by the States of Central and South America, Asia, and the Balkans.*

With these facts in mind it is possible to form some opinion as to the importance of constituting a permanent official international judiciary. One may begin by adopting, in a somewhat altered form, a statement of Mr. Baty's in his book on International Law. Our aim should be, he says, "arbitration which is obligatory in principle and voluntary in detail"; and he apparently advocates treaties which would bind nations in principle to accept arbitration in all cases, but would in every case leave open the settlement of the constitution of the arbitral body. We have given reasons for doubting the wisdom of nations binding them-

---

* It must be remembered that the States of Central and South America, Asia, and the Balkans were together in a large majority at the Second Peace Conference over the eight Great Powers *plus* the smaller European States. If one adds Honduras and Costa Rica, making at least forty-six sovereign States, Europe, excluding the Balkans, together with Japan and the United States provide eighteen, while Central and South America provide twenty, the Balkans and Asia eight. And then there are Abyssinia and Liberia, who might claim inclusion!

selves to accept arbitration in all cases, even in principle, and therefore we will alter Mr. Baty's statement, and say: "In principle the reference of a defined class of international disputes to a judicial tribunal should be obligatory, in detail it should as far as possible be voluntary." Many different kinds of international tribunal have already proved their worth, and there is every reason to believe that they will do so again in the future. The art of administering and interpreting International Law has only just been born, and we know so little about it that by trying to confine it to rigid lines we may easily kill it in infancy. We should aim, therefore, at making reference to a tribunal obligatory and choice of a tribunal voluntary.

But there comes a point at which the choice itself cannot be left voluntary, and that is the point at which the parties fail to agree upon the kind of tribunal to choose. For if failure to agree as to the tribunal is to make arbitration * impossible, then arbitration is obligatory neither in detail, nor in principle, nor in fact. The first necessity is, therefore, to give States the greatest possible latitude in choosing the tribunal before which they will bring legal disputes, and to provide a particular tribunal, of easy access, before which such disputes *must* be brought if the disputing States cannot agree to choose a tribunal. It is only in this way possible to make the refer-

---

* By arbitration in this and the following paragraphs I mean the decision of international disputes by a judicial body.

ence of certain disputes to arbitration smooth, automatic and indisputable, and at the same time to ensure to nations the widest freedom of choice in details.

It follows that on this view the primary importance of a central international tribunal is of a somewhat limited nature. All we want is that there should be *a* court to which, under certain circumstances, disputes can be easily referred. Our point of view is radically different from many of the diplomatists at the Hague Conference. Some of them envisaged the creation of two courts—the existing Hague Tribunal, which would decide *questions politiques*, and the new "Judicial Arbitration Court," which would decide *questions juridiques*. We are concerned only with *questions juridiques* and only with the problem of making arbitration in such questions really obligatory. Again, our view is essentially different from those whose object was to lure nations into a law court by building one. We do not aim at spreading the practice of arbitration by establishing an imposing permanent tribunal, but to make an agreement to arbitrate operative by providing a court in which that agreement can be carried out.

Our view of "some international authority" does imply the existence of an official permanent judiciary. Does the existing Hague Tribunal meet the necessities of the case? In a sense there can be no doubt that it does meet the bare necessities. Sixteen years have proved that it is possible to constitute a Hague Court competent to deal with important international disputes of a legal nature. An adequate procedure has been elaborated and laid down, and a workable system of selecting the judges or arbitrators. If the principle of obligatory arbitration of *questions juridiques* were admitted, all that we should require would be that nations should bind themselves to refer such questions to the Hague Tribunal in the event of their failing to agree upon any other tribunal to which it should be referred.

But though the non-existence of a tribunal, permanent in the sense in which the Judicial Arbitration Court would have been permanent, is not an absolute obstacle to obligatory arbitration, it is true that the existing tribunal is far from being completely satisfactory. It does not, for instance, make a reference to arbitration "automatic" or even "easy." As the Report of the First Committee of the Second Peace Conference says, quoting M. Asser, "Il est difficile, long, et couteux de la mattre en mouvement." This is obviously a grave defect in the Central International Judiciary, and it is a defect inherent in any tribunal which has to be constituted anew for every case brought before it. Moreover, there is no doubt that it is only by interpretation in a permanent tribunal with a tradition of continuity that a logical evolution of International Law will become possible. It is therefore extremely desirable, though not absolutely necessary, that the **problem over** which the Hague Conference failed should be solved, and that a tribunal of the nature of their Judicial Arbitration Court should be established.

It is clear that it is not possible—nor, one may add, reasonable—to establish it if between forty and fifty States are to have the right of appointing judges, and each State is to claim absolute equality as regards the right of appointment. And yet it does appear to be inevitable that the Central Judiciary of the International Authority should be composed of judges appointed by the constituent nations. It follows, that either the smaller States will have to be left out of the International Authority, or they must give up in some respects their claim to the complete equality of all independent sovereign States. For the small States to stand out of the International Authority would lead inevitably to an absolute world-hegemony of the Great Powers—a result which would be good neither for the morals of the Great Powers nor for the interests of the Small. The independence of weak States is in perpetual jeopardy as long as arms remain the constant arbiter in international affairs; it will receive an amazing increase of security if there can be established any pacific method of regulating those affairs. Nothing, therefore, could be more blindly foolish than for such States to stand in the way of, or outside, an international system because of some semi-technical, wholly unreasonable shibboleth of national honor or national sovereignty.

What is required, then, in the Central Judiciary

is a permanent court composed of a small number of jurist judges appointed by the constituent States for a long term of years. There are several good schemes in existence, any one of which would probably have been accepted by the Powers at The Hague if it had not been for the action of the small American States. The systems on which these different schemes would work may be distinguished as follows:

1. *The scheme recommended by the Sub-Committee of the Conference.*

A court of seventeen judges organized for a definite term of years. One judge nominated by each of the eight Great Powers to act as judge for the whole period. One judge nominated by each of the other Powers to act for parts of that period, varying in proportion to the population, etc., of each Power.

2. Each Great Power to nominate one judge. Nine other Powers to be selected by the Conference as representing all parts of the world and with the power of each nominating one judge. The Court to consist therefore of seventeen judges.

3. America as a unit to select four judges, the remaining nations to elect thirteen.

4. Various schemes of election of a small number of judges, each nation having one vote.

Of these schemes, No. 1 has two advantages: It gives each Power the right of appointing a judge, and it yet provides that the judges appointed by the Great Powers sit continuously. On the other hand, it suffers from a disadvantage in that a large

PREVENTION OF WAR

number of judges will be continually changing if there are many small constituent Powers. This disadvantage is very clearly seen in the scheme actually adopted by the signatory Powers to the Convention relative to the establishment of an International Prize Court. The Court is composed of fifteen judges, appointed for six years. The judges appointed by the eight Great Powers always sit, while the judges and deputy judges appointed by the other Powers sit by rota. The rota is given in an elaborate table annexed to the convention—for each year of the period of six years the nations supplying the seven judges and seven deputy judges are enumerated, and an analysis gives the following results:

One nation supplies a judge for four years and a deputy judge for four years.

One nation supplies a judge for three years and a deputy judge for three years.

Nine nations supply a judge for two years and a deputy judge for two years.

Three nations supply a judge for one year and a deputy judge for one year.

Four nations supply a judge for two years.

Six nations supply a judge for one year.

Fourteen nations supply a deputy judge for one year.

Scheme No. 2 gives a very permanent tribunal and ensures that the Great Powers are represented, but one has some doubts as to the feasibility of selecting nine States to represent the rest of the world in appointing judges. Nos. 3 and 4 both give us permanent tribunals, but they have this defect, that the small nations have an overwhelming voice in the constitution of the court, and therefore it is possible, if not probable, that it will be largely or wholly composed of jurists from small States. Nobody could, of course, legitimately object to citizens of Haiti, Siam, Paraguay and Panama forming the International Judiciary if they were persons of commanding judicial ability and legal eminence, but one may legitimately doubt whether such persons will be found as easily in those countries as in Germany, France, and the United States.

On the whole, it may be said that No. 1 is the most attractive of these schemes. But a still simpler system might be adopted combining parts of these four schemes. Thus, if the tribunal is to be composed of seventeen judges, eight would be appointed by the eight Great Powers, and nine would be elected by the other States from persons nominated by those States. A judge appointed or nominated by a nation would be debarred from sitting as judge upon any case in which that nation was a party. In this way the International Authority would obtain a permanent tribunal, composed of men best able throughout the world to interpret and apply a great system of International Law, "a court of law" (to quote America's representative at the second Conference) "for the trial of legal questions—questions involving the interpretation of treaties, questions which judges and lawyers are best able to decide." And there is no reason why the existing Hague Court should not go on existing side by side with this more permanent tribunal. Nothing should be done to restrict the choice of tribunal to which nations are to refer questions in dispute; and if States prefer a court in which judges are appointed by the parties themselves to try a particular case, the Permanent Court of Arbitration provides them with an easy method of giving effect to this preference.

CHAPTER VII

AN INTERNATIONAL AUTHORITY

THE point has now been reached at which it is necessary to pause and look back from it to our starting point in order to see how far—if at all—we have made progress to the goal. The starting point was the past, the goal an International Authority or organization, no longer qualified by that shadowy "some," but defined and solidified by dull facts gathered out of the past. The facts and conclusions which I have ventured to pick up from the roadside as useful for this purpose may be summarized as follows:

(1) A vague protoplasmic International Authority has made its appearance in the nineteenth century, a primitive organism with two rudimentary organs, one consisting of judicial tribunals and the other of Conferences of representatives.

(2) The judicial tribunals are capable of development into a regular organ of an International Authority. Their function is to decide international questions which can be reduced to a legal form, and such questions are capable of definition, and have been defined. International organization must begin with machinery through which the obligation to refer all such questions to a tribunal

(or alternatively under certain circumstances to a Conference) can be carried into effect.

(3) The past indicates the Conference of representatives as the most fitting organ for dealing with questions which cannot be reduced to a legal form. Its development must proceed by an extension of the principle which denies the right of any one nation, and asserts the right of the nations collectively, to settle such international questions when negotiation has failed and the only alternative is war. The extension of this principle raises problems, discussed and left unsolved in Chapter V, which will again have to be considered in this chapter.

(4) The past also indicates the Conference as the proper organ for performing the most important function of making, with authority and precision, general rules of international conduct or laws. The development of this function is attended with difficulties very similar to those referred to in the last paragraph.

It will be seen that these suggestions and facts have not brought us very near an International Authority or even an international organization. We have followed the footsteps of history, and the great lesson of the past is that diplomacy has not attempted any organization in the methods of settling international affairs. In almost every other branch of human activities—in national and municipal government, in industry and commerce and finance, in science and medicine, even in sport and games—the whole progress in modern times has been bound up with an enormous elaboration of parts and functions, an intricate machinery, and a conscious co-ordination of the parts of the machine. The relationships of States have no more escaped this elaborate complication than have the factory and the football field; but the diplomatist, unlike the manufacturer and the footballer, has not attempted to control this complication by co-ordinating the different parts of his machine. He has his various methods of regulating the relationships of States—negotiation, mediation, arbitration, Conference—but he has never co-ordinated them. There is no doubt that this has been a very serious obstacle to the pacific settlement of international questions. The most obvious result is, of course, that in times of sudden and acute dispute the difficulty even of getting his machinery to work is insuperable. When the ordinary methods of negotiation have suddenly ended in a deadlock, the diplomatist does not find in the co-ordinated international machinery any lever to pull in order to set in motion a mediator, a tribunal, or a Conference. He has to begin all over again negotiating by the ordinary methods as to whether mediation, or arbitration, or a Conference shall be set in motion. The machinery of peace itself becomes merely a counter in the diplomatic game; and, while Sir Edward Grey is proposing mediations and Conferences, the co-ordinated machinery of war is getting smoothly and automatically to work.*

---

* See the grimly illuminating passage in the telegram of the Austrian Ambassador at Petrograd to Count Berchtold (in the Austro-Hungarian

And it is worthy of remark that this system, or want of system, has a further and less obvious result. It is difficult to know exactly what the ordinary business is which takes place daily behind the mysterious doors of Foreign Offices and Chancelleries, but there is reason for believing that a very large number of international questions are raised but never settled by negotiation, and they remain, therefore, a constant source of official and a recurring source of popular irritation. Diplomatists themselves may be left to describe the actual state of affairs in their own words. The following is a quotation from the official report of the discussion at the second Hague Conference upon the proposal that the Cour de Justice Arbitrale should be permanent, and that the judges should reside at The Hague: "L'on ajouta q'une residence continue à La Haye serait aussi incommode pour les juges que peu favorable à la dignité de la Cour si dans les premiers mois ou les premières années de son existence peu ou point de causes lui étaient soumises. Mr. Choate et le Baron Marschall répondaient à cela que *les Chancelleries étaient encombrées d'affaires litigieuses qui attendent un réglement definitif et qu'une fois la Cour établie les puissances signataires s'empresseraient de les leur soumettre.*"

Red Book, No. 28, July 26, 1914): "Count Pourtalès has called the Russian Minister's attention in the most serious manner to the fact that nowadays measures of mobilization would be a highly dangerous form of diplomatic pressure. For, in that event, the purely military consideration of the question by the general staffs would find expression, and if that button were once touched in Germany, the situation would get out of control."

A deliberate co-ordination of the machinery of international relationship is therefore absolutely essential as a first step towards preventing war. It is in fact the A, B, C of international organization, the framework about which an International Authority can be built. Organization is preliminary to the constitution of an authority, and if it is to proceed along the lines indicated by the past, it must consist in the construction of a regular procedure under which the several kinds of international disputes can be necessarily referred either to a tribunal or to a Conference.

The simplest way of approaching the question is to begin with the minimum of organization possible and see what an extension of it would involve. At the last Hague Conference there were 44 sovereign States represented. If one adds to these Honduras, Costa Rica, Abyssinia, and Liberia (which did not send representatives), one gets a total of 48 independent sovereign States in the world. These 48 States might agree: (1) To set up a judicial tribunal on the lines indicated; (2) to refer all questions falling within the five classes defined as legal questions to a tribunal agreed upon by the parties or to the central tribunal (or alternatively under particular circumstances to a Conference); (3) to refer all other questions and differences for examination and report to a Conference.

This is, it will be seen, the least possible amount of organization of international machinery on past lines that can be conceived. But if it came into existence there would still be no International Authority. Each isolated State would simply be bound by a bare agreement with all the other States to follow a certain method of procedure. It is possible that even a primitive and simple organization like this might be a great advance towards the prevention of war, but it is obvious that it is a very fragile bond which in this way would be tied between nations. The very word "authority" implies something more than this— some right and power of the organization, as a whole, over the individuals which form its parts. An International Authority implies, therefore, some rights and power in the nations collectively over the individual nations which are the constituents of the authority.

We come back, then, from a different angle to those difficulties which were left unsolved in Chapter V; for if the future is to develop logically from the past, the central point in the international organization and authority will be the Conference. That means that the abstract conclusion arrived at in the last paragraph appears here as the particular and practical problems: "What shall be the competency of an International Conference? What rights can be given to the nations to settle questions and to make rules collectively in such Conferences? And what powers shall be given to the nations collectively to enforce the rights and the decisions of their Conferences?"

Before proceeding to reconsider these problems in detail, it is necessary to point out a fact which may appear to some people an abstract and irritating quibble, but which, I believe, is for all that of importance. A right, and the power to enforce that right, and the right to exercise power to enforce that right, are three entirely different things. Thus, an international organization might be constructed merely by States admitting the right of the nations to settle collectively by decisions in Conferences certain questions. That is one stage towards an International Authority. A second stage comes when the nations not only have the right to decide questions collectively, but the power to enforce their decision; and a third stage when nations not only have this right and this power, but also the right to exercise collectively the power to enforce collective decisions. The importance of the distinction becomes apparent when one considers what have been called "sanctions." It may be necessary or politic to constitute an International Authority with rights over the individual constituent nations and yet without any sanctions. And one may go still further and say that there is no reason why an International Authority should be in this respect uniform in all its parts. It may be politic to give an International Conference the right both to decide certain questions and to enforce its decisions, while in other classes of questions it may be necessary to give the right to decide and to withhold the right to enforce the decision.

If we return to the problem as we left it in Chapter V, it will be remembered that the question was whether Conferences could be transformed into Legislatures, and whether the rights of a majority to bind a minority in an International Conference can be admitted and defined. It is clear that our answer to these questions must to some extent depend upon our conception of the constitution of an International Authority. Many people at the present time seem to think that there is no half-way house between a federation into a world-State and the existing splendid isolation of independent States. If this is true, our alternatives are Utopia and chaos, and it is impossible to say which is the more unsatisfactory. For however attractive a world-State may be to our imaginations, a little reflection, aided by the sobering study of protocols, blue books and white papers, will show that in the world of actual facts there is no ground prepared for the reception of so strange a plant.

A federation of the world, or a federation of Europe, implies the construction of an International State—a Bundesstaat. It would be necessary strictly and accurately to define the respective spheres of Federal and State government. The model for the International State would be the German Empire or the United States of America. The International Conference would be transformed into a true International Parliament, in which sat, not the representatives of independent States, but the representatives of the peoples of those States. In this way we easily solve the question of the right of the majority to bind the minority, because the sphere of the federal body would be strictly defined, and within that sphere the majority of representatives would, *ex hypothesi*, bind the minority.

Unfortunately, it is only a writer of imaginative fiction who, with a wave of his pen and a row of dots across the page, can transport us from a world of Hague Conferences and Great Wars direct into a World Set Free. Before you get the nations of the world to enter into this International State, and before you set up this Parliament of Nations, you have got to solve those two difficulties of Chapter V in their most insoluble form—the difficulty of diverse national systems and ideals, and the difficulty of accurately defining the spheres of national and international government. The time for seriously considering an International Federal State will have arrived only when someone provides a draft constitution in which one can see legally defined the parts of their affairs which the British, and Persian, and American, and Chinese peoples are to be called upon to place in the hands of the federal body. And the person who succeeds in doing this will have to go on to show that there is any possibility of two nations with such different institutions and ideals as, say, Persia and Britain, uniting in so close a union as is implied in a Federal State.

One is therefore forced to the conclusion that an International Federal State—a Bundesstaat—is Utopian, and that an International Authority, if it can be constituted at all, must take the form of a

Staatenbund, a federation of States. There follows, too, the very important consequence that the representatives in the central organ of that authority will be representatives of independent sovereign States and not of the people of those States. His Excellency the Right Honorable Sir Edward Fry, G.C.B., and His Excellency Samad Khan Momtazos-Saltaneh could sit together at The Hague Conference, despite the difference between Teheran and London, between the weald of Sussex and the plains of Persia, simply because each of them came there as the representative of a single independent State, or rather of the Government of that State. This is possible because the *Governments* of all States are sufficiently homogeneous, even though the head of the one Government may derive his authority from the Sun, a second from an Act of Parliament, and a third from Jehovah or the Blessed Trinity. All that is necessary is that the State should have *a* Government. But, if the people are to be represented, there must be some homogeneity of ideals and institutions among the peoples. There must, for example, be a uniform system of choosing or electing representatives, and this implies a homogeneity which does not exist between the free American citizen and the Russian peasant, to say nothing of Persian tribesmen and the unintelligible millions of Chinamen.

Purely, therefore, for practical reasons, one must conclude that representatives in the Conference of the future must be, as they have been in the past, representatives of the Governments of different States. And the method of choosing and appointing such representatives must be left in each case to the State itself. We shall never get a State like Russia to come into an international system at all if we try to make it a condition of entrance that she adopt the institutions of democracy; and, therefore, though we may have (as I have) the profoundest belief in democratic control of foreign policy, it would be absurd to attempt to introduce that principle into the international organization itself. In our own State we should insist upon democratic control, and we should take the steps necessary to make, not only the Government, but its international representatives and diplomatists, the responsible servants of the people instead of irresponsible servants of little classes and castes. But we have not yet shown that we are sufficiently democratic to send Mr. Bernard Shaw or even Mr. Ramsay Macdonald as representatives of the British Empire to an International Conference, so that we hardly have the right to object to his Excellency Samad Khan Momtazos-Saltaneh.

The representatives at International Conferences must, then, remain representatives of the Governments of independent States. Now, this fact is commonly assumed by diplomatists to have consequences which, if true, would inevitably cut at the root of any development of Conferences into true International Legislatures. In such a Conference, it is argued, a majority can in no circumstances bind a minority, and a decision can only be arrived at if the Conference is unanimous; and this principle is not a mere matter of form or agreement, but is a kind of natural law of international relationship. But if one examines the reasons with which diplomatists support this view, one finds that it is really founded upon confusion of thought. The clearest expression of the theory is given in a speech by the President of the second Hague Conference at a meeting of one of the committees: "The first principle," he said, "of every Conference is that of unanimity; it is not an empty form, but the basis of every political understanding (*toute entente politique*). In Parliaments, majorities can impose their will upon minorities, because the members of those assemblies each represent only one and the same nation; but in an International Conference each delegation represents a different State of equal sovereignty. No delegation has the right to accept a decision of the majority which would be contrary to the will of its Government." It will be seen that M. Nelidow's reasoning is vague and confused. In the first place, the members of a Parliament do not represent one and the same nation, but parts of, or parts of the people of a State. There is no more reason why Northumberland should allow Lancashire and Middlesex to impose their will upon it than why Belgium should allow Germany and England to impose their will upon it. Northumberland sends a representative to Parliament on the understanding that the majority of representatives can bind the minority. The Government of Belgium might similarly send a representative to an International Conference on the understanding that the decision of a majority of the representatives will be binding on the minority. Such an understanding or agreement in no way destroys the independence or the sovereignty of Belgium. It is only an agreement which limits the freedom of action of the State of Belgium. M. Nelidow's argument would mean that any agreement or treaty limiting the future freedom of action of a State destroyed the independence or sovereignty of the State, which is absurd. When a State signs an arbitration treaty it agrees to accept the Court's decision, which may or may not be contrary to the will of its Government, and it still remains an independent sovereign State. Similarly, a State can sign a treaty by which it will agree to accept the decision of a majority of representatives in an International Conference, even though such decision be contrary to the will of its Government, and it, too, will still remain an independent sovereign State. M. Nelidow's confusion arises from the fact that he regards the delegation as accepting a decision contrary to the will of its Government. But it is not the delegation which accepts the decision at all; it is the Government itself, which sends the delegation, having agreed to accept the decision of a majority of the delegates. While, therefore, agreeing that the delegations at International Conferences must represent the Governments of States, one need not accept the conclusion that the States cannot agree to be bound by the decisions of a majority of the delegations. The question is, in what cases is it practicable and reasonable for States to agree to be bound? Chapter V showed that it is impossible, in an at-present imperfect and unequal world, to expect nations to bind themselves generally to accept the decision of an International Legislature, and also that it is not possible to draw a broad line between international and national questions. It is therefore necessary to approach the problem from a different direction.

If one studies carefully the words of people who raise objections to universal arbitration and other universal methods of pacific settlement, one finds that their real and ultimate objection is that by submitting to such methods States will lose their two most precious jewels—independence and sovereignty. Now, independence and sovereignty, though they are not easy to define, are very real things. They are not only the theme of publicists and diplomatists, but are closely connected with the springs of that dangerous and complex passion called patriotism. The existing international system of the world is founded upon the theoretical sacredness of the independence and the sovereignty of independent and sovereign States. That is why, in my search for an International Authority, I have assumed that the constituents of that authority will be independent sovereign States. It is certain that to-day, in this demi-civilized world, no State will agree to come into an international system unless its independence and sovereignty are safeguarded; but—and this is the important point—it is just as certain that no one would object to his country entering such a system provided that he was absolutely convinced that its independence and sovereignty could not thereby be impaired.

We have, in fact, reached in these characteristics those fundamental things which to-day convert 48 mixed and mongrel populations into 48 distinct nations. Translated into emotions, or the objects of emotions, they become the stuff out of which springs the flame of patriotism. August, 1914, showed clearly that modern Europe could not be made to fight at all unless it was made to believe in every hill and valley of it that it was fighting for national existence. And national existence is only the politician's or the journalist's *cliché* answering to the lawyer's independence and sovereignty.

Again, there can be no doubt that, with some vague idea that they are protecting these characteristics of States, diplomatists have inserted the "vital interests and honor" clause in arbitration treaties. "If we look closely," writes Sir Thomas Barclay,* "into the meaning of a vital interest, we can only find, as typical instances, cases in which the independence of the State itself, its own territorial integrity, or a deliberate breach in the established usage of nations of fundamental importance are involved." And later he gives the still more explicit and comprehensive definition:

---

* "The Problems of International Practice and Diplomacy."

"A State's territorial independence or integrity, its freedom to determine its own mode of government, legislation and institutions, its power to receive political refugees from other countries, its right to grant absolute freedom of thought, and of its expression as regards matters beyond its boundaries, etc." He therefore makes the very valuable and interesting suggestion that, instead of the clause reserving matters of vital interest and honor, there should be inserted in arbitration treaties a clause reserving matters affecting "the independence," "territorial integrity," and "the internal laws and institutions" of the contracting States.

Now, under the system of obligatory arbitration recommended in Chapter VI such a reservation is unnecessary. A reference to a tribunal is only obligatory where the international dispute can be decided by interpreting an international contract or law. The whole of International Law has been built up about the principles of independence, integrity, and sovereignty of States. They are, therefore, absolutely protected by the judicial system itself, provided that it is strictly limited to the questions defined in Chapter VI. For instance, we feel impelled to protect the territorial integrity of our State, and we mean by that the integrity of the territory which legally belongs to our State. A tribunal which can only take cognizance of the law must protect, and cannot impair, this territorial integrity. It is only by extra-legal means, such as the arbitrament of arms, that an Alsace-Lorraine can be lost or gained.

But, though this is true of our judicial tribunal, it is not true of an International Legislature. The International Conference, with its right to decide in non-legal questions, does not interpret, it makes International Law. If its competence and scope were unlimited, independence and territory and the mysterious sovereignty of nations might theoretically be lost in the council chamber, just as in the past they have been lost upon the battlefield. Here, then, for the present, we can draw the true and the rational line between nationalism and internationalism. Every independent sovereign State must affirm the right of the nations collectively to settle questions and to make law, except in three cases; and every such State can send its delegation to a Conference at which the majority shall bind the minority, except in three cases. Those three cases are: Where the law or the decision would affect the independence, or the territorial integrity of the State, or would require an alteration in the internal laws of the State.

And now it is possible to see how the Conference can develop logically and at the same time, without cutting across the passions and prejudices of human beings, into a real organ of an International Authority. These occasional and tentative assemblies of national representatives must become regular and permanent. They will have the right and the power to make general rules of international conduct, and to consider and pronounce decisions upon all differences and disputes which are not referred to a judicial tribunal. The rule that every dispute in which negotiation has failed must come before either a tribunal or a Conference will be the pivot of the international system, and this co-ordination of machinery will be the foundation of international organization. But, since the units of the International Authority are independent sovereign States, they alone are masters, and must retain that mastership of their own independence and sovereignty. They can, therefore, without fear of endangering their "vital interests" or "national honor," agree to be bound by the decisions of such Conferences, and to maintain the right of the majority to bind the minority only where the decision would not affect the independence, or territorial integrity, or would not require an alteration in the internal laws of the State.

"And what about those sanctions?" the publicist will most undoubtedly be asking. This unpleasant and inappropriate word has a peculiar fascination for him. The whole question of sanctions is of theoretical rather than practical interest. Where there is power to enforce a right or an obligation, little in practice is gained by a formal declaration of the right to exercise the power. If the International Authority, the Society of Nations, has the power to compel a member to comply with its obligations, and if it has the will to do so, a way in which to exercise the power will be found. The important point is that the rights should be clearly defined and the obligations explicitly acknowledged. Now, one can set down as follows the international rights and obligations which would be defined and acknowledged under the proposed system:

(1) The obligation to refer all disputes and differences not settled by negotiation either to a tribunal or to a Conference.

(2) The obligation in certain defined disputes and differences,* referred to a Conference, to accept and abide by the decision of the majority of the representatives.

(3) The obligation to accept and abide by the judgment of a tribunal.

(4) The obligation of a State to abide by every general rule of law and every decision made by a Conference and agreed to or ratified by that State.

(5) The obligation to abide by certain defined general rules of law* made by a majority of the representatives in a Conference.

It might no doubt prove to be an amusing task to devise methods of putting into the hands of the International Authority the power of compelling its members to comply with these obligations. It would be quite possible upon paper to build up your divisions or squadrons of an armed international force without going quite as far as the gentleman who has already proposed an international fleet with its base on the West Coast of Africa and its general staff upon the land-locked lakes of Switzerland. But it is hardly practical,

---

* *I. e.*, those which would not affect the independence, or the territorial integrity, or which would not require an alteration in the internal laws of a State.

in the present condition of the world, to discuss the possibility of anything like a permanent international police force. The only practical question is whether, given these obligations, the States of the world can agree beforehand upon the methods to be adopted to enforce compliance with them. Those methods may be of two kinds: They may consist in a use of the combined military and naval forces of individual States, or in those measures which are adopted in wars between States of bringing economic and social pressure to bear upon the population of States. Now, clearly, in every particular case it would depend among other things upon the nature of the obligation broken whether it was possible or politic to use this or that method of enforcing it. We are a very long way from the time when it will be possible to draw up beforehand a list of pains and penalties for all imaginable international delinquencies. We are only just feeling about for an International Authority, and all that we can hope for at this stage is that the nations will agree upon and declare what methods the Authority has the right to use in order to enforce those fundamental obligations upon which this system of international society rests.

The five obligations given above are the fundamental obligations upon which the International Authority outlined in this chapter would rest. But one has only to read them to see that they are not all equally important, so far as the preservation of the peace of the world is concerned. A nation might, therefore, reasonably agree to declare the right of the Authority to use force in order to enforce compliance with, say, the first, the third, and the fourth obligations, but refuse to do so in the case of the second and the fifth. These are, in fact, questions of detail, and can only really be settled when the representatives of Siam and Haiti are once again sitting face to face about the Conference table with the representatives of such other States as the present system of regulating international affairs shall have left in existence. There is, however, one right so fundamental that, unless it is affirmed and enforced, one may conclude beforehand that the international organization will accomplish nothing towards preventing war. That right is the right of the nations to insist upon the use of the pacific machinery of international organization before any warlike operation or preparation by any individual State. Thus our International Authority will vanish into the thin air of theory or Utopia, unless the nations which compose it are agreed to enforce, and actually enforce, by every means in their power the obligation of each individual State to refer a dispute or difference to tribunal or Conference before resorting to force of arms.

There remains one other question to trouble anyone who is considering as a practical problem of to-day the construction of some International Authority. It is the problem, already touched upon in Chapter VI, of the inequality of equal independent sovereign States. In the society of States, one has at one end the British Empire, with a population of 435,000,000 and an area of 13,-000,000 square miles; at the other, Luxemburg, with a population of 260,000 and an area of 1,000 square miles. And yet in that society and in its most fully developed organ of the past, the Hague Conference, "none is afore or after other; none is greater or less than another." The practical result of insisting upon this mystic equality of things radically unequal, of trying to make thousands balance millions in the international scales, has already been noticed. It made a fair representation of international interests impossible, and therefore a reasonable settlement of any question in which those interests were really involved became equally impossible.

But the difficulty becomes far more obvious in any system or organization in which the principle of a majority binding a minority is recognized. The eight Great Powers at an International Conference speak for, roughly, three-quarters of the inhabitants of the world. If the principle of the absolute equality of independent States, set up by the smaller nations at The Hague, were applied to a Conference in which the rights of a majority to bind a minority were admitted, then one-quarter of the earth will be given five times greater voting power than the other three-quarters. Such a system is, on the face of it, an absurdity, and anyone, by the exercise of a little common sense, will see that the United States of America, for instance, will never submit its interests to a body in which its voting power is no greater than that of any of the other twenty States of the American Continent. And it is not, of course, mere size or power that has to be considered, but the whole network of individaul and racial qualities from which spring the political, commercial and artistic activities of nations. States undoubtedly do stand upon different levels of civilization, however much we may disagree as to which are the high and which the low levels. The French Republic moves and troubles the world more, impinges more upon its surface, and stirs its depths more deeply than that Republic in the West of which José Bordas is President, or even than that other in the East with its four hundred millions ruled over by President Yuan Shih-Kai. It will continue to do so as long as a Frenchman remains a Frenchman, a Dominican a Dominican, and a Chinaman a Chinaman. It is through not recognizing and providing for such hard, unchangeable facts that a stable international society becomes impossible, for you can no more expel nature by a diplomatic or legal fiction than by a fork.

If, then, the world is ever to organize itself for the peaceful regulation of international affairs, that organization must provide for the essential inequality of States. If such inequality is not reflected in the pacific machinery, it will make itself felt in war, while the machinery will be left to rust unused. Common sense, which is always practical and conservative, will say at once: "Yes, and that's why you'll never be able to do without war. You'll never in practice be able to weight

France against Dominica, China against Luxemburg, and draw up a table of international weights with a voting power assigned to each State according to its weight in international society." The answer to this objection is that, as a matter of fact, such a table has already been drawn up, not by a theorist in his study, but by "practical" diplomatists themselves at the Hague Conference. The table was constructed for the purpose of giving inequality of representation upon the International Prize Court, the representation being proportioned to the population, commerce, maritime interests, etc., of the various States. The differences are therefore not assigned as differences of voting power, because the question of voting power did not arise; but it is possible, and may be of interest, to show how the differences of representation assigned by the diplomatists to the States of the world can be translated into differences of voting power. It is not suggested that the table is, as it stands, suitable for the purposes of an International Legislature, because where the question was the constitution, not of a Conference, but a Prize Court, a special weight was given to particular characteristics of States—*e. g.*, maritime interests.* It only shows that it is possible to make such a list for practical purposes.

In the Convention relative to the Establishment of an International Prize Court adopted by the Second Hague Conference, the method of consti-

---

* This accounts for the unduly high position in the list of such States as Norway.

tuting the Court is really that recommended by the Committee for the Judicial Arbitration Court, and described briefly in Chapter VI. Its object is to allow representation on the Court to be proportioned to population, commercial interests, etc., of the different States. The judges are appointed for six years. This period of six years is then divided into six periods of one year each. The eight Great Powers are given absolute equality of representation, the judges appointed by them sitting for the whole period of six years. But the judges and deputy judges of the other Powers sit by rota, as shown in an elaborate table annexed to the Convention. Their representation varies from a deputy judge in one of the six periods up to a judge and a deputy judge in four of the six periods.

	Representation on Prize Court.	Equivalent Voting Power.
Austria, the British Empire, France, Germany, Italy, Japan, Russia, the U. S. A.	Whole period.....	18 votes each
Spain	4 judges, 4 deputy judges	12 votes each
The Netherlands	3 judges, 3 deputy judges	9 votes each
Belgium, China, Denmark, Greece, Norway, Portugal, Roumania, Sweden, Turkey	2 judges, 2 deputy judges	6 votes each
Argentine, Brazil, Chile, Mexico	2 judges	4 votes each
Switzerland, Bulgaria, Persia	1 judge, 1 deputy judge	3 votes each
Colombia, Peru, Serbia, Siam, Uruguay, Venezuela.	1 judge	2 votes each
Bolivia, Costa Rica, Cuba, Santo Domingo, Ecuador, Guatemala, Haiti, Honduras, Nicaragua, Panama, Paraguay, Salvador, Luxemburg, Montenegro	1 deputy judge...	1 vote each

Now, if one takes a deputy judge sitting for one of the six periods as the unit of representation power, and a judge sitting for one of the six periods as two units of representation power, it is possible to translate into voting power the variations of representation power assigned to the nations of the world by the diplomatists who framed the Prize Court Convention. The table works out as shown on the opposite page.

CHAPTER VIII

CONCLUSIONS

IN the preceding pages I have tried to sketch in briefest outline a possible structure for an International Authority. That structure is by no means ideal; it is full of ugly corners, and often degenerates into mere rickety and dangerous scaffolding which may or may not betoken a future building in more solid and more beautiful material. The result is curiously unsatisfactory and unsightly to anyone who desires ardently to see a world ruled by order and reason. That, one may be bold to claim, is a distinct merit. Man in national or international masses is not yet an orderly or a reasonable animal. He is an animal of passion and prejudice. Any system, or organization, or machinery for governing his affairs must, if it is to be accepted by him, allow play to these passions and prejudices. It is no good building him a brand new, beautiful, international institution. The human institutions really used by him are secreted by him much in the same way as some small repulsive insects secrete a kind of building around themselves. And the only way of influencing him is by tickling him to induce a more copious secretion on one side than on another, just as ants for this purpose tickle their cow-like aphides with their antennæ. There would be no grounds for deploring the uselessness of human effort if, by a judicious process of intellectual and emotional tickling, human beings could be induced to divert some of the energies which they devote to the construction of armies and armaments to the construction of this feeble and faulty system of pacific machinery. It will, however, be useful to point out clearly to ourselves in what respects such a system falls short of our hopes and desires, and I propose, therefore, to recapitulate shortly the results arrived at, and to bring out at the same time in what respects they would, and in what respects they would not, make for the prevention of war.

Our international system takes, just as the present system does, the independent sovereign State as its unit. It admits that, within the sphere of its independence and sovereignty, every State must remain absolute master of its own destiny. It receives within itself, therefore, a medley of dangerous national systems, under which nationalities are bound together by all kinds and varieties of stupid and irrational and unjust bonds. It does not attempt to deal at their roots with all those causes from which, during the last hundred years, the great wars have sprung, the administrative, political, and economic relationships of States. It is a system which must fall far short of any sane man's hopes and desires. It falls far short of a cosmopolitan system or a world State. But cosmopolitanism or a world State presupposes that the world is convinced of the truth—namely, that the interests of France do not necessarily conflict with the interests of Germany any more than those of Paris do with those of Bordeaux, and that the violent but narrow passions that pass under the name of patriotism are not the noblest forms of human and social emotions. The world, or the people who, unfortunately, have most to say in governing the world, believe no such thing, and will not believe it when the representatives of States meet again to decide how to fill up the graves which they helped to dig in Europe.

We take things, therefore, as we find them, however melancholy and dangerous they may be. The cosmopolitan or International State implies a cosmopolitan or international patriotism; it is, therefore, useless at present to disturb its long rest upon the dusty shelf reserved in libraries for Utopias. But that does not mean that there are no practical steps which can be taken for preventing war by improving the machinery of international relationship. We can do something by providing that the complications of modern existence do not, merely because they are complicated, tie us into inextricable international knots, and still more by developing and extending that international machinery which has in the past encouraged and given scope to those factors in human society which have tended to the drawing together of nations and the pacific settlement of international disputes.

Now, there are two such factors of the greatest importance. One is the growth of International

Law and of the principle that the relations of States shall be regulated by general rules of conduct. Society, the whole system of European civilization, all that we are accustomed to regard as good in our way of life, our hopes and our ideals, have grown about and depend upon the governing of human relationship by law and general rules of morality. The last two years have shown that it would be as easy to destroy that civilization by attempting to regulate international relationship merely by erratic violence and brute force as it would be within a State to destroy society by abandoning it to lawlessness. We have, in fact, reached the point in the history at least of Europe where continued progress depends upon the growth of International Law and morality as certainly as upon the policeman in Piccadilly Circus and all that he stands for. The binding force of law where law exists, and the binding force of contracts where contracts exist, are the foundations of a stable system of international relationship. But the last 1,915 years seem to show that such a system is not going to spring into sudden and full-blown existence by a special act of creation on the part of the Deity. It requires for its operation in this complex world humanly devised and consciously devised machinery. The conception of an International Authority, sketched in these chapters, simply recognizes these facts. It aims only at providing the machinery without which the system will remain "in the air." It presumes merely that nations are to be bound by law where law exists, by contracts where contracts exist, by the bare minimum of international good faith. It would apply legal machinery only to legal international differences, to those disputes which are concerned with rules of law and conduct to which the disputing nations have themselves subscribed, and with contracts to which they have themselves agreed. It proposes, therefore, that the reference of such legal differences and disputes for decision to a legal tribunal should be compulsory. Again, by extending and elaborating International Conferences, it would provide machinery for making International Law of wider application and of greater precision. On the one side it would strengthen the obligation, on the other side extend the range, of International Law.

The other factor is the growth of the principle which denies the right of any one nation, and asserts the right of the nations collectively, to settle questions which imperil the peace of the world. The world is so closely knit together now that it is no longer possible for a nation to run amok on one frontier while her neighbor on the other is hardly aware of it. We are so linked to our neighbors by the gold and silver wires of commerce and finance—not to speak of telegraph wires and steel rails—that a breeze between the Foreign Offices of Monrovia and Adis Ababa would be felt the same day in every Foreign Office from Pekin to Washington, and every war threatens to become a world war. And the closer the interconnections of international life become, the more necessary becomes this principle to save international society from dissolution. And one must face the fact that what stands in the way of the acceptance of this principle in the regulation of international affairs is the diplomatic, governmental and, to a less extent, popular view of the independence and sovereignty of States.

It is necessary sometimes to accept the universe as a fact, to make the best even of a divine bad job. Such action in this case would seem to consist in devising machinery which would give the fullest scope for extending this principle without infringing the independence and sovereignty of States. That is the aim of the system sketched in these chapters. It proposes to recognize the right of the nations, collectively at least, to discuss and express an opinion upon any and every question before any one nation independently takes action to settle such a question by force of arms. It proposes, therefore, that the reference of non-legal differences and disputes to an International Conference shall be compulsory. But, because it has to provide for the stubborn fact of the independence and sovereignty of States, it allows the principle full force only in those questions which do not affect independence and sovereignty. It therefore proposes that the decision would not affect a State's independence, integrity, or the control of its internal affairs.

One must meet the chorus of practical men and their sceptical criticism: "You're never going to make war impossible like that by means of spider webs. You're never going to prevent war by machinery of tribunals and Conferences. Even if the world had agreed to this system or machinery, you can't be so simple as to believe that Germany and Austria, who have torn up every scrap of paper which bound them, would have paid any attention to it in July, 1914." At the cost of repetition, this criticism requires an answer. In the first place, it is impossible to make war impossible. The Ulster question shows that in no quarter of the globe has human folly been sufficiently exorcized to make even civil war impossible. None the less, history proves that human institutions and machinery for government by restraining political folly, and giving scope to political wisdom, can make, and have made, civil war improbable. Our aim is not to compass the impossibility of war, but merely to increase its improbability.

And so with July, 1914. Machinery for settling disputes co-ordinated in the form of an International Authority *would* have made war less probable. It is a very good case to consider, because the strain would have come upon the very weakest link in the system proposed in these chapters. The dispute between Austria and Serbia was not a legal dispute, and it did affect the independence and sovereignty of a State. Under our system, all that would have been required was that the question should be referred to a Conference for examination and report. Austria would not have been bound by the decision of that Conference, and would have been legally and morally free to bombard Belgrade as soon as the Conference had expressed its opinion.

Would Austria have waited for a Conference? If the system had been instituted in June, almost certainly not. But suppose the system had been working ten years, that several disputes had been referred automatically to and settled by tribunal or Conference? We should have had one more and a serious obstacle in the path of war lords; we should have made—and that is all we can make—war more improbable, less "inevitable." The very people who are most insistent that war was "inevitable" in July, 1914, forget that they have asserted the truth—namely, that there would have been no war if Germany had realized that the breaking of her treaty about Belgium would bring in Great Britain. If we are really to consider that kind of inevitableness in human affairs, the only rational action is complete quiescence and fatalism. The happening of every event was inevitable after it had happened. If a man got drunk yesterday, it was in this sense inevitable that he got drunk, but it does not follow that we cannot make it more difficult for him to get drunk by closing the public-houses to-morrow.

People are always prophesying international bad faith and dishonesty. When their words come true they shout, "I told you so"; but, like Old Moore and other prophets, they forget and are silent about the innumerable cases in which they turned out to be wrong. After the Russo-Japanese war it was commonly said that no nation would ever again conform to the international obligation of declaring war formally. The advantage of catching your opponent off his guard and by the throat before he is ready for you is so great under modern conditions, it was said, that a sudden undeclared war is "inevitable." The patriotic Briton was exhorted to live in daily terror of going to sleep in profound peace and waking up next morning to find his Fleet at the bottom of the North Sea. In the British Empire, France, Russia, Japan, Italy, Serbia and Montenegro, it is a fact that Germany and Austria deliberately planned the war at the time and under circumstances most favorable to those two Powers; in Germany and Austria, it is a fact that Great Britain, France and Russia planned the war at the time and under circumstances most favorable to the Triple Entente. And yet in no case did any of these Powers omit to comply with an international obligation, a formal declaration of war, an obligation which deprived them of the enormous advantage of sudden warlike action.

This system, if it had been in existence for, say, ten years before 1914, would have been an additional and a serious obstacle to war in July, 1914. It would have helped those people who wanted peace, and would have hindered those people who wanted war. That is the function, and no negligible function, of pacific machinery. It would have made an immediate war improbable and a Conference probable. And it is almost certain that if a Conference had taken place there would have been no war, even though no nation was bound by the decision of the Conference. War between two nations under modern conditions is impossible unless you get a large number of people in each nation excited and afraid. Now, people can only be made excited and afraid in large masses by springing something on them suddenly which they do not altogether understand. War-mongers know this well enough in every country. That is the real objection to secret diplomacy. It enables the war-mongers to work up excitement and fear. They allow it only to be known that a crisis has occurred, "negotiations are proceeding, but a deadlock is feared." Nobody knows what is happening, what the real question is, what the worst is to be feared. "Panic on the Stock Exchange" is the inevitable newspaper placard in our streets —a little straw which shows how the psychological wind must blow in a nation before it can be induced to go to war. Suddenly we are told that the crisis is acute. Into this atmosphere of fear, ignorance, doubt, excitement, a complicated international question is flung to us in the speech of a politician which gives us the minimum of evidence and explanation and the maximum of patriotic and fear-inspiring *clichés*. Naturally, when that point is reached, ninety-nine people out of every hundred will take the lead given by "the people in authority." Peace and war no longer depend upon finding a reasonable settlement in a dispute, but upon whether in some country those in authority **do or do** not want war.

Now, a Conference works in two ways upon the psychology of nations to counteract these tendencies. In the first place, it prevents excitement by being so intolerably dull. When a score of diplomatic gentlemen have been sitting round a green baize table discussing an international question for a fortnight, they have killed all interest in that question for at least a year. The Algeciras Conference killed the Morocco question in this way. Before it met, Germany and France were boiling with excitement; long before it finished its work, everyone was so bored with it that it was quite impossible to use Morocco as a *casus belli* for five years. Even a Serbian or a German would lose interest in a question of Serbian and German nationality if he saw it discussed by diplomatists at a Conference, and not one person in a thousand would ever have thought of Serajevo again if a Conference had met in July, 1914.

But Conferences and the whole co-ordinated machinery for the pacific settlement of disputes would act on national psychology in another way. They would prevent fear, and the exploitation of fear, by people who are quite ready to attain their ends at the risk of war. The great advantage of Conferences and judicial tribunals is that they bring things out into the light. The diplomatist is compelled, to some extent, to put his cards on the green baize table, or to show his hand to the Court. The real question in dispute is really discussed, instead of being lost on the back stairs of Foreign Offices and Embassies. And as soon as a question is discussed, reasonable men see that there is a reasonable method of settling it. It is darkness, doubt, and ignorance which breed fear, and fear which breeds war. To prevent war, what is wanted in diplomacy and international relationships is light, said M. Hanotaux, himself a statesman and diplomatist. Light not only dispels fear and suspicion, but makes dishonesty difficult. Even the most cynical diplomatist dare not openly avow and practise bad faith in international relations; and if we could compel him to act in the light, we should compel him to act honestly.

Therefore, even in a case in which our International Authority is weakest, even where we have most conspicuously failed to solve those difficulties which appeared in Chapter V, its machinery could do much to prevent war. It would allay unreasoning excitement; it would let in the light; it would strengthen the hands of those persons who were working for peace. But perhaps its most potent influence would come from another side. The holding of Conferences whose decisions would be binding in questions which did not affect the independence and internal sovereignty of States would involve a formal recognition of that principle upon which the future stability of international society depends—the principle that the nations have the right collectively to settle questions which imperil the peace of the world. It is true that the recognition of that principle would apply only to a small and comparatively unimportant class of questions. But, at least, we should have made a beginning, have laid foundations out of which a more rational system of international relationship might grow. We have now tried for one or two centuries, with lamentable results, a system admirably described by Swift in the epigram at the head of this report. We have adapted our international machinery solely to the hopeless task of balancing Europe in armed and hostile groups. It will be some gain if we have at least the machinery and the power to regulate some international affairs upon a more rational system.

PART II

INTERNATIONAL GOVERNMENT

CHAPTER I

INTERNATIONAL GOVERNMENT, INTERNATIONAL AGREEMENT, AND INTERNATIONAL DISAGREEMENT

EVERYONE is born either a "practical man" or an "amiable crank," and by their words, oddly enough, you shall know them. In the first category one may place Thrasymachus, Kleon, Pontius Pilate, Bismarck, General Boulanger, Queen Victoria, the late Mr. Chamberlain, and all the nameless gentlemen who write leaders in the daily Press; in the latter, Socrates, Plato, Dædalus, Jesus Christ, Voltaire, Miss Jane Addams, *et id genus omne*. Now it is a curious fact that the practical man of to-morrow almost invariably says exactly what the amiable crank is hanged or laughed at for saying by the practical man of to-day. Thus a *Times* leader-writer in 1916 has a profound admiration for Socrates; yet there can be little doubt that if he had been born some 2,300 years ago he would have written: "We yield to none in our determination to uphold the right to freedom of speech, which is the common inheritance of Athenians; but a right implies a duty, and the people of this country, unlike the Government, is determined in these critical times not to allow its young men to be corrupted by the pernicious doctrines of amiable cranks and men who hide their sinister motives under a cloak of idealism. We believe the country to be right, though we are inclined to think that this was a case in which justice might have been tempered with mercy, and the death sentence commuted to one of penal servitude for life." Again, Bismarck and Queen Victoria were both devout Christians in the nineteenth century, yet they certainly would not have been so in the first, if the one had been sitting on the throne of Cæsar and the other had been Cæsar's Imperial Chancellor.

We do not, of course, mean by these reflections that every amiable crank is always right and every practical man is always wrong. What we suggest is that all through the history of the world people calling themselves plain and practical men have been led into the most hideous and disastrous errors by accepting false inferences and false standards as obvious and fundamental truths, while other men have been reviled and humiliated as cranks and charlatans precisely for insisting upon the falsity of these standards and inferences. These considerations are relevant because anyone who expresses a belief in the possibility of International Government, the efficacy of international agreement, or the illusion of international rivalry, is in danger of being shouted down as a crank or worse by a chorus of plain and practical men. All round us to-day are people, like Mr. Maxse and Mr. Blatchford, who hold up to execration or contempt anyone who denies the premises of their arguments, the premises that International Government is a dream, that international agreement is a delusion and snare, and that national interests demand a perpetuation of international warfare, the open warfare of bayonets and blood, or the suppressed warfare of tariffs and armaments. But these premises, which are thundered forth as self-evident truths, are nothing of the kind; whether they are true or false depends upon a mass of extremely complicated and unfamiliar facts and inferences. I propose in the following chapters, therefore, to examine some of the more important facts, and to suggest some of the more important inferences that can be drawn from them.

What does one mean by International Government? In the broadest sense—and the one in which I propose to use it—International Government means the regulation of relations between States, Nations, or Peoples by international agreement. When the world and man were young, international relations were confined almost exclusively to physical contiguity of frontiers, and to periodical and mutual killing and pillaging of neighbors. Communication was so difficult that intercourse of individuals scarcely existed, except in the case of a few traders, or an amiable crank like Herodotus, who had a dangerous passion for foreign travels. The supremely important question of international relationship was, therefore, in those days one of frontiers, and for centuries it was regulated almost entirely by armed warfare. Probably more wars have arisen as attempts to settle frontier questions by force than from any other cause. But apparently the world gradually learned that this was not a very efficient method of settling the physical relationship of States. At any rate, it has become more and more usual to regulate frontier questions by international agreement, and the last century saw the custom of settling such disputes by agreement to arbitrate established as an almost universal rule. Thus it is correct to say that for frontier questions and international relations which result from physical contiguity, a system of International Government has evolved in the regulation of those relations by agreements, and in the last resource by judicial decisions.

This is one example of the substitution of International Government for international warfare as a method of regulating inter-State relations. In the first part of this book I considered the question of the possibility of the creation or development of machinery through which all the relations of States might be submitted in the same way to International Government rather than to the arbitrament of arms. In other words, I was considering the possibility of regulating international relations by agreement, and, as the task set myself was strictly limited, I confined myself to the question of the kinds of machinery—international law, treaties, conferences, judicial tribunals, and an international authority—which, in the case of international disputes, were likely to lead to agreement, and so prevent war. I was, therefore, in those chapters mainly concerned with those differences and disputes of a legal, economic, or political character which have in the past led nations into war. My conclusion was that the deliberate creation of organized machinery for settling such differences and disputes in the shape of an international authority would go far towards ensuring agreement and towards making war extremely improbable. But I did not generally or in detail deal with the wider question of the possibility of International Government and international agreement, and, therefore, with the contention of the "plain and practical man" school of writers that the application of government by agreement to international relations is the dream of the idealistic fool. In this part I propose to deal with this wider problem.

This is by no means a question of theoretical interest only. The dogma that war is a natural and necessary corollary of the existence of States, and that, therefore, International Government is not practically possible, has been and will be continually used as an argument against particular proposals and attemps to develop international agreement. The whole history of diplomacy is one long tale of this disastrous process, of men consciously or unconsciously saturated with this theory struggling against the natural tendency of the world towards International Government. The Hague Conferences, in so far as they failed, were not failures of impossible ideals before hard facts, but the triumphs of this dogma over facts—

the facts which I propose to enquire into in this part. The reasons which the large numbers of persons who hold and preach this dogma give for believing in it may be divided into three classes, and it is only with the third class that it is necessary to deal in detail. The first class is purely mystical. It is frequently asserted or assumed that there is some mysterious property or quality in States and nations which makes them mutually and inevitably hostile; that this natural and irrational hostility, though it lie dormant for years, must break out and spend itself periodically in bloodshed, and that, therefore, any effective system of government by agreement between States and nations must be impracticable. This theory, the result of confused thinking, has given rise to an immense amount of mystical philosophy and history, under the title "crowd-psychology." Thus Sir Martin Conway asserts that nations are crowds, and that, apparently by a divine dispensation of Providence, the only relation that one crowd can have to another crowd is the emotional one of hatred: *ergo*, nations must hate one another. But Sir Martin's assertion and the whole theory is the result of confusing metaphor and fantasy with facts. A national emotion can only be used metaphorically of the emotion of hatred felt by the individuals who make up a nation; in other words, there cannot be an emotion outside the individuals who feel it. The fact that each individual forms one of a crowd, or of a nation, does, of course, influence his emotion; but there is no composite emotion of the crowd. Now, it is certain that ordinarily the individuals who make up a nation feel no emotion at all towards those individuals who form other nations; but when States and the individuals of which they are composed are brought into frequent contact and relation with one another, the individuals of one nation acquire feelings towards those of another which may vary from hatred and repulsion to affection and attraction. But these "national" emotions are not a mysterious property of crowds; they can be traced, just as the emotions of one individual towards any other, to community or divergence of circumstances in the relations of the individuals themselves. International feeling in Germany, Great Britain, and the United States of America will afford clear proof of this. The position of Germany and America towards Britain in the latter part of the nineteenth century was in many ways identical. Each of the first two was a young nation with a rapidly increasing population, with no colonial empire; they were, too, the chief commercial and industrial competitors of Britain. Yet it would be absurd to pretend that the national emotion in this country towards the other two was in 1913 the same—namely, one of hatred and opposition. The Englishman's feeling towards the German was nationally one of suspicion and hostility; this was due partly to a consciousness of differences of language, customs, institutions, and ideals; partly to the belief that the German was aiming at a colonial empire, which he could only obtain by depriving us of ours; in other words, to a belief in the divergence of German and English interests. The Englishman's feeling towards the American was nationally one of friendliness; this was due partly to a consciousness of common stock, language, customs, and ideals; partly to the belief that the national aims of America in no way threatened our own; in other words, to a belief in the community of English and American interests.

There is, then, no mysterious property in crowds and nations which makes national hatred inevitable. The national feeling of Englishmen towards Frenchmen was as real after the entente as before it; it had changed from hostility and fear to affection and reliance because a belief that French aims and interests were on the whole the same as ours was substituted for a conviction that French ideals were hostile to us and French interests threatened ours. But people who hold the dogma of international hostility often support the mystical line of reasoning by a second class of scientific or pseudo-scientific reasons. The Darwinian theory and the biological law of development through the struggle for existence are enlisted to prove a ceaseless and inevitable struggle for existence between "waxing and waning" nations. This doctrine has become notorious as "made in Germany," because it forms the basis of the popular books of General von Bernhardi; but it seems to commend itself to many English writers who would be the first to execrate the logical conclusions of the German cavalry officer to which it leads. The doctrine is itself based upon a misunderstanding of Darwin and a misapplication of a misunderstood "scientific law" from one set of facts to another; but to prove this assertion would involve a long scientific argument which would carry us far afield. Moreover, the whole fallacy has been fully dealt with and conclusively exposed in *Evolution and the War*, by Dr. Chalmers Mitchell, to which I must refer the reader who desires proof.

The third class of reasons is entirely different from the other two, though it is often confused with them. It is clear, as I have just pointed out, that international hostility does spring very often from the *consciousness* in individuals of one nation that their ideals, language, institutions, etc., differ from those of the individuals of other nations, and also from a *belief* that their own national interests are opposed to or threatened by the national interests of others. The existence of such a consciousness and belief is used frequently as an argument to prove that International Government and international agreement are impossible or undesirable. All kinds of ramifications and elaborations of this argument are continually being evolved. For instance, it is often asserted that national differences of custom, language, institutions, etc., actually do make government by agreement impossible—an argument which is obviously quite different from the fact noted above, namely, that hostility springs sometimes from the consciousness of such differences—and which is disproved by the existence of the Swiss Confederation alone. Or, again, the assertion is made, or it is assumed as a self-evident fact, that the interests of nations actually are irreconcilably opposed, and therefore that government based upon international agreement must either be illusory or, if real, must result in a betrayal of our national interests.

Here, then, is the real crux of Internationalism, no matter what particular form it takes. Is it true that the regulation of international relations, whether of the governments and administrations or of the individuals and groups of individuals of States, is impossible, because of an impassable gulf of differences in national laws, customs, languages and ideals, or because national interests remain, and must remain, irreconcilably opposed? The answer to this question is certainly not self-evident; it must depend upon a knowledge and correct interpretation of a vast number of intricate, little-known historical and other facts. If we desire to know how far it is possible and by what methods it is most practicable to apply government by agreement to international relations, we must turn to facts and ascertan what has been the history of such government, and how far the divergencies of national life and the clashing of national interests have withstood or have yielded to systems and methods of obtaining international agreement. It is these questions and these facts which I now propose to examine.

Historically, the facts, when fully examined, will, I believe, show first that a profound change in international relations has been taking place since the beginning of the nineteenth century, and that the people who repeat and repeat again that International Government is Utopian, and international agreement must betray national interests, simply shut their eyes to the fact that in every department of life the beginnings, and more than the beginnings, of International Government already exist, and that in every department of life, even where the conflict of national interests ought to be most acute, international interests are far stronger and far more real than national interests, and the latter can be and have been successfully harmonized, combined, and merged in the former by means of international agreements. It must be remembered that in early times States were commonly regarded as water-tight compartments of conflicting interests. *Ex hypothesi*, therefore, what was one State's gain must be every other State's loss. This extraordinary theory, which a moment's calm reflection will show to be false, still forms the basis of the art of diplomacy, and influences the thoughts and actions of many people who ought to know better. To give one and a striking example, only the other day a learned writer in the *Times* solemnly used an argument which implied that if Great Britain bought goods from a foreign country and that country benefited by the trade, the other's benefit must be the measure of Britain's loss. This gentleman would certainly have agreed that if Lancashire exchanged cotton goods for coal from

Northumberland, the benefit derived by Northumberland might well be the measure of the benefit derived by Lancashire; but substitute Britain for Lancashire and Germany for Northumberland, and immediately the light of his intelligence is snuffed out by the fog of old superstitions about "irreconcilable national interests."

But though these old superstitions are still strong in the world, thousands of people in the last century began to lose or to doubt them. The recognition of international interests, and that national interests are international interests, and *vice versâ*, was the great social discovery of the last 100 years. This discovery has operated in many different ways, all of which throw light upon the problem of International Government. In the first place, it has led to the spontaneous creation and evolution of a large number of new organizations, international organs and organisms, the functions of which are either to regulate through agreements the relations of States or administrations, or individuals or groups of individuals, belonging to several States; or, looked at from another point of view, to promote international interests and harmonize national interests. The result has been, at least, two clearly defined lines of human progress. The first has been the establishment of direct International Government for many departments of human affairs in which separate national governments and organizations have proved unable to watch over and promote international interests. The International Administration applied to Posts and Telegraphs, to

Railways, to Currency and Coinage, to the prevention of diseases, to agricultural interests, and to the collection and publication of information, is the most obvious example of this tendency. A study of the working of these administrations throws much light upon the dogma of the anti-internationalist, for in these already highly developed forms of International Government one can see the real relations of national to international interests, and the possibility or impossibility of harmonizing them by agreements. But direct International Government is in process of establishment not only by these "official" international administrations, but also, as I shall show, by unofficial bodies or groups of individuals in the different countries. When national groups of capitalists, manufacturers or merchants organize themselves internationally, and proceed to regulate the production and distribution of commodities throughout the world by international agreements arrived at in these organizations, we have in this as true a type of International Government as in the Universal Postal Union—and the same problems of national and international interests have to be solved. And this is true of the similar organizations of Labor, of science, of professions, or even of criminals.

The second line of development is no less relevant to the dogma of anti-internationalism. The dogma rested upon an exaltation of the differences of national laws, customs, education, and ideals. Now, it is precisely in breaking down these differences that the spontaneous international movement of the last century has been most successful. In the most widely separated fields of human activity this process has been taking place simply because it has become clear that these differences are themselves inimical to international interests *and, therefore, to national interests*. This result has been achieved by international agreements arrived at, in or through international organizations. A knowledge and understanding of this tendency is, therefore, essential before any judgment on the possibilities of International Government is made.

I propose, therefore, in the next chapter to deal generally with the history and structure of the various International Organs and Organisms which made their appearance in the last century. In the following chapters I shall deal in detail with their achievements, tracing in particular these two great international tendencies—first the growth and operation of true International Government which has been the natural result of the consciousness of international interests; second, the internationalizing of laws, science, customs, thought, industry, commerce, and society.

CHAPTER II

INTERNATIONAL ORGANS AND ORGANISMS

IT is common to regard "government" as always connected with "official" or "State" organization or organs. The Houses of Parliament, the Courts of Justice, the policeman, and the Borough Council are all in this sense organs of national government. But the complexity of modern society has made this conception far too narrow. National government is the regulation of relations between individuals living within the territory of the nation. It may be true that when the structure of society was simpler those relations were regulated, in so far as regulation existed at all, by State organizations and rules and laws emanating from organs of State. But even in those early times the Church and the Guild, to take two examples only, were as obviously organs of government as the Legislature and the court of law. They were so because they were associations of individuals whose decisions regulated the conduct and mutual relations of individuals. And in the same way to-day the regulation of industry and labor by associations of manufacturers, consumers or workers, the regulation of science by associations of scientists, of professions by associations of professional men, or of sport by associations of cricketers or football players or swimmers, are all no less parts of the system of national government than the regulation of sanitation by a borough council or of bankruptcy by the Bankruptcy Court.

The narrow vision of government and the functions of government as limited to State or Municipal organization leads to much misunderstanding of the history and the future of International Government. In the eighteenth century no regular organs of International Government existed at all. The relations of sovereign States were confined to diplomatic conversations, and were regulated only by a few treaties concluded at rare intervals to meet particular circumstances, or by a small and vacillating code of customary law known as the Law of Nations. This lack of International Government was not felt to any very great extent, simply because, owing to the want of adequate means of communication, there were very few international relations which required regulation at all. In the eighteenth century the number of persons in these islands who had any relations with any inhabitants of Sweden could probably be counted on the fingers of two hands; to-day, any person who buys a box of matches is linked by an intricate chain of relationship with hundreds of Swedish woodcutters, factory workers, employers, railway men, and shippers. In the eighteenth century, therefore, because relations between the individuals of the two countries scarcely existed, interests common to Englishmen and Swedes did not exist, or, at any rate, could not become apparent to the people themselves; to-day, the continual intercourse between the two countries produces a network of Anglo-Swedish interests which affect the every-day life of hundreds of persons in the two countries. And a similar network of international intercourse and interests has been woven, mainly by the railway, the steamship, the telegraph, and the telephone, over the whole face of the earth.

It is impossible to have any highly organized system of human relationship without government—that is to say, without regulation of the relations through agreement or agreements. Man adapts his institutions to his needs, and, if he did not, he would have remained with the simple needs and under the simple institutions of his cousins of the jungle—the gorilla, the chimpanzee, and the ourang-outang. Thus the system of International Government which has developed in the last 100 years has not been the perverse invention of international cranks, but a spontaneous growth to meet international needs, and without which every-day life, as we know it, would have been impossible. The development of the system has proceeded along four different lines, entailing the growth of four different kinds of international organization or organism.

The first line has been to develop the ordinary diplomatic methods of obtaining agreements between the governments of independent sovereign States. As I showed in the previous part, the diplomatic conference or congress, as a means of regulating by agreements embodied in treaties the relations of States or of the individual citizens of States, was really the invention of the last century, and is clearly a rudimentary international legislature. By the twentieth century we had reached a stage at which no year passed without several such conferences meeting, and at which between 50 and 100 treaties, embodying international legislation, were signed annually. A glance at the subjects of these conferences and treaties shows the extent of the field of international relationship to which they have by agreement applied legislative regulation. They deal with international trade, industry and finance, international communications, health, science, art, literature, morals and crime, emigration and immigration, besides the "political" relations of States. Steadily, under the pressure of public opinion, which inevitably voices and insists upon the satisfaction of the needs of an evolving society, this system of international legislation has, as I shall show, been working in two directions: First, towards the recognition and protection of international interests; second, towards the unification of administration and the unification of law throughout the world.

But the Conference and Treaty system of the last century suffered from several serious defects. It ordinarily provides no regular or permanent organ of International Government. A conference only met when the governments, or rather the diplomatists, of the different States agreed that one should meet. The result has been very much what would happen if the House of Commons broke up at the end of a session without any rules as to reassembling, and only met again when all the members agreed to meet, or, rather, yielded to the pressure of their constituents who wanted the government of the country attended to. The isolated international conference could only pass isolated measures of international legislation. But many international interests had attained such a degree of permanence, intricacy, and urgency that continual revision of international legislation and, in some cases, some form of international administration, were necessary. The result has been that various more or less permanent associations of the Governments or Administrations of States have made their appearance.

These associations are sometimes called Public International Unions, and in standard works on International Law a few meagre details about them will be found under such headings as International Unions, International Offices, International Commissions, etc. A detailed study of their forms and constitutions would be of great interest, for, as any reference to lists of them in the few books which deal with them will show, they vary from being merely an ordinary diplomatic conference, meeting at irregular intervals, to highly elaborate organs of International Government and administration. In the chapters that follow I shall only incidentally be concerned with them as *formal* organs of governments, for my chief object will be to trace their effects upon national and international interests and the kind of International Government which they have produced. But I propose here to deal very briefly with the number and variety of their forms.

In an American work, "Public International Unions," by Paul A. Reinsch, the statement is made that "there are in existence 45 Public International Unions, composed of States. Of these, 30 are provided with administrative bureaus or commissions." The "Annuaire de La Vie Internationale" for 1910–1911 (an extraordinarily complete Belgian publication which deals with all forms of international organization) contains a list of 41 such public Unions. But a very little enquiry into the form of the organisms included in these lists shows that they differ so widely among themselves that a general classification of this kind is not of much value. Thus, in the 41 Unions of the Belgian list, and presumably in the 45 of the American, the Automobile Conference and Convention of 1909 is included side by side with the Universal Postal Union. But the first, regarded merely as an organ of International Government, or as a "Union composed of States," differs in no way from any other diplomatic conference or convention; the convention sets up no permanent organ of government or administration—it is merely an agreement between States or administrations by which each is bound individually to take certain administrative measures; it is not so much a union of States as a unification of national administration; it is unification of national government rather than the creation of International Government. The Automobile Convention is of great importance and interest in its effect upon International Government, but it does not create an organ of International Government as did the International Postal Convention of 1874. The Universal Postal Union, the offspring of that Convention, is a true union of States (or rather of administrations). The Convention did not merely bind the signatory Powers to do or not to do certain administrative acts; it created two new, permanent organs of International Government—the Postal Congress, whose decisions are binding upon the different States, and the Postal Bureau, which is a purely administrative organ. This Convention, therefore, sets up international administration for the transport of letters, etc., between different States, and it provides new organs through which the regulation of that transport by agreement may be carried out.

If a proper appreciation of the forms which these "State" international organisms have taken is to be given, a more detailed classification of them is required. Such a classification would, I suggest, distinguish the following varieties:

I.—Permanent Deliberative or Legislative Organs Working in Conjunction with Administrative Organs.

1. The Telegraphic Union.
2. The Radio-telegraphic Union.

3. The Universal Postal Union.
4. The Metric Union.
5. The International Institute of Agriculture.
6. La Commission Pénitentiaire Internationale.
7. The Sanitary Councils and International Office of Public Hygiene.
8. The International Geodetic Association.
9. The International Seismological Union.
10. The Pan-American Union.
11. The Central American Union.

II.—Periodic Conferences in Conjunction with Permanent International Bureaus or Offices.

1. Railway Freight Transportation.
2. Industrial Property.
3. Literary and Artistic Property.
4. Pan-American Sanitary Union.
5. Slave Trade and Liquor Traffic in Africa.

*III.—Conferences and Conventions with Object of Unifying National Laws or Administrations.**

1. Conférences Internationales pour l'Unité Technique des Chemins de Fer.

---

* There have been numerous other conferences and conventions which have had the same object, and should rightly be included in this list. Many of them will be referred to in the following chapters. The ten are given in this list only because they are usually classified as Public International Unions. There is, however, no valid reason why the Convention of 1909, unifying the administrative regulations in different countries regarding motor-cars, sign-posts, etc., should be considered to have produced an "International Union," while the conventions of 1910, unifying the regulations of maritime law (*vide* page 272) in the different countries, should not be so considered.

2. Automobile Conference.
3. Latin Monetary Union.
4. Scandinavian Monetary Union.
5. Central American Monetary Union.
6. Conference on Nomenclature of Causes of Death.
7. Legal Protection of Workers.
8. Submarine Cables.
9. Commercial Statistics.
10. White Slave Traffic.

*IV.—Special International Organs of a Permanent Character.**

1. Sugar Commission.
2. Opium Commission.
3. Plague Surveillance in China.
4. International Committee of the Map of the World.
5. Hague Tribunal and Bureau.
6. Central American Court of Justice.
7. International Bureau for the Publication of Customs Tariffs.

It would be possible to write a considerable volume merely upon the variations in form which the machinery of International Government has

---

* There are, or were, a considerable number of other international organs set up by special conventions which ought strictly to be included in this list, *e. g.*, the European Danube Commission, the International Commission of the Congo, the Suez Canal Commission, the Financial Commissions in Turkey, Greece, and Egypt, etc. They have not been included because they are not usually regarded as organs of Public International Unions.

taken in these thirty-three international organisms. Even within each of the four classes there are marked variations of form. The machinery devised in the Telegraphic and Postal Unions, which have brought the exchange of telegrams and the transport of letters, etc., under International Government, is absolutely different from that which, through the International Sanitary Conventions, the Sanitary Councils, and the International Office of Public Hygiene, has superimposed international upon national government in the prevention and control of epidemic diseases. The most important varieties of form will become apparent in the following chapters, and I propose, therefore, here only to point out the distinguishing features of the four classes. In the first class the convention or conventions upon which the union of States is founded itself provides for the creation of some permanent deliberative or legislative international body, and also for an administrative body working under the direction of the former.* The Telegraphic Unions, the Postal, and the Metric Union are constituted on the same model, the deliberative organ being a conference or congress, and the administrative a permanent bureau. The Institute of Agriculture has a very elaborate constitution, with two deliberative bodies, the General Assembly and the permanent committee and a permanent bureau. In the Commission pénitentiaire, the Geodetic Association, and the

* The Sanitary Councils are in this respect anomalous (*vide infra*, page 240).

PREVENTION OF WAR

Seismological Union, the deliberative organ is a permanent Commission. The two American Unions are highly developed associations of States, with several legislative and administrative organs. The second class differs from the first in that the convention upon which the union of States is founded does not provide for any permanent deliberative or legislative body. The convention concluded at an ordinary diplomatic conference is revised periodically by a similar conference, while it is the function of the permanent bureau or office, created by the convention, to watch over the carrying out of its provisions. The third class consists of conferences and conventions which have not resulted in the creation of any special international organs of government, but which have tended to unify the laws and methods of administration in the several States. The fourth class consists of a variety of special international organs created by conventions for specific purposes.

As regards the history of this development in International Government, it is important to notice that not one of these thirty-three unions or organisms existed eighty years ago. This whole system of regulation by international agreement between States and administrations, which has been applied, as the list shows, to communications and transport, to agricultural and commercial interests, to public health, science, arts, literature, morals, law and order, evolved *ex nihilo* in the nineteenth century. The evolution began with the creation in 1838* of the Conseil Supérieur de Santé in Constantinople, an international body appointed for the purpose of preventing the introduction of cholera into Turkey. But the real impetus towards the formation of International Unions dates from 1855, when the first International Telegraph Convention was signed, which led directly to the formation of the Telegraphic Union in 1865. This Union formed the model for the most important of the eleven associations of States in the first class, though it was nine years before another—the Postal Union—was established. It is, therefore, true to say that the whole of this movement towards the regulation of international relations by agreement, arrived at through permanent associations of governments and administrations or through permanent international organs, has been built up in the last fifty years.

This new international organization which we have just been considering is essentially one of States. It has grown out of the ordinary diplomatic relations of State to State, and it has strictly maintained its "official" character. But, side by side with it, and in close connection with it, has appeared another and a no less important movement towards International Government. In 1840, for the first time, I believe, in the history

---

* The new Internationalism really began with the Congress of Vienna in 1815. The first appearance of special international organs created and appointed to carry out specific international purposes is in the Commissions appointed under the Treaty of Vienna to carry out the provisions regarding navigation on certain European rivers.

of the world,* there assembled an International Congress, not of representatives of the Governments of States, but of individuals of different nations who realized that they had an interest to serve or an object to attain which was international rather than national. This was the World Anti-Slavery Convention, which met in London. Between 1840 and 1847 three more International Congresses were held, two in London (a religious Congress of the Evangelical Alliance and a Peace Congress) and one in Frankfort, the Congrès internationale pénitentiaire. After 1847 such Congresses were continually held, until to-day there is hardly a profession, trade, occupation, object, or interest which does not periodically gather together in these voluntary associations the persons engaged in or interested in them in the different countries of the world. The extent to which this kind of international intercourse has developed may be gathered from the fact that no less than 135 International Congresses were held in the year before the war.

The congress, though interesting in itself as a new means of international intercourse, is most important as having developed into a new organ of International Government. The isolated congress very early gave birth to permanent international

* It is interesting, perhaps, to note that the "congress" of private individuals is itself a very modern invention. The idea seems to have originated with Alexander von Humboldt, who assembled and presided over a congress of German scientists in Berlin on September 18, 1821. From Germany the congress spread to England (1831), France (1833), and Belgium (1847).—*Vide La Vie Internationale*, 1913, Vol. III, p. 123.

organisms, composed of the members or delegates who had attended the congress and of persons or associations interested in the subjects or questions discussed. Since 1840 over 500 such voluntary international associations have been created, and over 400 have a permanent existence. In the following chapters I shall show in some detail how these organisms have contributed towards the solution of the problem of International Government; in this chapter I am concerned only with their general character and form.

In the *Annuaire de la Vie Internationale*, referred to above, some details are given of 371 such associations. A mere glance at the list opens one's eyes to the fact that there is hardly a sphere of life in which a consciousness of international interests has not penetrated, and led to men of every tongue and race joining together in order to promote those interests. Practically every profession, from engineers and architects to nurses and commercial travelers, is represented. Industry and commerce, from Chambers of Commerce to bird-fanciers and cinematograph film makers; Labor, in some forty separate International Federations; Science, from the powerful Electrotechnical Commission to the International Society of Psychical Research; Medicine, with as many as thirty-nine distinct associations; Art, Literature, Learning and Religion have all entered the field of international organization. Finally, there are innumerable associations of persons working for some special social object, like Women's Suffrage, Temperance, or the suppression of prostitution, and who are seeking to attain that object by international action. In this division Morals, Education, and Feminism provide the largest numbers, but the catholicism of internationalism is well shown by the existence of an "International Association for the Suppression of Useless Noises" and an "International Association for the Rational Destruction of Rats."

The form of these organisms is scarcely less various than their objects and names. In order to coordinate their activities there was established in Brussels in 1910 an international association formed of international associations—L'Union des Associations Internationales—and the definition of an international association adopted by the Union lays down that it must have three characteristics:—

(1) It must have individual or collective members belonging to different countries, and membership must be open to similar elements of different countries.

(2) Its object must be one which interests all or some nations, and which is not profit.

(3) It must possess a permanent organ.

It will be observed that this definition is very wide. However, the great majority of the organizations that fall within it conform to the following type. They have a general assembly or supreme legislative organ, which meets in Congress every year, two years, or even at longer intervals. The function of the Congress is confined to passing resolutions. An executive body, usually called a permanent Committee, Council, or Commission, and elected or appointed at a Congress, carries on the work of the Association in the intervals between Congresses. In close connection with the executive is a permanent paid secretariat, called either a Bureau or an Office. But there the resemblances end; in membership, in organization and constitution, in the relations of the different organs, in rules as to procedure and voting, every kind of variation is to be found. With the majority of those variations I do not propose to deal, but there are one or two points which deserve notice as bearing upon the problem of International Government.

The most important point is the membership, for through it the International Association seems to be working towards a new type of human association and a new method of human government. The membership of most international associations is composed either of individuals, or of associations of individuals, belonging to various countries, or of both. It is when associations adopt the two latter types that their scope and their influence can become considerable. But there are important variations even within the types themselves. For instance, some international associations are really federations of national associations, which had, and have, an independent existence of their own, but which become conscious of pursuing the same object in their several countries. Many associations whose object is social reform, and all Labor associations, are of this type. Thus the

International League Against the Abuse of Spirituous Drinks, created in 1897, is a federation of anti-alcoholic societies, while the International Federation of Miners, the International Union of Woodworkers, the International Federation of Metalworkers, and the thirty-six other international associations of workers are federations of national federations, themselves composed of the trade unions which organize the workers in the mining, wood, metal, and other trades. On the other hand, many international associations are not so much federations of national groups, which existed for specific national purposes before the constitution of the international group, but are composed of national groups, sections, or associations which have been formed specifically for international purposes. Thus the Commission Electrotechnique Internationale is composed of representatives of local Electrotechnical Committees appointed in each country by the governments or technical societies, and the Inter-Parliamentary Union of twenty-four national groups of members of the Parliaments of twenty-four different countries.

These two kinds of international association follow the lines of many national voluntary associations. But a new development of a remarkable kind has taken place in recent years. It has long been customary for the Governments of States and the municipal authorities of towns to send official representatives to the more important international Congresses and to make contributions to the funds of many international associations.* But lately in more than one case States and municipalities have themselves become members of some influential international organizations. The membership of such an association often presents an extraordinary and novel spectacle, for it sometimes consists of States, municipal authorities, private individuals, and every sort and kind of national group, society, and association. The most striking example of this new type and experiment in human co-operation is the International Association to Combat Unemployment (Association Internationale pour la Lutte contre le Chômage), which numbers among its members eight Governments, seventeen national official bodies, eight provinces, two federations of towns, fifty-nine towns, fourteen official municipal bodies, three fédérations nationales de placements, twelve bourses de travail, twelve fonds de chômage, three international associations, fifteen scientific societies, six national federations of employers, three professional federations, four local federations, thirty Labor federations, and individuals belonging to twenty-three different countries.

The fact that these associations are voluntary should not blind anyone to the importance of this new phenomenon—the gathering together into a single association of every kind of human organi-

---

* *E. g.*, thirty countries sent official representatives to the sixth Congress of the International Association for Testing Materials, and twenty-nine Governments contributed to the finances of the Association Internationale du Froid.

zation. The real difficulty with which internationalism has to contend is the extreme complication and ramification of international interests. Even within the boundaries of a single country any question of government affects a vast number of different individuals and groups of individuals, and it is clear that the regular organs of even national government are far too simple and rigidly set to allow adequate representation to these heterogeneous groups and their interests in our tangled modern world. A measure introduced into the House of Commons to-day affects millions of people, not only as individuals, but as members of small and large groups and organizations, municipalities, churches, trade unions, federations of employers, co-operative societies, clubs, associations, etc. A member of Parliament is physically and mentally unable to represent the net views of constituents regimented in such diverse ways, and we are faced with a serious gap between the organization of life and the organization of our government. Representation is still based upon geography, which used to be the most important thing in a man's life—for it determined to a great extent his position in society—but it is now among the least important. It is interesting to see how in national government tentative measures are being taken to bridge this gap. When a Bill is being passed in the House of Commons it is customary now for Ministers to confer with all kinds of groups and organizations and classes, either in deputations or regular conferences. At these conferences of bankers, shipowners, federations of employers, trade unions, etc., pledges are given or extracted which materially affect the proposed legislation. Members of Parliament often complain that information is given to such groups which should rightly be first given to Parliament, and that the Government makes "concessions" to such groups behind the back of the House of Commons. This is true; but the real meaning of the fact is that here we have the beginning of social group—or class—representation in national government, which is absolutely essential if the gap between the organization of our life and the organization of our Government is to be filled in.

If this be true of national government, it is far more true of international government. As soon as any attempt is made to deal with unemployment, for example, it becomes clear that this is not merely a national but an international question. Its ramifications touch the interests of a vast number of national and international groups, States, municipalities, employers, workers, statisticians, economists. The whole question of emigration and immigration, with its accretions of political and racial controversy, is involved, no less than the fluidity of labor and the maintenance of trade-union regulations. It is a question which cannot be adequately dealt with as one merely between the Governments of independent sovereign States, nor as one merely of economic interest between capital and labor. If the political and racial interests are in some cases nationally vertical, the economic are internationally horizontal. These criss-crossing interests can only be reconciled into a harmonious pattern if that pattern can be worked out by study and discussion in an international body composed of State, town, capitalist, worker, and scientist. That is what l'Association Internationale pour la Lutte contre le Chômage and several other international associations have spontaneously achieved.

How such International Associations in many cases have resulted in the regulation of relations between States and other international groups by agreement will be shown in detail in the following chapters. Here it will be useful to give a brief and general indication of the nature of this tendency. In the first place, over and over again in them is to be found the source of international legislation proper. It is in them that the consciousness of international interests and of the inconvenience of divergence in national laws and customs becomes articulate. The individuals or groups of individuals interested, whether traders or workers or artists or scientists, become aware of the necessity of International Government, and set themselves to working out practical methods of establishing it. Many of the diplomatic conventions establishing the Public International Unions, dealt with above, and many conventions which have unified the Laws and Administrations of States have in this way originated in and been worked out by international associations. Thus, the Metric Union was due to action taken by the International Congress of Weights, Measures, and Moneys in 1867, and of the International Association for the Measure of the Degree in Europe; the Copyrights Conventions of 1886, 1888, etc., which established the International Union and Bureau of Literary and Artistic Property, originated in the International Literary and Artistic Association founded in 1878 by Victor Hugo; the Conventions of 1910, which have established a uniform commercial law of salvage and collisions at sea for practically the whole world, were first worked out in the International Maritime Committee.

But these associations of individuals or groups of individuals belonging to different countries are not only the initiators of agreements between States, establishing international administration or regulating the relations of States in other ways, they are themselves often organs of International Government. Whenever they are representative, that is to say, whenever they bring together groups which in each country really control or influence some department of human life, whether it be science or education or commerce or labor, the agreements arrived at in the association actually regulate the relations between the national groups or substitute for the different national customs, methods, or institutions of the groups one international method, custom, or institution. Many of the international associations are composed, as their titles show, of amiable cranks and enthusiasts who live so far ahead of their age that they have little or no influence upon it, but many others are fully representative in this sense. The International Association of Academies, for example, is a body composed of the chief scientific societies of all the important countries of the world; the Congrès international des Ephémérides astronomiques in 1911 united in one body the directors of practically all the astronomical observatories of the world. The object of the former, according to its statutes, is to prepare or initiate scientific work and to facilitate scientific relations between countries; the latter, by agreements embodied in resolutions, unified methods of astronomical work and observation in the different countries. By these two representative associations, therefore, first science generally and then a highly-specialized department of science are clearly being internationalized or subjected to international rather than national regulation. Or, again, take two associations of a very different kind, the International Association for the Testing of Materials and a great International Labor federation like the International Metal Workers' Federation. The first, with some 3,000 members in all the great industrial countries of the world, is engaged in unifying methods of testing materials. Its members are engaged in the practical prosecution of industry; the work of their association and the agreements embodied in their resolutions tend to establish international standards of industrial materials, metals, cements, stone, and other products. Similar associations are in almost every department of industry and commerce establishing, by similar international agreements regarding analysis or methods of production of commercial products, international rather than national standards of production. In other words, the kinds of things which we use and wear and eat are being standardized internationally by international agreement between the producers. On the other side, the labor side of industry and production, we find all the great metal workers' trade unions of the world united for international action in the International Metal Workers' Federation. That action consists in an attempt to regulate by agreement between the national groups the conditions of employment, and in particular to regulate the international movements of labor in the metal trades. Such international organization of labor has its weak points, but, as a later chapter will show, it has already succeeded to some extent in applying International Government to the relations (1) of employer and worker, and (2) of the different national groups of workers.

The three kinds of International Organism with which we have so far dealt are: (1) The Diplomatic Conference, (2) Permanent Associations of Governments or Administrations, sometimes called Public International Unions, (3) International Associations of which the members are individuals or groups of individuals. The fourth and last kind is one which is connected only with a particular department of life, namely, commerce, industry, and finance. Everyone has heard or read such phrases as: "Capital is international," or "finance is international"; but few people realize the extent to which not only finance but industry has been internationalized in the last 100 years. A large part of the production and distribution of commodities throughout the world is regulated by agreement between the groups of producers and suppliers in the different countries; in other words, International Government has been extensively applied to national and international trade. A study of this phenomenon is peculiarly relevant, because this regulation of relations by agreement has appeared spontaneously among national groups engaged in competition and in a sphere of life where national interests are always assumed to be most violently in conflict. The organisms or organization through which this government has been established take many different forms. In the simplest form there is merely an agreement between national companies or individual producers and traders—each an "independent sovereign" commercial or industrial entity —to regulate competition or production or price or to divide the world into "markets." In other cases the national groups surrender some of their independence and sovereignty, and form international trusts and cartels, which may be very elaborate international organisms; in others, again, the groups merge their own individuality completely in one International Company, which would answer in the political sphere to an International State. Details will be found in Chapter VI of many of these different types and of the functions which they have performed.

CHAPTER III

THE INTERNATIONALIZATION OF ADMINISTRATION

ADMINISTRATION must be regarded as the most precious flower and fruit, the essential mark and prerogative of the independent, sovereign State. It is, then, not wonderful that those who regard such a State as an isolated entity, a water-tight compartment of "national interests," should postulate the absolute independence of its administration as a condition of its existence as a State. This is well understood in those subterranean regions where the evil spirits guide diplomatists toward inevitable war. They know that, whatever the real causes which would induce civilized men to massacre one another by the hundred thousand, the men themselves must believe that a demand had been made by one independent sovereign State to interfere in the administration of another independent sovereign State before the process could begin. Nothing could make a war between Austrians and Serbians so inevitable as a demand on the part of "Austria" to interfere in the administration of "Serbia."

That Austria's demand was unjustifiable cannot alter the fact that this conception of the State and of administration is false, for it does not mirror the realities of life and the world as they exist to-day. History is continually getting ahead of the conceptions and beliefs of human beings, including diplomatists and international lawyers; and the catastrophes and miseries of humanity are often caused by the attempt to apply these obsolete conceptions and beliefs to a world which they no longer fit. Such is the present catastrophe, and it shows that either our conceptions must go forward and conform with an advanced world, or the world will be dragged back into line with our primitive beliefs.

Administration, as we know it to-day, is part of national government. In most civilized countries the maintenance of law and order, the regulation of health and sanitation, of means of communication, of many commercial and industrial relations and operations, is intrusted to or controlled by the State. All the practical steps which from day to day the State takes to maintain law and order, and to regulate health or the dispatch of telegrams or the coinage and issue of money, are part of the administrative function of State government. These functions are not the result of any sudden discovery, of any new theory or crank; they have grown naturally to meet the needs of a changing society. Life as we know it in cities like London and New York—where men live so close that they have had to tunnel into the earth in order to be able to move about, and build high into the air in order to find room to sleep—would be impossible if the maintenance of law and order were left in the hands of the individual, or to any organization not coextensive with the whole population. But precisely these latter conditions exist where, as in Arabia, the normal life of society is different, and can proceed with every man a law unto himself. And the same is true, though perhaps not quite so obviously, of the State organization of the medium of exchange or postal communications. Certainly modern industry and commerce, as well as other sides of life, could not exist in Great Britain without the uniformity of organization which public administration alone can give to our currency and post office.

The infinite complication of life brought State Socialism into existence; immediately men began to quarrel about its theory. But while they were quarreling, life itself was moving on and changing, and, therefore, calling into existence something beyond State Socialism—the beginnings of inter-State Socialism. The needs of human society in large parts of the earth can no longer be met by organization rigidly confined to administration of independent States. In innumerable ways the condition of society in England is so dependent upon that of society in Germany, and *vice versâ*, that either the fabric of society or the complete independence of German and British administration had to break down. In the years between 1815 and 1914 it was not the fabric of society, but the independence of States, which, in fact, gave way. Take the case of trade alone. In the twelve months before the war the peoples of the two countries exchanged goods the value of which was £120,000,000, or half again as much as the value of our whole foreign trade in 1820. In the same time our exports to and imports from Asia amounted to £210,000,000, or more than 150 per cent. of our whole export and import trade in 1820. It requires little imagination to realize what these figures mean in the coming and going of men and ships between the different countries, in the rapid and regular dispatch and receipt of telegrams and letters, in the constant and smooth working of the machinery of credit. And while the diplomatists and three-quarters of the inhabitants of civilized countries, deluded by the fetish of national interests, still believe in the absolute independence of the individual sovereign State, the most subordinate clerk in any of our public offices, if he paused to think before signing his name to many an official document which passes across his table, would see in it how impossible the intercommunication of peoples would be if this independence of States really existed. How could the German and the Chinaman buy our coal and our cotton goods to the value of millions of pounds per annum, how could we buy the German's iron and the Chinaman's tea, unless the uniformity and regularity and certainty of postal and telegraphic communication had been assured by international rather than national administration? And how long would the perpetual coming and going of our ships continue, if there were no international regulation and administration of sanitation and quarantine, if Asia were allowed to export its plague and its cholera, and European countries were allowed to import them as freely as its rice and its silks and its spices?

Here are international interests in trade and industry and public health to which all purely national interests have, in fact, had to give way. As a result of international agreements between States, two processes have taken place, either international administration has been set up with international administrative organs, or the several States have undertaken to introduce uniformity into their several administrations. The process has been applied to four departments of life and government: (1) Communications, (2) Public Health, (3) Industry and Commerce, (4) Morals and Crime. The process is, as I have said, of very recent date, and it has been checked and thwarted by the obstinate affection of Foreign Offices for the theories of "irreconcilable national interests," and of the absolute independence of national government. Nevertheless, what it has achieved is of so great an importance that I now propose to examine in detail this internationalization of administration in the four departments of life. For the examination will, I believe, show, first, how much has been accomplished in this way towards regulating the relations of States and administrations by international agreement, and second, how the establishment of such International Government for the sake of international interests has affected particular and peculiar national interests.

A.—Communications

It has often been pointed out that life in 1900 differs enormously more from life in 1800 than life in 1800 from life in 800. This rapid revolution has been made possible only by a revolution in communications. The civilizations of the first 1800 years of the Christian era at different times rested upon the Empire, the Church, Feudalism, the Land, or the Hierarchy of Classes. Our civilization rests ultimately upon the Post, the Telegraph, the Telephone, the Railway, the Steamship, the Motor Car, and the Aeroplane. If you cut the communications of Europe we should fall back plumb in twelve months from the 20th century to the 10th. But these communications are international; they cease to exist unless they are made independent of the frontiers of States. They are the greatest of all international interests, and they cannot perform their functions without international administration. Consequently we shall find that the most complete internationalization of administration has occurred in the case of communications.

Before proceeding to show how this has in detail been accomplished, there is one point of great general importance which should be noted. Everyone can see that the interests in the international uniformity of the Postal Services are international. "Of course," it will be said, "it is to the interest of every nation to unify the administration of such services, and even to sacrifice some independence of national administration in order to obtain this uniformity. This is an international interest. It is also in the interest of each individual nation. Therefore there is no sacrifice of national interests in taking part in such associations as the Universal Postal Union. But they have no bearing upon the political and economic problems of international relations in which great national interests are involved." Such arguments have, in fact, caused the importance of the object-lessons in International Government displayed by the Postal and other unions to be ignored; but, despite their superficial plausibility, they are good examples of the ignorance and confusion of thought which prevail on the subject of international relations.

The ordinary view is that national interests demand the jealous maintenance of complete independence of government for each State. Here are international interests so compelling that they have led every State to sacrifice some of its independence of government. The fact that this sacrifice is so obviously in the national interests only shows more clearly the falseness of the ordinary view of national interests and the independence of States. But it is historically quite untrue that these international interests are so completely also national interests that the adoption of International Government for their regulation did not involve the sacrifice of what are ordinarily thought of as "national interests." The formation of the Postal Union was delayed because France refused to join it, believing that it would involve a sacrifice of her peculiar financial interests. Great Britain refused for some time to enter the Radiotelegraphic Union on the ground that it would involve the sacrifice of vital Imperial interests, just as she refused for long to sign any general Sanitary Convention on the ground that it would involve the sacrifice of interests vital to her as a great maritime Power with a great carrying trade. And when these associations of States and administrations have been formed and international administration is operating, within the organizations or associations themselves, diverse "national interests" are, as we shall see, continually showing themselves. Within the Postal Union the interests of Germany and Britain are no more identical than they were in the Algeciras Conference. All government which is regulation of relations through agreement involves compromise, a give and take between not identical interests. It is sheer confusion of thought which leads people to believe that such compromise is rational when applied to so useful and palpable a thing as a national postage stamp, but would be national suicide if extended to a priceless but impalpable thing like national prestige.

(1) *The Universal Postal Union*

The Universal Postal Union after a life of over forty years remains the most complete and important example of international administration. As soon as economic and commercial relations on a large scale became possible—and this happened in the nineteenth century—in order that that possibility might be utilized, some international regulation of postal communications between countries was necessary. During the first half of the century this regulation was attempted, and this attempt was made strictly in accordance with the ordinary theory of the absolute independence of the independent sovereign State. Individual States concluded treaties with one another, regulating the interchange of correspondence between them. A considerable number of such treaties were made, and they were made in accordance with the ordinary "diplomatic" theory of national interests. The object of State A in concluding a postal treaty with State B was to advance the interests of A at the expense of B, and the object of B was to advance the interests of B at the expense of A. The aim of these treaties was not to advance the international interest of international communication, but "to make the foreigner pay."

This system, however advantageous it may have been to the State, was by no means satisfactory to its citizens. Making the foreigner pay is a game at which two can play, at any rate where a Postal Convention is concerned. The foreigner did pay, but, as everyone was a foreigner, everyone paid —ridiculously high foreign postage rates. The rates were also uncertain, extremely variable, and could only be ascertained in many cases by complicated mathematical calculation. They were made up of a payment to the country of dispatch, a payment to the country of destination, a payment to any intermediate country through which the letter had to be transmitted, and a payment for sea transit. For instance, there were three different rates between Germany and Austria, and a business man sending a letter from the United States to Australia was confronted with the fact, arrived at after some calculation, that the postage would be 5 cents, 33 cents, 45 cents, 60 cents, or $1.02 per ½ oz., according to the route by which it was sent.*

After a system of this kind had been tried for some fifty or sixty years, it became clear that the development of modern commerce required an attempt to be made to organize international postal relations on uniform principles. In 1863, at the suggestion of the Postmaster-General of the United States, fifteen States sent delegates to a Conference in Paris, at which agreement upon certain general principles was found possible. The principles were, however, not made obligatory. Meanwhile, the International Telegraph Convention, the basis of the Telegraphic Union, had been signed in 1865, so that everything was conspiring to push the several States into a union for the purposes of postal communication. The final impetus came from Dr. Von Stephan, the Director-General of Posts of the North German Confederation, who, in 1868, having just successfully introduced unification of postal administra-

---

* Reinsch, *Public International Unions.*

tions in the German States, published a scheme for a similar unification in the greater international world. The proposal met with considerable hostility in nearly all countries. There were people who argued that national interests would suffer financially, when they thought of the few millions of revenue which they believed they "made the foreigner pay": they forgot the few millions of revenue which the foreigner believed that *he* "made the foreigner pay," and they overlooked the many millions from which efficient international communications would flow into the national income from foreign trade. Then, too, it is interesting to notice that there were other people who foresaw in a Postal Union just those dangers to the independence and sovereignty of the State which we are told to-day threaten us from any proposal which would make for International Government.* Finally, those national interests of France, which, in the region of politics, the French nation believed at the time that they were advancing by fighting the German nation in the Franco-German War, intervened and proved conclusively to the French that they had no national interest in international communications.

But, despite of wars and independent sovereign States, the world of everyday life and everyday men proceeds to develop in its own way. By 1874 the pressure of this development had overcome all obstacles, and on the invitation of the

---

* "Nationalists of all countries saw in the proposal a menace to national sentiment and national glory."—*The Post Office and Its Story*, by E. Bennett.

Swiss Federal Council and the suggestion of the German Government, a Postal Congress, at which twenty-two States were represented, met at Berne. As a result, the General Postal Union—which in 1878 became the Universal Postal Union—was formed by a Treaty which was ratified and came into force on July 1, 1875. Since that date the Governments of practically all civilized and even uncivilized countries have adhered to the Convention of the Union, so that it is hardly an exaggeration to say that international postal communication throughout the world is regulated by its provisions.

The Universal Postal Union establishes an elaborate form of International Government, and I propose, therefore, first to examine in detail its constitution, and then to show how in practice that constitution has worked. The constitution of the Union is contained in a Convention and a Règlement; the provisions of the former establish the organs of government, and, roughly, lay down the fundamental principles and the more important details of the administration to be applied to international postage; the provisions of the latter are concerned solely with the details of that administration. These provisions apply to letters, post cards, printed papers of every kind, commercial papers, and samples entering into the international service. The most important of them contained in the Convention * are as follows:—

---

* The provisions which follow are those contained in the most recent Convention and Règlement concluded at the last Congress of the Union held at Rome in 1906.

1. The countries in the Union form a single postal territory for exchange of correspondence.
2. Freedom of transit is guaranteed throughout the territory of the Union. The transit charges are fixed according to the total net weight and according to the mileage of transit. The basis for charges is obtained by weighing mails during four weeks every six years.
3. Uniform postal rates for foreign correspondence are fixed.
4. In case of loss, the responsibility of Administrations is established.
5. Acceptance for transit through the post of certain articles is forbidden.
6. Restricted unions for special purposes are allowed.
7. Arbitration in disputes between Administrations is provided for.

Further, the Convention and the Règlement together prescribe limits of weight and size of postal matter, govern the charges to the public for postage, registration, express delivery, collection of value on delivery, and coupons for the prepayment of reply postage. They also lay down rules for the treatment of letters, etc., for the making up of mails, for the transport of mails, for the accounting in respect of intermediary transport services, and for the settlement through a Central Clearing House of such accounts as the Administrations mutually agree to liquidate in this manner.

The original Convention also established the

following three organs of International Government:—

1. *The Congress* of plenipotentiaries, which is to meet every five * years or when demand is made by two-thirds of the Governments. Each country has one vote. The Congress has power to alter or amend both the Convention and the Règlement, and a majority vote of the delegates is sufficient to secure the amendment of any clause of either or the insertion of a new clause. The Convention and Règlement, when amended by the Congress, is signed by each delegate, and requires, like other diplomatic instruments, subsequent ratification by the several Governments.

2. *The Conference* of Delegates of Administrations.—It is to meet on the demand of two-thirds of the Administrations when any question of minor importance has to be considered. Its rules of procedure are similar to those of the Congress.

3. *The International Bureau.*—This is a permanent administrative organ, maintained under the supervision of the Swiss Postal Union at Berne. Its expenses are shared among the Administrations, which are divided for this purpose into seven classes. Each member of the first class contributes 25 units, and members of the other classes contribute smaller proportions. The different countries, at the time of their entry into the Union, come to an agreement with the Swiss Government as to their classification. The Bureau collects,

---

* This provision is not strictly observed in practice. The interval between the last two Congresses was nine years.

publishes, and distributes information, circulates proposals, and notifies alterations adopted; publishes a journal in three languages; acts as a Clearing House for the settlement of accounts; arranges for the manufacture and supply of reply-coupons; gives an opinion upon questions in dispute at the request of the parties concerned.

The Convention provides a further procedure for obtaining decisions as to the government of the Union. In the intervals between the meetings of Congresses or Conferences, proposals concerning the working of the Union or the amendment of the Convention or Règlement may be made by any Administration (provided that they are supported by at least two others) through the International Bureau. Observations are first invited. The answers received are tabulated and circulated, and the Administrations are then asked to vote either for or against the proposal. The following are the rules * as to the proportion of votes which proposals must obtain in order to become binding:—

(a) In the case of modification of 16 out of 39 articles of the Convention, or the addition of new stipulations, the voting must be unanimous.

(b) In the case of modification of the other 13 articles, a two-thirds majority of votes is required.

(c) In other cases (*e. g.*, where the question is one of interpretation) a simple majority suffices. Such is the constitution of the Universal Postal Union in outline. But its full significance can

---

* These are taken partly from the latest Convention and partly from the actual practice of the Union.

only be understood by an examination of how it works in practice, for all human organizations will be found to differ considerably in practice from what they appear to be in the skeletons of their paper constitutions. First, it should be observed that the Union has successfully applied complete International Government to all those relations of States which are connected with postal communications. It has done so by forming a Union of Postal Administrations. And in doing so, however much in theory and on paper each State has guarded itself, actually it has destroyed the independency and sovereignty of the State over its own administration of the foreign post. The delegates who go to the Congresses are delegates from the national Administrations. They are, of course, instructed by their Governments as to how they shall vote upon important matters. But when they have recorded their vote, their Administration is upon every question bound by the decision of the majority of Administrations voting.* It is true that in theory the delegate might refuse to sign the Convention, or, even if he signed it, his Government might refuse to ratify it. In practice, neither of these courses is ever contemplated, simply because our Governments have accepted

---

* Writers on the subject do not seem to realize that in the Congress a majority vote is sufficient in every case to make a decision binding. Thus, Professor Reinsch (*Public International Unions*, p. 26) seems to imply that fifteen articles of the Convention require unanimity of votes for their modification by the Congress. But this really refers only to the procedure for amending the Convention in the intervals between Congresses. The Congress itself always decides by a majority vote.

International Government for this department of life. At one Congress the majority of the delegates were in favor of a change in a foreign postage rate. The French Government was strongly opposed to any change, and the French delegate announced that he would not only vote against, but refuse to accept it. The proposed change obtained a majority of the votes; the new Convention was signed by the French delegate and ratified by his Government; and the rate was changed. Thus, the French Government was faced by the alternative of withdrawing from the Union and asserting the independence of its own Administration, or of surrendering its independence for the advantages of International Government. It did not hesitate twenty-four hours to choose the latter. In fact, so far has the surrender of independence to International Government gone in the Union, that the theoretical right of the State to refuse ratification to the Convention and Règlement as voted at a Congress in practice hardly exists. The Administrations, adhering to the Union, never wait for formal ratification before putting the new regulations into operation, and the decisions of a Postal Congress are acted upon whether they are ratified or not.

The result is that the nations of the whole world have for everything connected with the international exchange of letters and other postal matter submitted to International Government. Each national Administration can no longer determine the rates it will charge, the matter which it will or will not receive, or the methods on which it will conduct the foreign postal service. On all these subjects the national Administration is in practice bound to accept the decision of the majority of the Administrations adhering to the Union. In other words, the administration of postal communication between States has been internationalized.

There is one minor point as to the development of the Union which is worth recording, because it has not been noticed or understood [*] by writers on the subject. The framers of the constitution gave the Union two legislative organs, the Congress and the Conference, and it was clearly their intention that the former should meet periodically to revise the Convention and Règlement, and be summoned to settle any matter of importance, while the latter should be called together when any question of minor importance had to be decided. But in practice the Union now acts only through the one organ, the Congress, and the Conference has ceased to exist. A Conference was held once in 1876, and that is, I believe, the one solitary instance in the whole history of the Postal Union. The reason is obvious. Any question of small importance that arises in the interval between Congresses can far more conveniently be disposed of by circulation of the proposal to the Administra-

---

[*] *Public International Unions*, by Professor Reinsch, p. 25:—"The Congress is composed of plenipotentiaries empowered to introduce changes both in the Convention and Règlement; whereas the Conference is an administrative body, which deals only with the latter." The statement is not, it will be seen, accurate.

tions by the procedure described above than by calling a Conference. Hence, in practice the Union works through two, not three, organs, namely, the Congress and the Bureau.

We have seen that the adherence of a State to the Postal Convention results in a surrender of its independence and sovereignty in the realm of postal communications, in its voluntary submission to International Government.* The most interesting question raised by this event is: What have been the practical effects of this surrender and submission? Have they resulted in ruin and disaster to the fabric of States and of international society? And have they involved, as all the doctrines of all the patriots would lead us to expect, the surrender of national interests? It may be said at once that none of these terrible disasters appears to have resulted. The Postal Union, having by its birth effected a revolution in the constitution of the society of nations, has had a forty years' history of placid obscurity, unworthy of the notice of patriots, and rarely recognized as a herald of the Millennium by an occasional pacifist.

Yet a very little enquiry would show that the problem of conflicting national interests contin-

---

* It is safer to forestall criticism by remarking that a good case could be made out theoretically for the assertion that the independence and sovereignty of the State are not impaired by adherence. Personally, I believe that a view of independence and sovereignty which implies that they are impaired by voluntary submission to international government is in need of revision. But that cannot alter the fact that the practical working of the Union is not compatible with the independence and sovereignty of a State as they are ordinarily conceived (*vide supra*).

ually arises and is continually being solved by agreement within the Union. The interests of all the nations of the world are no more identical in postal communication than they are in the exploitation of Morocco. And it might even be argued that the interests involved in the methods of such communication are no less "vital" than those involved in the rights of a few capitalists to build bridges for, sell gramophones to, or work the mines of some African potentate. At any rate, as soon as the Postal Union began to devise a uniform system of international postal administration, it found that the national interests in that administration differed profoundly. I propose to show briefly how agreement has succeeded or failed to harmonize such conflicting interests.

The Union was very soon faced with the difficulty, discussed in an early part of this book, of applying International Government to States, each of which ranks as a unit of government, but which vary enormously in size and importance. The interests of the forty million Frenchmen, represented by the French Postal Administration, are certainly greater in the international post than the ten million Persians, represented by the Persian Postal Administration, especially when the difference of French and Persian societies is taken into consideration. In Part I of this book, in considering a particular problem of International Government, I argued that if in such circumstances the same voting power were given to both nations, irrespective of the difference in the interests which each had at stake, the system would in practice be found unworkable. At first sight this argument would seem to be disproved by the fact that the Postal Convention does give one vote to each State, no matter what its size or the size of its interests may be. But a closer view of the working of the Convention shows that it has been found necessary in rather roundabout ways to give States of great size and larger interests voting power proportionate to their size and their interests.

This has been achieved in the first place by giving Colonies and Dependencies of the Great Powers separate representation in the Union. Thus, not only the French Postal Administration is a member of the Union, but also the Postal Administrations of (1) Algeria, (2) Indo-China, and (3) other French Colonies. France has, therefore, in practice not one but four votes in the Congress, and in the same way Great Britain, including her Colonies and Dependencies, has eight votes.* But there is still another method by which the more important States have been given a preponderating voice. The preliminary work of the Congress is shared between Committees appointed at the first meeting of the delegates. In these Committees the proposals submitted by the various Administrations are discussed, and a report is then made to the Congress, which confirms or

---

* Similarly, Germany had three and the U.S.A. two votes. It is interesting to note that whereas the colonies and dependencies, etc., of other States always vote the same way as the Mother Country, this has not always been the case with the British Empire.

amends it. Finally, each Convention, Agreement, or set of Regulations is voted upon by the Congress as a whole. Anyone with any experience of the working of the machinery of human organizations will see at once that the real work of the Postal Congress is done in Committee. There were in the full Congress of 1906 over eighty delegates; such a body is not suitable for considering in detail in a limited time highly technical proposals. The result is that the Reports of Committees are generally accepted by the Congress. Now, by a certain amount of manipulation, it has become customary practically always to give the Great Powers representation upon the Committees, and in this way they have obtained very considerable opportunity for getting their views accepted. This arrangement has not been allowed to continue unchallenged, and at the last Congress the smaller States protested against their exclusion from Committees, and it was agreed that in future every Administration should be entitled to be represented at least once upon a Committee at every Congress.

The point is of real importance, for it shows how conflicting national interests emerge in the Union, and have been successfully dealt with. The great battles of the Postal Congress have been fought over the question of transit charges. At present when a letter is dispatched from the territory of one Administration to the territory of a second, but in the course of transmission has to pass through a third Administration, the intermediary is entitled to make a transit charge. There are, however, two groups of Administrations in the Union—one in favor of a charge being made for transit, the other in favor of free transit. It will readily be understood how it has come about that the interests of the larger and the smaller nations are in conflict on this question, and that the large nations are in the former, and the majority of the small nations in the latter group. It is to the interest of a country like Persia or the many small South American Republics that no charge should be made for transit, for, being outside the main highways of the world, very little postal matter passes through their territory *en route* for some other Administration, while much of the correspondence dispatched from their territory is obliged to pass through that of a third Administration. They, therefore, are payers but not receivers of transit charges. The case is very different with the great nations which are themselves the highways of international life by reason of their position and the network of railways which covers them, or are centers from which many shipping lines radiate across the seas to connect all the nations of the world. These countries are the carriers of the world's correspondence, and are, therefore, not only the payers, but also the receivers of transit charges. And so it would be all to the advantage of the majority of smaller nations for transit to be free, since the cost of carrying a considerable amount of international correspondence would fall upon the larger nations, the payment for which would go to the smaller nations. So far, the result of this conflict of interests in the Union has been that the supporters of free transit have not carried their point, while, on the other hand, the transit charges have been kept distinctly moderate.

There is one other point regarding the working of the Union which has a great bearing upon International Government. No government, international or national, which is based upon agreement or submission to collective decisions, is possible unless compromise, where interests conflict, is widely resorted to. In the House of Commons, in the County Council, and in the Trade Union it is in the power of a majority every day to vote down a minority and its interests uncompromisingly. But everyone knows that if this power were so used, if every unit in these associations regarded its own interests with a kind of religious veneration as something from which no abatement could be made in the interest of another unit, then neither national nor municipal nor trade union government would be possible at all. The theory of all modern government, including that of the State, implies an agreement between the units of an association to abide by the collective decisions of the associated units. But that agreement will in practice not be kept unless the decisions are themselves to a considerable degree in the nature of agreements. Each unit of the association must be prepared in some measure both to give and to take, to recognize that the interests of other units have at least a fractional importance of its own in the eye of God. This, in other words, means the dreary, but sacred, duty of compromise and recognition of the rights of minorities.

If this be true of national government it is far more true of the beginnings of International Government in which the bonds between the units of the association are still green. Yet here precisely patriotism and the popular and diplomatic theories of national interests might be expected to make for a ruthless prosecution by each unit of its own interests and a ruthless over-riding of minorities. It is therefore interesting to note that in the Postal Union compromise has been the rule, together with an extreme tenderness to minorities, and yet it has never been suggested that this tenderness on the part of one State for the interests of another has really harmed its own. The proof that, in actual practice, considerable allowance is made for the special circumstances and views of minorities may be found in the large number of exceptions and options allowed in the Postal Convention. It would take too long to deal with these in detail, and I therefore propose to give only one, but an instructive, example.

By Article 12 of the Convention (of 1906) each Administration retains the sums which it receives from postal matter dispatched by it, and letters, etc., cannot in the country of origin be subject to any charge other than the uniform postal rates. The result is that each Administration receives payment only for letters, etc., dispatched by it, not for those received by it. The theory, which on the whole works out fairly in practice, is that the number of letters dispatched will equal the number received by an Administration. But now it is found that the kingdom of Persia stands in a curious relation to the kingdom of Great Britain and the Republic of the United States. The former is inhabited by Mohammedans, the two latter by Christians. British and American Christians have a passion for sending Bibles to the Persian Mohammedans, while the Persian never sends his Koran to Britain or America. Moreover, in Persia there are no railways, and transport is by camel, and extremely expensive. At one of the last Postal Congresses the Persian delegate, in an eloquent and moving speech, drew attention to the injustice wrought to his Administration in these circumstances under Article 12. The British and American Administrations retain all the postage on the hundreds of Bibles dispatched by their Christian subjects. All the year round the Persian Administration has to provide at great cost strings of camels to convey the stream of foreign Bibles to its subjects. For doing this it gets no return, and meanwhile the Persians neglect to send either letters or Korans to foreigners, the postage on which would be retained by their own Administration. The justice and eloquence of the Persian plea had its effect, and the following Article V is added in a final protocol to the Convention of 1906: "Par exception aux dispositions du §3 de l'article 12 de la Convention, la Perse a la faculté de percevoir sur les destinataires des imprimés de toute sorte arrivant de l'étranger une taxe de 5 centimes par envoi distribué."

(2) *International Telegraphy*

The necessity for uniformity of administration is even more pressing in the case of international telegraphy than in that of the international post. And so, though the telegraph boy made his appearance centuries later than the postman, the International Telegraphic Union was formed at a Conference in Paris in 1865, nine years before the Postal Union. The international administration resulting from the Convention signed at that Conference is in so many respects similar to that which results from the Postal Convention that a detailed examination of it would entail much repetition. I propose, therefore, to deal very shortly with its chief characteristics and in particular with the points in which it differs from the Postal Administration.

The constitution of the Union is contained in a Convention and a Règlement, and it owes its present form to the Conference at St. Petersburg in 1875, which revised the original Convention. Unlike the Postal Convention, the Telegraphic Convention is strictly confined to the fundamental stipulations or general principles of the Union, while all the details are contained in the provisions of the Règlement. As a result, while the Postal Convention has been revised periodically by the Postal Congresses, no revision of the Telegraphic Convention has been found necessary since 1875. The fundamental stipulations bind States to recognize the right of all persons to correspond by means of the international telegraph and to provide special wires for the international telegraphic service in sufficient numbers to insure rapid transmission. They also insure the right of transit of telegrams,* and a uniform charge between telegraphic offices of different States.

The Convention establishes two organs of International Government—the Conference and the Bureau. The functions of the Bureau are similar to those performed by the Postal Bureau for the Postal Union. But the Telegraphic Conference differs in one important respect from the Postal Congress: the latter has the power to amend both the Convention and the Règlement, the former can only deal with the provisions of the Règlement. Thus, while the Postal Convention created a new international legislative organ which has the power to alter the constitution and fundamental principles of the Union, the legislative organ of the Telegraphic Union has no power to alter the constitution or fundamental stipulations, but is confined to regulating international telegraphy within the limits of the general principles laid down in the Convention. This, however, does not prevent the Conference from substituting In-

---

* Subject to certain reservations.

ternational for National Government in the widest sense. The decisions of the Conference bind the different Administrations on such important points as the following, which are contained in the Règlement:—

(1) The provision of apparatus necessary for rapid transmission.

(2) The hours during which telegraph offices shall be open.

(3) The form in which telegrams are to be written, the classification of telegrams, and the counting of words.

(4) The tariff of charges for transmission and transit; the settling of accounts between Administrations.

(5) The signals of transmission to be employed, and the methods of transmission.

(6) The international telephonic service.

The procedure of a Telegraphic Conference is in all important respects the same as that of a Postal Congress, and a similar * procedure to that of the Postal Union exists for amending the Règlement or Tariff in the intervals between Conferences. The union is not quite so universal as the Postal Union, since the United States of America

---

* The procedure differs in the following points: When proposals are circulated, counter-proposals and amendments are allowed. These, if made, are circulated, and each Administration is asked to vote for or against the original proposals and the counter-proposals. Unanimous assent is required for any modification of the Règlement, and the assent of the Administrations concerned for any modification of tariffs, but a majority vote is sufficient for an interpretation of the provisions of the Règlement.

still remains outside, though it sends a representative to the Conferences with the right to take part in the proceedings, but not to vote. The fact that very few of the telegraph lines of the United States are under federal control stands in the way of its becoming a member of the Union. It is interesting to observe that private telegraph companies are admitted to quasi-membership, *i. e.*, they are admitted to Conferences, but cannot vote. At the time of the last Conference there were thirty-one private companies "adhering" to the Union.

But the Telegraphic Union has not proved sufficient by itself to protect the international interests which telegraphy has created. The first submarine cable was laid in 1851, and the first transatlantic cable in 1858. Now, submarine cables are laid in the international territory called the sea. They are liable to many kinds of damage, but particularly to damage from fishing-boats and dredgers. But while it is to the interest of every State that submarine cables should be protected from damage, it is impossible that this can be adequately done by independent legislation and administration in the different States, in view of the fact that the territory in which the cables are laid is international and is used by vessels of all the different nations. As early as 1863 the need for international action was recognized, and a Conference of seven States was held in Paris, and resulted in a Convention for the protection of a submarine cable. Action on a large scale was not, however, taken until 1882, when a Conference of over thirty States met at Paris, and, after sitting again in 1883, produced a Convention, which was signed in 1884.

The method adopted for introducing International Government to protect this international interest differs considerably from that adopted in the two Unions with which I have just dealt. What is required in this case is to make by legislation certain acts of damage, whether voluntary or the result of culpable negligence, punishable, and then by administration to take the necessary steps for catching and punishing offenders. This might have been most easily attained by making the offenses international offenses, and offenders subject to arrest by the public officers and punishable in the Courts of any signatory State. But for some reason the idea of international jurisdiction for an international offense always seems a more dangerous encroachment upon nationalism than the far more drastic encroachments of organs like the Postal Congress. The method, therefore, adopted in the Convention of 1884 was a compromise between International and National Government. The signatory States agree that damage, done voluntarily or by culpable negligence, to submarine cables shall be punishable (Article 2), and that ships laying or repairing cables and boats engaged in fishing shall take certain precautions with a view to preventing damage (Articles 5 and 6). The several States bind themselves to introduce legislation "pour assurer l'éxécution de la présente Convention et notamment pour faire punir, soit de l'imprisonnement, soit de l'amende, soit de ces deux peines, ceux qui contreviendraient aux dispositions des articles 2, 5, et 6. Jurisdiction to try offenses is confined to the Courts of the country to which the offending ship belongs, but any vessel of war of any State, or any vessel specially commissioned by any State, may arrest any ship suspected of offending, and the officers of the former may examine the ship's papers and make a procès-verbal, which can be used in evidence in the Court before which the case eventually comes for trial.

Thus in the Convention of 1884 International Government is recognized in three different ways. The signatory States bind themselves by agreement to introduce a uniform national law (a subject which rightly belongs to the next chapter), thereby rendering certain actions not only national, but also international, offenses. The result of this cosmopolitan legislation is, further, to introduce some measure of uniformity into the several national Administrations. Thirdly, the actual apprehension of offenders is put under international administration, for the commissioned vessels of the signatory States are given powers of an international police for the protection of cables.

The Convention of 1884 recognized that isolated and independent action of States in this matter was useless. No harm seems to have resulted to national interests from the measure of International Government which was set up; in fact, there is evidence that the protection is not international enough to be efficacious. In 1908 the British Government, in consequence of damage caused to thirteen transatlantic cables, set up a National Commission, composed of representatives of cable companies and fishing interests. The Commission exercised surveillance over the construction of fishing boats, and the effect was to reduce the damage done to cables. But the effect could only be partial so long as other countries neglected to adopt similar measures, and so the British Government summoned a Conference in 1913 with a view to getting the Governments of other States to adopt uniform administrative measures of this kind. The object of the Conference was not to conclude a new Convention, but to arrange for the organization of a common system of inspection and other measures by the different Administrations.* The resolutions adopted at the Conference provide, among other things, for the establishment in each country of a central authority occupying itself with all questions relating to demands for indemnities for damage, these authorities to be in direct communication with one another. Another resolution provides for the direct exchange of information, etc., between the Administrations of the various countries which deal with the protection of cables.

The invention of wireless telegraphy introduced a further complication of international interests.

---

* *Vide La Vie Internationale*, V, 1914, p. 136.

The international interests of communication clearly prescribed the exchange of wireless messages between the installations of various countries, and the international interest of safety at sea even more clearly required the exchange of messages between ship and ship, and ship and coast. As soon, however, as a proposal was made to attain these objects by International Government through a Union on the model of the Telegraphic Union, the usual parochial cry of vital national interests was raised. "The British Marconi Company secured an exclusive contract with the British Lloyd and with the Italian Government for telegraphic service between vessels and coast. Under this arrangement the wireless stations in these two countries would refuse to receive or send messages of any other system than that of Marconi. The political advantages of such an arrangement to a Power like Great Britain are apparent at first sight, and the relinquishment of such a privilege through any Convention met with much resistance in England, because it was believed that, under the Marconi monopoly, the British Government would have obtained a great advantage over its rivals." *

In other words, we had to weigh the advantages of free international communication regulated by international agreement against the interests of the Marconi Company, national isolation, and a monopoly which might or might not prove of value

---

* Reinsch, *Public International Unions*, p. 128.

in war.* After a considerable struggle we sacrificed the "vital interests" of the British Marconi Company and the British Empire to the international interests of wireless communication, and it is a curious fact that neither the one nor the other seems to have suffered any visible harm, in peace or in war, by the sacrifice of its vital interests. Marconis stand at about 40s., and the British Navy after a few months of war was supreme in every sea.

The British surrender to internationalism took place, *horresco referens*, at Berlin in 1906, when twenty-nine States sent delegates to a Conférence internationale pour la réglementation de la télégraphie sans fils. The result of the Conference was the signing of a Convention and Règlement which establish a Radiotelegraphic Union on the model of the Telegraphic Union. The Convention contains the fundamental stipulations, the Règlement the details. The chief stipulations of the former were:—

---

* It was argued by British "Nationalists" that the possession of a wireless monopoly by Britain, even in foreign countries, would be a tremendous weapon in war. The *Times*, quoted by Reinsch, wrote:—"The existence of a world-wide commercial organization, with its headquarters in England, in closest touch with the Admiralty, largely operated, even in foreign territories and on foreign ships, by English operators, would be an invaluable asset to the Admiralty in a great war." But the Marconi system was, and is, not the only system of wireless telegraphy, and it is practically certain, therefore, that other countries would never have quietly acquiesced in the establishment of this British monopoly and wireless hegemony. It is interesting, as throwing light upon "Nationalist" psychology, to imagine what the *Times* would have said, and would say, of a similar attempt by Germany to establish, by means of peaceful penetration and commercial monopoly, a wireless hegemony over the whole world in closest touch with the German General Staff!

(1) The dispositions of the Convention are to apply to all wireless stations, whether on the coast or on ships, whether belonging to the States or to private companies (Article 1).

(2) All stations on the coast and all stations on ships must exchange messages without distinction of the system adopted by the stations (Article 3).

(3) Each State must connect its coast station with its main telegraphic system by special wires.

(4) General stipulations as to charges.

The organs of the Union are (1) A Conference of Plenipotentiaries, (2) An Administrative Conference, (3) A Bureau. The Conference of Plenipotentiaries is to deal with proposals to amend or alter the Convention, and it decides itself when and where it shall meet again. The Administrative Conference deals with the Règlement. The Telegraphic Bureau at Berne acts as the Bureau of the Radiotelegraphic Union.

The second Conference of Plenipotentiaries was fixed for 1912, and was held in London in that year. The experience of six years seems to have shown that national interests had not suffered under the International Government established by the Union. At any rate, everything which the Conference did was directed to the extension of the sphere of International Government. This was most remarkable in the attention devoted by the Conference to the question of wireless installations on ships. The *Titanic* disaster had just shown the world that safety of ships at sea is an international interest which can only be safeguarded by international action. An iceberg does not distinguish the national flags under which ships sail. If a vessel under the British flag is sinking or in distress, the safety of its crew or passengers may depend upon its ability to exchange wireless messages even with a German vessel in its neighborhood. That ability would itself depend upon the exchange of messages between all ships being always compulsory. But the Convention of 1906, although it laid down the rule that all coast stations and all ships must exchange messages, no matter what the system of installation adopted, had not applied this rule to the exchange of messages between ship and ship. The Conference of 1912 amended the Convention by making the exchange of messages between ships in all cases obligatory. It also added stipulations regarding the provision of wireless installation on certain classes of ships, the maintenance of wireless communications on ships, the number of operators to be carried, and the provision of an uninterrupted line of wireless installations on the coasts of the signatory States. It stated its adherence in principle to the employment of wireless installation on vessels of certain classes being made obligatory, and declared the desirability of the unification of national legislation by international treaty.

The Convention of 1912 also made a slight alteration in the constitution of the Union. By the original Convention every State was given one vote in the Conferences and by Article 12 the right in certain cases to separate representation of colonies and dependencies was recognized, with the proviso that the number of votes at the disposal of a Government, including its colonies and dependencies, should not exceed six. In the Convention of 1912 the number of colonies and dependencies to which representation and votes were accorded was finally decided.

(3) *Railways*

When two States with a common boundary have reached the stage of civilization which France and Germany had attained in the last century, complete independence of railway administration is incompatible with the modes of life and the requirements of the men and women who are called Frenchmen and Germans. An imperious Franco-German interest accordingly arises which requires the abolition of the national frontier so far as the railway traffic in men and goods is concerned. That "through traffic," under such conditions, should be impossible would be felt to be an absurdity and an anachronism. And this applies to nearly the whole of Continental Europe. "Through traffic" becomes an international interest. But this international interest is not compatible with many "vital national interests," for it can only be properly served by the internationalization of railway administration and the substitution of International for National Government.

The first step towards such a substitution was

taken in 1878,* when an international Conference met at Berne. A second Conference was held in 1881, a third in 1886, and a fourth in 1890. The fourth Conference resulted in the signing of a Convention internationale sur le transport des marchandises par chemins de fer by nine States —Germany, Austria-Hungary, Belgium, France, Italy, Luxemburg, Holland, Russia, and Switzerland. The Convention, although it does internationalize the administration of railways so far as concerns the transport of merchandise, does not set up so advanced a form of International Government as the Unions previously described. It establishes an Administrative Bureau, but no legislative organ with quite the same powers as the Postal Congress and Telegraphic Conference. It provides for modification and amendment of the Convention by stating that Conferences of delegates of signatory States shall be held at regular intervals or on demand of at least one-fourth of the States.

The Convention does, however, effectually abolish the independence of national administration. This can best be shown by giving some of its more important provisions†:—

(1) The acceptance and transport of all merchandise, other than certain defined classes, is

---

* It is said that the idea of an international agreement was first advocated in a pamphlet by two lawyers, MM. Seigneux and Christ, published at Bale in 1875.

† The original Convention, as the result of conferences of revision in 1896 and 1905, has been amended by additional Conventions. The provisions which follow are taken from the amended Convention.

obligatory on all railways, provided that the consignor conforms with the requirements of the Convention.

(2) A uniform system of through transport is established under a "lettre de voiture." Detailed uniform regulations as to the form of the "lettre de voiture," and as to the packing, transport, etc., of certain articles, the recovery and payment of charges, the settlement of accounts between railways, are imposed upon all administrations.

(3) The responsibility of administrations for loss or damage is established. The amounts recoverable from railways for delay are fixed.

(4) The court competent to try cases is the court of the domicile of the railway, but all judgments are executory in all the signatory States.

(5) Disputes between railways are, on the demand of the parties, subject to arbitration of the Bureau.

The Convention has thus applied international administration to the transport of merchandise. The results have been so satisfactory that a proposal was soon made to extend the international system to passengers and baggage, and a draft Convention was under consideration when the great war broke out. But in another direction the further internationalization of railway administration has been found to be both necessary and possible. On the Continent modern conditions of through traffic require some uniformity of gauge and rolling stock, and in 1882 a Conference for the "Unité technique des chemins de fer" met in

Berne. Two further Conferences were held in 1886 and 1907. Conventions have been concluded at these Conferences, and have been ratified by nearly all the Continental States, regulating for all railways:—
 (1) The maximum gauge.
 (2) The construction of rolling stock.
 (3) The loading and marking of wagons.
 (4) The type of lock on carriages used in the international service.

(4) *Other Means of Communication*

The Post, the Telegraph, and the Railway are in most countries subjected to State control and are State enterprises. Their internationalization has therefore largely consisted in a unification of administration by means of an international authority, established by international agreement, and by whose decisions as regards the international services national administrations are bound. Other means of communication, such as shipping and road transport, are usually left to private enterprise, and, though they are often the subjects of national legislation or the objects of national administration, they do not themselves form a department of the administration of the State. Nevertheless, so important are the international interests in the uniformity and freedom of all such means, that neither for shipping nor for road transport by motor-car has independent administration by independent sovereign States been found possible under modern conditions.

To deal in detail with the internationalization of administration applied to shipping and motor-cars would, however, occupy so much space that I propose here simply to give references to some of the more important agreements. As regards shipping, there are in the first place a large number of agreements insuring freedom of navigation on rivers, and either subjecting national administration in connection with navigation to uniform regulations or setting up organs of international administration. Thus, the navigation of the Rhine is regulated by Article 5 of the Treaty of Paris of 1814, and by two Conventions of 1831 and 1868. The regulation of navigation of the Danube has been laid down in Articles 15 to 19 of the Treaty of Paris of 1856, in a protocol of the Conference of London of 1871, in the Treaty of Berlin of 1878, and in the Treaty of London of 1883. By the Treaties of Paris and London, an international organ, the Commission européenne, was created to carry out work necessary to render the river navigable and with power to levy international navigation dues to cover the cost of the work. Navigation of the Scheldt was regulated by Article 9 of the Treaty of London of 1839, and of the Congo by Articles 13 to 25 of the Treaty of Berlin of 1885, in the latter case through an International Commission with wide powers.*

---

* Other rivers to which freedom of navigation has been applied by international agreement are the Meuse, Elbe, Oder, Pruth, Dniester, Niemen, Vistula, Guadiana, Tagus, Douro, in Europe; the St. Lawrence, Amazon, Rio Grande, Rio de la Plata, in America.—*Vide Annuaire de La Vie Internationale*, 1908–1909.

The Automobile Convention of 1909 also deserves mention. It was signed by sixteen States, and it introduces a considerable measure of international administration. It prescribes uniform conditions, by compliance with which cars and drivers can claim the right to use the roads of all signatory Powers, international road certificates and number plates are to be issued by all the different administrations, and four international signposts marking cross-roads, etc., are adopted.

B.—*Public Health and Epidemic Diseases*

Anyone turning over the pages of a collection of treaties signed in the last twenty years will find at intervals some fifty pages occupied by an International Sanitary Convention, a most elaborate international agreement in nearly 200 articles, signed by most of the civilized States of the world. The history which lies behind that document, if it could be fully written, would be of immense value to the student of International Government and of human prejudices, for the conflict fought by the theory of national independence, isolation, and national interests against the facts of international life and international interests has nowhere shown itself more persistently and clearly than in the struggle of human beings against the scourges of cholera, plague, and other epidemic diseases. That history cannot and never can be fully written, for much of the conflict has taken place behind doors closed by diplomacy, in International

Councils and Conferences and in documents buried securely in the archives of public departments. Yet sufficient facts can be ascertained regarding the conflict to show that the ordinary conceptions of the independent State and of the independence of national interests have proved as inapplicable to sanitation and shipping as to communication by post, telegraph, railway, river, and motor-car. Those facts I now propose to give in some detail.

For centuries Europe has been liable to devastating invasions of epidemic diseases, and in particular plague and cholera. They came from the East, from Asia, where in some places they are endemic. The growth of communications and international intercourse through trade in the nineteenth century profoundly affected the question of the spread of these diseases. Modern science tells us that cholera is mainly a water-born disease, and that it is spread usually through the drinking by healthy persons of water which has been contaminated by diseased persons. Bubonic plague is communicated by rat fleas, which have bitten a diseased person, subsequently biting a healthy person. The danger of international epidemics is, therefore, certainly increased by anything which increases the movement of people, rats, or fleas from infected to uninfected areas. It is also increased by anything which increases the rapidity of communications. The incubation period of cholera does not exceed ten days, and of plague fifteen days. In the days of slow sailing vessels the presence of an infected person would often become apparent during the voyage, where to-day, traveling in a fast steamer, he may reach his destination without detection, and start a center of infection in some densely populated place. Facts confirm these *à priori* statements. Cholera and plague epidemics follow the great trade routes between Asia and other continents, and in Asia itself the trade and the great pilgrimage routes. The enormous increase in the volume and rapidity of the streams of humanity which flow along these routes soon warned Europe in the nineteenth century by facts of the increased danger of infection. In 1830 cholera entered Europe for the first time; in 1832 it arrived in Britain, and the same year crossed the Atlantic to America. In 1848–1851, 1851–1855, 1865–1874, 1884–1886, 1892–1895 Europe again suffered from its invasions.*

The safeguarding of Europe against these Asiatic invasions has existed as an international problem since 1830. The problem is twofold, for, since the epidemics follow both the pilgrimage and the trade routes, measures for defense must be applied to the pilgrim traffic to the great Mohammedan shrines at Al Medina and Mecca, as well as to the shipping traffic of men and merchandise from Asia to Europe. These two sides of the problem affect different national interests in different ways; they have for the most part been dealt with by different methods; and it is con-

---

* Manson, *Tropical Diseases*, p. 389.

venient, therefore, to consider them at present separately.

First as to the trade routes. The prevention of the export of cholera from Asia to Europe is clearly for the latter continent an international interest, and the history of the six European epidemics of the last century has proved that isolated and independent action by isolated and independent States is absolutely useless. The rapid diffusion of cholera from one country to another in those epidemics was due solely to the rapidity and frequency of communication by sea between the different countries. The cause of that rapid and frequent communication was international trade, and without freedom for ships to come and go in the ports of the world, international trade as we know it is impossible. Therefore, in dealing with the problem, there are, broadly, only two alternative and mutually exclusive policies available. The first is to take steps which will stop the freedom of shipping and with it both the diffusion of cholera and the international intercourse of commerce; the other is to find some means of preventing the entry into ports of cholera without preventing the free entry and departure of ships. Over these two policies a long and bitter international controversy raged throughout the nineteenth century, for while many Continental States attempted to enforce the first, Great Britain, with her vast "commercial and shipping interests," clung tenaciously to the second. It is in the history of this controversy that the hopelessness of attempting to apply the theory of national independence to the facts of modern life becomes particularly clear.

The first policy is the policy of quarantine. It applies in its extreme form the theory of national isolation and independence. It attempts in each country to keep out epidemic diseases entirely by national action and administration. Theoretically there is no reason why it should not succeed. If there are three countries, A, B, and C, and cholera exists in A and B but not in C, then if C, by administrative action, closes its ports and frontiers to all men, goods, and ships from A and B, C will undoubtedly remain free from disease. Many Continental States in the earlier part of the nineteenth century attempted to apply such a system by quarantine regulations. Men, goods, and ships were detained in ports for a period which was thought to prove that they could not be infected with disease. In some cases the period of detention was as much as twenty days.* Such regulations under which passengers or perishable cargo are liable to three weeks' interment in a southern port, are obviously incompatible with international commerce and intercourse of any kind. A nation which adopts them is electing to withdraw from the international life of the twentieth century into the national isolation of the tenth.

But no State can go back ten centuries unless the individuals of which it is composed are also

---

* *E. g.*, Greece, in 1865 (*vide* Sir John Simon's *Public Health Reports*, Vol. II, p. 246).

willing to go back, and from 1830 to 1914 men and women were, on the whole, unwilling. Consequently, the attempt to keep out cholera by independent national administration, by isolation and quarantine, practically always failed.* It failed primarily because persons refused to suffer the loss of international intercourse and trade, and, to quote Sir John Simon, who was a member of the General Medical Council and Medical Officer of Her Majesty's Privy Council, and one of the first authorities upon Public Health, "contraband of quarantine, like ordinary smuggling, is developed as soon as the inducements for it are considerable. And thus, practically speaking, where great commercial countries are concerned, it can scarcely be dreamt the quarantine restrictions will be anything better than elaborate illustrations of leakiness." But a second cause of their failure was the fact that nations are so dependent upon one another that no isolated action by one Administration could be efficacious. The most stringent quarantine laws are useless unless the Administration of the country knows when to apply them. But it cannot do this unless it has immediate notification of the presence of cholera in other countries. Such notification can only come from the Administrations of those countries. Thus a con-

---

* Sir John Simon (*Public Health Reports*, Vol. II, p. 284) notes only two proved cases of successful quarantine, and they were both cases of small islands, Sicily and Dominica, in which quarantine could be applied with the utmost stringency. In Dominica health-guards with loaded muskets were stationed all round the island to prevent anyone setting foot on it.

dition precedent to effective quarantine is the establishment of an effective and universal system of international administration for the notification of the appearance of disease. It is not unnatural that people so wedded to the theory of national independence and isolation as the adherents of the quarantine policy did not realize this. The result was that over and over again cholera was carried from one port to another port before the National Administration in the second knew of the presence of the disease in the first. This is clearly shown in Sir John Simon's account of the epidemic of 1865. It originated in the return of pilgrims from Mecca to Suez, and Suez handed the disease on to Alexandria. But "before Alexandria confessed itself to be infected it had infected Marseilles. . . . Then before Marseilles confessed itself infected Valencia had received a most disastrous infection from or through it." Altenburg, in the middle of Germany, received its infection from Odessa before it learned that Odessa was infected, and from Altenburg the epidemic spread through Central Europe.

The great opponent of the quarantine system was Britain. She had tried it with most discouraging results in 1832, and ever after that date medical expert opinion and the desires and interests of the trader and shipowner have been in harmony on this matter. It became a plank in British foreign policy that her national interests required an unbending resistance to any interference with shipping. But her reaction against the quarantiners drove her along the path of "national interests" into the opposite extreme, and for years she put forward no reasonable alternative policy. Her fear of damaging her "peculiar interests" became an excuse for refusing to agree to any international action at all. Thus essentially Britain's policy was the same as the quarantining States—"every State for itself, and God protect us all"—the only difference being that, while the latter believed that God would protect from cholera the State which restricted international trade, Britain believed that God would protect the State which left shipping absolutely free. As a matter of fact, God protected neither, and cholera entered equally the closed ports of Greece and the open ports of Britain.

The steps by which the quarantiners were driven by facts into an international policy, and Britain was driven by the same facts to formulate a national policy, which subsequently had to become an international policy, are most instructive. The latter country faced at last the problem of keeping out cholera by independent administrative action without interfering with shipping. It gradually adopted a system which became a national policy. This consisted in inspection of suspected ships, the provision of hospitals at ports and the removal to them of all diseased persons, the disinfection of infected ships, and the improvement of public sanitation in the country. The essence of the system was to detect the presence of the disease and to deal at once with all cases of disease by isolation in properly equipped hospitals, but in this process to subject the movement of men and goods to as little restriction and inconvenience as possible. Accordingly, only persons actually infected were detained; suspected persons were allowed to enter the country freely, provided only that they could furnish an address in order that the medical authorities could keep in touch with them. But this system itself proved ineffectual without international action. In the first place, it suffered from exactly the same defect as the quarantine system in clinging to independent administration. If the presence of cholera in Marseilles was not immediately notified to Southampton, cholera might already be in the heart of England before the British system had begun to work in our ports. Again, the refusal to enter into international agreements and to take international action from fear of endangering shipping and trading interests really contributed to bring about the results which we hoped to avoid. When every country went its own unfettered way there was no limit to the inconvenience and damage which quarantine regulations could impose upon us in foreign ports. These regulations varied in every conceivable way, and it was no consolation to the English traveler interned for days in a death-trap somewhere in the Mediterranean, or to the British shipowner whose ship was detained for days in a French port and its cargo destroyed by disinfection, to know that men and ships could freely enter and leave all British ports.

For sixty years European States continued to maintain the obsolete independence of their National Administrations, and to follow blindly what they called vital national interests. Meanwhile trade and international intercourse suffered, and cholera entered freely quarantine and non-quarantine countries at regular intervals. Each epidemic after 1851 was followed by an International Diplomatic Conference, but for forty years "conflicting national interests" made agreement impossible. But those forty years were not fruitless, because all the time the inevitable logic of facts was destroying the fictions of national diplomacies. Every epidemic showed more clearly that the British view of the futility of quarantine was correct, and that the British system was equally futile without international agreement and action. When, therefore, the last European epidemic of the century broke out in 1892 the two opposing parties found that they had drawn together, and that all the interests of all the nations required common international action. The immediate result was the signing of the first International Sanitary Convention at a Diplomatic Conference in 1892, and this was followed by another Conference and another Convention in the following year.

The provisions of these first international agreements are well worthy of study. That of 1892 [*] is perhaps more concerned with pilgrim traffic than with trade. It deals with one particular

[*] Signed by thirteen States, including Germany, Austria-Hungary, France, Great Britain, Italy, and Russia.

locality—the Suez Canal—and lays down international sanitary and quarantine measures to be applied to ships passing through the Canal. It also deals with the functions of an international organ, the Conseil sanitaire, maritime, et quarantenaire d'Egypte, which had been established in 1881 to act as an international guard at that dangerous passage for disease between Asia and Europe. This Convention is a recognition of the necessity of the establishment under international administration of a barrier against disease at that spot where the streams of pilgrim traffic and of trading traffic approach one another. The Convention signed at Dresden in 1893 is of more general application, and its provisions affect the question not of pilgrim but of commercial traffic. It deals with two questions—the international notification of the existence of cholera and international prophylactic measures. In the first place, it makes the international notification of the outbreak of disease obligatory. It then deals with the vexed question of quarantine. And it is remarkable that the Dresden Conference, the first to reach an agreement upon this subject, proceeded, as the Austrian and German delegates foreshadowed in their opening speeches, to lay down not the minimum of prophylactic measures which each country must adopt, but the maximum of such measures which European States were not to exceed. It was recognized that, in order to establish uniform international administrative action, a beginning must be made by stating those measures which had been proved "excessive and useless," and by forbidding their adoption by national administrations. This was, of course, in one sense a victory for British national policy, for it involved the acceptance of our contention that the vital interests of no one State required that it should impose regulations making international trade impossible. On the other hand, it also involved the abandonment of the British contention that the vital interests of British trade made it impossible to enter into an international agreement limiting our freedom of administrative action on questions affecting shipping. When we signed the Convention of 1893 we admitted that the freedom of international trade could itself not be secured without some international regulation of the relation of States as regards the administration of prophylactic measures in ports—in other words, without International Government. The Convention of 1893 marks one more breakdown of national government when applied to international and, therefore, to national interests created in the nineteenth century.

I do not propose to give the detailed provisions of the Conventions of 1892 and 1893, because the diplomatic conferences held regularly since then, in 1897, 1903, and 1911–1912, have modified them, and I shall later briefly deal with the Convention of 1903,* which is a complete code of the International Legislation applied to epidemic diseases,

---

* The Convention of 1911–12 has not been ratified, owing to the war.

and expressly repeals previous Conventions. Before doing so, it is necessary to say a few words on the question of pilgrim traffic and the history of the attempts to apply international administration to its regulation. The problem of cholera and the Mohammedan pilgrimages is not quite the same as that of commercial shipping. The pilgrimages take place within the Turkish Empire very near to the meeting-place of three continents: the whole world must, therefore, be endangered by any laxity on the part of the Turkish Government in applying sanitary regulations to this dangerous traffic. But that Government is typically Eastern, and is incapable of and hostile to any system other than that of *laissez-faire:* and so it very soon became clear to the civilized States of Europe that the coexistence of the modern steamships and railways with Turkish ideas of sanitation and sanitary regulation must infallibly subject European countries to periodical invasions of cholera. Here again we find the growth of a peculiar international interest in the sanitation of the Turkish Empire, and again resort has to be made to international administration. As early as 1838 the Sultan was induced to agree to the establishment of an international organ, the Conseil supérieur de Santé of Constantinople, composed of delegates of the Turkish Empire and the chief maritime Powers, to which the task of supervising the sanitary regulation of Turkish ports was entrusted. In 1881, when Egypt was entering the orbit of the British Empire, a special and similar Council, the Conseil sanitaire, maritime, et quarantenaire d'Egypte, was established for that country in Alexandria, and international councils of the same type have been created at Teheran and Tangier to perform the same functions for Persia and Morocco. After 1892, when agreement was at last arrived at as to the form which the international administration to be applied to diseases should take, the Sanitary Conventions contain most elaborate particulars of the administration to be applied by these councils.

The history of the four international councils will probably be claimed by the "Nationalist" as proof of the futility of international action and of the inevitable submission of international to national interests. On the contrary, I believe that the little which we are permitted to know of what has happened at Constantinople, Alexandria, Tangier, and Teheran goes to prove the truth of everything which I have said regarding national and international interests, their relations and relative values. The charge of failure against internationalism will rest upon the proceedings at Constantinople and Teheran. For many years before the war the Conseil supéricur de Santé of Constantinople and the Teheran Council were simply hotbeds of political intrigue. The details of these intrigues are not available, but it seems to be indisputable that Germany, with the help of Austria, deliberately set out to oppose Britain on every conceivable opportunity within the councils. The campaign was carried out without any regard to the objects of the sanitary conventions and the protection of Turkey, Persia, and Europe from disease. It was part of a larger campaign inaugurated by the German Government for establishing the political predominance of Germany in the Near East, and for destroying the political position of Britain in the Persian Gulf. The Constantinople Council furnished an admirable *terrain* for this kind of politico-diplomatic manœuvring. The funds of the Council were provided by taxation of shipping, and since British commerce is predominant, the work of the Council was being financed mainly by British shipping. It was naturally peculiarly exasperating for our diplomatists, who, in such circumstances, identify British shipowners and their interests with Great Britain and her interests,* to feel that "Great Britain" was always paying the piper and never being allowed, owing to German intrigues, to call the tune. And so, when the German delegate contrived to prevent the Turkish Government from putting up urgently needed hospital accommodation in some Turkish port because the proposal came from the British delegate, he had the satisfaction of feeling that he was not only exasperating the British diplomatists, but "dealing a blow at British prestige in the Near East."

---

* This is one of the commonest "Nationalist" fallacies. It is worth remarking that the Nationalist diplomatist rarely, if ever, identifies the British working classes and their interests with Great Britain and her interests.

Matters eventually reached such a pass that in 1914 the Turkish Government, presumably with the approval of Germany, issued a declaration denying the right of the Council to act in Turkey.

International administration, it may be at once admitted, has proved in these two Councils a failure, but it does not follow that International Government is impossible. Under slightly different circumstances the similar Council has in Alexandria experienced none of the Constantinople difficulties. Here we have an international administrative organ with a technical staff of eighty-seven international health officers, etc., with an expenditure annually of £80,000, derived from an international tax levied upon ships and pilgrims. But the true significance of the failure of International Government in the Constantinople and Teheran Councils can only be grasped by considering what part national interests played there. The objection made to International Government is that it is incompatible with the prosecution by each State of its real interests. But is it possible to argue that International Government was rendered impossible in the Sanitary Councils by Germany and Britain prosecuting anything which a sane man could call a "real interest" of either? It was certainly a vital interest not only of Germany and Britain, but of every State in Europe—if the "State" has any connection with the individuals who compose it —that Turkey and Persia, by their lack of administration, should not be allowed to infect themselves with cholera from Arabia and the Persian Gulf, and then spread it along the trade routes over Europe, as they had done more than once in the nineteenth century. And what were the "vital national interests" for which Germany and Britain abandoned these vital national and international interests? They are interests of a political and diplomatic nature so vague and illusory that it is almost impossible to define them at all in the language of ordinary men. First and foremost, there is national prestige—that extraordinary idol of the diplomatic cave. The directors of German and British policy really believed that if Germany contrived perpetually to defeat British proposals in the Councils at Constantinople and Teheran, British prestige would suffer in Asia Minor and the Persian Gulf. But anyone with any knowledge of the life of the *people* in the East or, for that matter, anywhere else, would know that not one in a million inhabitants of Asia Minor or the Arabs of the Gulf would ever hear of what took place in a Sanitary Council in Constantinople or Teheran. In the Persian Gulf British prestige, in so far as it exists at all, rests upon the lighthouses which we set up and maintain in its waters; on the British India Steam Navigation Company's steamers, which regularly call at its ports; and H.M.S. *Highflyer* and *Hyacinth*, which used to police its waters and capture its dhows when engaged in illicit traffic in arms. The British prestige which Germany struck at by thwarting British proposals in the Councils and by inciting

Turks and Persians not to carry out sanitary measures suggested by Britain was a reputation for firmness and diplomatic adroitness confined to a tiny circle of Government servants and diplomatists. Thus in this case the national interests of Germany and England, covered by the names of prestige and political predominance, under analysis appear to be nothing but the maintenance of a reputation among half a dozen deorientalized Orientals and European diplomatists for diplomatic obstinacy and unscrupulousness.* Then there are the national interests of political power and commerce. A moment's consideration will show that in these spheres, too, the diplomatic view, which we are asked to adopt and act upon in foreign policy, is founded upon delusion. If the German delegate had succeeded in out-manœuvring and outvoting the British delegate on every question which came before the Councils for ten centuries it could not possibly have increased the political power of Germany or decreased that of Britain one jot, nor could it have produced the transference of one cargo from a British to a German firm or ship. The only practical effect that it could have was upon the sanitation of Turkish ports and the spread of cholera from Asia to Europe.

---

* This is a very good example of the emptiness of national prestige. Diplomatists naturally look upon prestige as the result of diplomatic triumphs. They labor under the common human delusion that their own personal triumphs and failures are noticed by or affect anyone other than themselves.

In other words, the national interests which Germany and Britain prosecuted in these Councils, and which made the International Government impossible, were delusions and illusions. The real national interests were the international interests. And that is all which at present I am concerned to establish. If the civilized peoples of twentieth-century Europe are determined to pursue illusory and imaginary national interests rather than true national interests, then, of course, International Government may really prove impossible. But that is a very different thing from the statement that International Government is impossible because it does not allow nations to prosecute their own peculiar interests. It may be quite true that the dog in the fable lost his bone by snapping at its shadow in the water, but no canine argument could alter the fact that the real bone was in his mouth, and only the shadow of a bone in the water. And the future of the dog in his relation to bones, and of man in relation to the universe, depends upon learning by experience the difference between shadows and reality.

It remains to indicate briefly the International Administration as regards sanitation, which had been evolved at the time of the Sanitary Convention of 1903. That Convention, which applies both to plague and cholera, consists of three parts, of which the first deals with the general problem of shipping and commerce, the second with ordinary shipping in the Suez Canal and Persian Gulf, and the third with that of the pilgrimages. Part

I imposes certain uniform international rules upon the National Administrations. It establishes obligatory notification of disease to the different Administrations, and prescribes the method of notification and the detailed information to be notified. It prescribes what articles and merchandise may, and what may not, be treated as capable of conveying plague or cholera, and may be subjected to disinfection or restriction, the measures to be adopted at ports in the case of infected ships, the maximum period of quarantine, and the provision by each Administration of at least one port with an organization and equipment sufficient for the reception of a ship, whatever its health conditions may be. Parts II and III set up an elaborate system of International Administration in places outside Europe, such as the Suez Canal and Persian Gulf, and for pilgrim traffic. The international regulation and inspection of shipping in these places is laid down in great detail, as well as the methods of disinfection and quarantine, the provision of buildings, hospitals, and apparatus, the number and the salaries of the medical officers to be stationed at particular places. The International Sanitary Councils are recognized as the authorities for carrying out these regulations, and their constitution is defined.* Provision is

* The "composition, functions, and the manner of discharge of the functions" of the Conseil Sanitaire, etc., d'Egypte as fixed by Annexed III of the Sanitary Convention of Venice of 1892 and by Khedival Decrees of 1893 and 1894 and a Ministerial Order of 1894, but the provisions of all these are "confirmed" by Article 162 of the Convention of 1903. Article 165 of the 1903 Convention lays down that "the framing of the

made for meeting the cost of the sanitary services by taxes on shipping and a quarantine charge on each pilgrim, and the proportion of expenses to be borne by the Turkish and Egyptian Governments and the Sanitary Councils respectively are fixed. Chapter III of Part III, Articles 151-161, defines the penalties to which ship captains and others shall become liable for infringement of the various regulations of the Convention—one of the very rare examples of the creation by International Convention of international legal offenses. Articles 173 and 174 set up a Consular Commission, an International Appeal Court to try cases in which in Turkish ports contradictory statements are made by sanitary agents and incriminated captains regarding infringements. The fines levied under the penalty clauses of the Convention are paid to the Sanitary Councils.

It remains to deal with one other question connected with the international interest of Public Health. Article 181 of the Convention of 1903 decided to create an International Office of Public Health in Paris. Accordingly, in 1907, the Office international d'Hygiène publique was established by an Arrangement signed by twelve States. At the end of 1915 thirty-two States, including colonies, etc., with separate representation, adhered. This Union has suffered by the refusal of Germany

---

measures to be taken with a view to prevent the introduction into the Turkish Empire and the transmission to other countries of epidemic diseases devolves upon the Constantinople Superior Board of Health." The following articles, 166-175, deal with its composition, etc.

and Austria to take any part in it, because the Office was not established in Berlin—another case in which an imaginary national interest has been preferred to a real international interest by a diplomatic service. The principal object of the Office is to collect documents and information regarding Public Health, and to bring them to the notice of adhering States. It publishes a valuable Monthly Bulletin containing Public Health Statistics, the Sanitary Conventions, Laws, and Regulations made by the different countries, and other information, which could hardly be produced except by public international action. Another of its functions is to propose modifications in the Sanitary Convention. It corresponds direct with the Sanitary Councils. It is controlled by an International Committee, composed of technical representatives of States. Its staff consists of a Director and Secretary, appointed by the Committee, and subordinates. The number of votes allowed to each State in the Committee is inversely proportional to the number of the category to which such State belongs for the purpose of determining its contribution to the expenses of the Office. The number of categories is six, those States placed in category Number 1 contributing twenty-five units, and those in category Number 6 three units.

C.—*Industry and Commerce*

Industry and Commerce nowhere form part of the administrative activities of States to the same extent as either Communications or Public Health. The internationalization of these departments of life could not therefore take place through internationalization of public administration, though, as we shall see in a subsequent chapter, it has taken place under other forms of International Government. Yet administration in the individual State necessarily touches the industrial system at many points and is ancillary to it: in fact, it is difficult to conceive how our industrial system could continue at all unless the State continued to perform certain Public Services. And here, as elsewhere, the need for international rather than national administration has subsequently appeared, the inadequacy of the ordinary conception of the isolated independent State is manifest, and the relation of international interests to the apparent interests of individual States is worthy of study.

In international, industrial, and commercial relations, etc., loss and inconvenience necessarily result from uncertainty or lack of uniformity in the machinery of commerce. Where the State regulates or controls any part of that machinery, uniformity of administration becomes an international interest. There are several such cases in which already international administration has taken the place of national. The Latin, Scandinavian, and Central American Monetary Unions unify the monetary systems or coinage of the States which adhere to them, and the independence of the national administrations as regards their coinage is materially limited by the international administration which the various Conventions set up. In another sphere, that of weights and measures, by the establishment of the Metric Union under the Convention of 1875, the twenty-six States which now adhere have adopted in the international kilogramme and mètre, the prototypes of which are deposited with the International Bureau of the Union at Paris, international instead of national units of mass and length. This Union again has directly led, since 1905, to the adoption by nearly all countries of a uniform legal metric carat of 200 milligrammes in place of a carat which varied from 188.5 milligrammes in Italy to 254.6 in Arabia. I do not propose to consider in detail the International Government which, in these cases, has produced uniformity of administration, partly because the lessons to be learnt from it are much the same as those already learnt from the history of the Postal and Telegraphic Union, partly because I desire to devote my space to an "International Union," the Institute of Agriculture, which at first sight appears to have accomplished far less, but the history of which throws more light upon the relations of national and international interests.

Before dealing with that Institute there are, however, two points which deserve a passing mention. The first is this: As to the relative value of international or national administration, where administration touches industry and commerce, the business community of the world seems to be in no doubt. The business man in every country is a confirmed internationalist. The unanimous resolutions of the International Congress of Chambers of Commerce,* at which practically all the important Chambers of Commerce of the world are represented, show this. These Congresses are Parliaments of the leading commercial opinion of all countries, and they prove that commercial opinion is far more favorable towards internationalism than opinion in the diplomatic and administrative services of the different States. The resolutions are almost entirely occupied with pressing the Governments to take steps to internationalize administration, legislation, etc. Thus, the question of uniformity in the compilation of customs statistics is of great importance to commerce. Ever since 1853 it has been pressed upon Governments by individuals and associations of individuals. In 1870 a diplomatic Conference was at last summoned, but led to nothing. In 1890 a very small step was taken when the International Union and Bureau for the Publication of Customs Tariffs was established by a Convention to which over forty States now adhere. This Union sets up international administration for the purpose of a regular and comprehensive publication of all customs tariffs, laws, and treaties, and so makes indirectly for uniformity. But the uniformity desired by commercial men was very far from being attained. Pressure from them and from various

---

* *Vide* also page 328.

international associations * led to an International Conference of twenty-six States meeting in 1910, at which certain principles were accepted and products divided into five large classes for tariff purposes. A special Commission was appointed, and after some study sub-divided the five classes into 185 sub-classes. This classification still awaits the calling of another Conference, and its embodiment in an international agreement. Meanwhile, the business men in the Chambers of Commerce are still asking for an International Bureau of Statistics and for international administration which will ensure "uniformity in the compilation of customs statistics, and particularly in regard to methods of valuation of imports and exports." And the same business men were in 1912 pressing the Governments to establish a Uniform International Calendar and a fixed date for Easter, an international law of cheques, a uniform international system of Consular invoices, etc.

The second point which merits a brief reference is the significance of that curious and anomalous international organism, the Permanent Sugar Commission. Into the rights and the wrongs and the details of the Sugar Convention of 1902, which was eventually signed by fourteen States (including Germany, Austria-Hungary, France, Great

---

* Besides the International Congress of Chambers of Commerce, the Congrès Internationale de la Règlementation douanière, the Congrès d'Expansion Economique mondiale, the International Statistic Institute, and the Union Economique internationale have all pressed for Governmental action.

Britain, Italy, and Russia), I do not propose to enter, but the Convention clearly violates all the ordinary doctrines of independent national action. It was an attempt to deal with the abuses of the bounty system, and it was a confession that those abuses—which are themselves the results of the extreme individualist view of national interests—could only be dealt with by drastic limitation of national independence and an advanced form of international administration. The signatory States bound themselves to abolish sugar bounties, not to impose import duties exceeding a certain maximum, and to impose a countervailing duty upon imported bounty-fed sugar. It set up an international administration in the Permanent Commission to carry out these provisions. The Commission determines whether sugar is or is not bounty-fed, and, if it is, the rate of countervailing duty to be imposed upon its importation into the several signatory States. These States are bound by the decisions of the Commission, which are arrived at by a majority vote. But certain exporting countries, *e. g.*, Russia, also bound themselves not to authorize exportation of sugar exceeding a certain quantity per year, and the yearly quantities to be authorized were revised by the Commission. Thus here we find the power of the State over its own tariff and its right to export its own produce subjected to International Government. The independence of the sovereign States had worn very thin in the provisions of the Brussels Convention of 1902.

We have the authority of the Book of Genesis for saying that agriculture is the oldest of all human industries. It still remains probably the most important. The proposal of an eminent American citizen of the twentieth century to set up an organ of International Government in order to watch over and promote the international interests of this industry, and the fate of that proposal, throw much light on the problem which I have been considering in this chapter. Mr. Lubin was struck by the fact that the interests involved in agriculture, so far as the human race is concerned, are for the most part uninfluenced by national frontiers. The nineteenth century revolution in international communications has also revolutionized agriculture. The material earth upon and about which men have built their theoretical conception of the individual State is international in the sense that its produce is grown to feed foreigners in all the ends of the two hemispheres. A heavy crop in Asia, a hailstorm in America, the knowledge of agricultural science on the steppes of Russia, may all vitally affect millions of Western Europeans. The diffusion of the knowledge of scientific inventions and new methods affecting agriculture is an international interest which cannot adequately be served by isolated national action. Moreover, just as we saw that the growth of international intercourse enormously increases the danger of the spread of human epidemic diseases, so the exchange of agricultural produce between nations leads to the introduction and diffusion of pests and diseases disastrous to agriculture—and in this case, too, only international action can afford protection. Lastly, the internationalization of food production has created a new complication of interests. When Adam delved and himself consumed the produce of his delving—a condition of affairs which obtained in many parts of the world even in comparatively recent times—or even when the inhabitants of small areas relied for their food mainly upon the agricultural produce of those areas, group interests were simple, and were closely connected with geographical boundaries. In such a state of society group interests did for the most part follow national frontiers. But when the inhabitants of Lancashire depend upon the wheat growers of Asia and America for their bread, innumerable intermediaries between the groups of agricultural producers and consumers are interposed, and the interests of these many groups refuse to follow national boundaries. The interests of the American farmer and the Lancashire consumer, as against those of the cosmopolitan shippers, agents, brokers, merchants, and speculators, may be identical, namely, that the wheat shall be transported from America to Lancashire for a reasonable sum which will cover the cost of carriage and distribution. The price which the original producer can demand and the final consumer ought to pay is influenced by the state of the world's crops at any particular moment, and also by *their* knowledge of the conditions of supply and demand. It is the superior knowledge of these conditions possessed by speculators and other intermediaries which allows them to promote their own interests by making the original producer take less and the consumer pay more than he should. Thus the interests of the millions of Russian, Indian, and American wheat-growers are identical when opposed to the group interests of the British, German, and American shipowners, or the group interests of the cosmopolitan speculators; the group interests of British and German consumers, again, are opposed to the group interests of British and German shipowners, and are identical in this respect with the group interests of Russian, Indian, and American wheat-growers. Now, our ordinary conception of the nature of States, and of the system of national government and of international relations which is founded upon that conception, refuses any recognition to these complicated groupings of interests: it is a fundamental assumption of "foreign policy" that the interests of all Englishmen in relation to all Germans and Americans, and of all Germans and all Americans in relation to all Englishmen, are identical. (This results from the fact that our conceptions of the "State," of "government," and of "international relations" belong to a condition of society which finally passed away in the eighteenth century.) Hence national government breaks down and proves to be incapable of dealing with a question like this of agriculture because its rigid lines cut right across those lines in which the vital interests of human groups now run. Only some form of International Government which ensures representation of these vast group-interests could deal with these problems.

Perhaps it was the air of his native place, California—where, if anywhere, the oldest industry should be touched by the spirit of the New World—that impressed some of these considerations upon the mind and imagination of Mr. Lubin. At any rate, in the year 1904 he laid before the King of Italy a scheme under which the nations of the world were to unite in establishing a system of International Government to promote and protect international agricultural interests, and he so fired the imagination of the monarch that the Italian Government invited the other Governments to send delegates to a Diplomatic Conference upon the subject at Rome. Mr. Lubin's scheme was conceived on a wide and revolutionary scale. His Union of States was to collect and publish and distribute information of all kinds regarding agriculture. In this way he hoped not only to promote the knowledge of agricultural science, but, by disseminating broadcast at regular intervals accurate information as to the condition and yield of the world's crops, to check that speculative manipulation of the markets of the world's food which allows a tiny minority to profit at the expense of an enormous majority of human beings. Then he drew attention to the heavy freights and railway charges which handicap producers, pointing out that between producer and consumer are dealers, etc., in command of adequate information and capital, who are in a better position than the producer to anticipate the future course of the market. His idea was that some form of International Freights Tribunal should be constituted, analogous to the Interstate Commerce Commission of the United States, to which questions in dispute between producer and carrying agency or dealer might be referred. In other words, he contemplated international regulation of freights for food products. He also proposed that the Union should concern itself with measures for the protection of the common interests of agriculturists and the improvement of their conditions, and, therefore, with such questions as the prevention of plant diseases, agricultural co-operation, insurance, and credit.

It is very instructive to read the opinion of the British administrative officials on this proposal. The Board of Agriculture, when consulted by the Foreign Office, is not opposed to our sending representatives to the diplomatic Conference to consider the creation of an International Institute of Agriculture, but it points out that British members of such an Institute, if appointed by Government, "could not well take any active part" in, *e. g.*, "examination and criticism of the legislative and administrative proposals of the Government by which they were appointed," nor "assist in the organization of measures of defence, not provided by law, against what might be considered by the Bureau to be an excessive and arbitrary use of the rights and powers possessed by railway trusts and corners." This curious statement seems to ignore the fact that, of course, the members appointed by the British Government to represent that Government in an organ of International Government would, and could, take an active part in the examination and criticism of legislative proposals, etc., provided that they represented the views of the British Government in that organ in accordance with their instructions. This is a daily occurrence in all organs of International Government, from the ordinary Diplomatic Conference to the Congress of the Postal Union. Then the Board of Agriculture went on to point out the respects in which "the position and interests of this country differ materially from those of other Powers." They are: (1) Exceptional position of the United Kingdom as a market for foreign agricultural produce; (2) the increasing extent to which our requirements are satisfied by our Colonies; (3) advantages derived by our insular position in regard to such matters as the prevention of the introduction of disease and examination of imported food products. In all this, it will be observed, there is no recognition of those "agricultural international interests" of which Mr. Lubin was thinking. For instance, the "exceptional position of the United Kingdom as a market for foreign agricultural produce" is precisely what makes the international improvement of agriculture and the international protection of agriculturists of immense importance to an enormous number of the inhabitants of the United Kingdom. This exceptional position, instead of making us hesitate to take international action, as the Board implied, ought to have made us all the more ready to do so. The Board, which would have identified the interests of a small number of British shipowners in high freights, or of a small number of British farmers in high prices, with "national interests," entirely failed to identify the interests of the millions of British consumers in low freights and low prices with "national interests."

The British Government appointed their delegates to the Conference, and their instructions incorporated all the recommendations of the Board, with the additional statement that "H.M.'s Government cannot be parties to any action which would be likely to impair the favorable position of British agriculturists." The Conference assembled in Rome, and Mr. Lubin's proposals were submitted to it with the significant exception of the one which dealt with freights. On the other hand, the Organizing Committee of the Italian Government presented a report in which the existing conditions which could be ameliorated by International Regulation are so fully and yet succinctly indicated that they are worth quoting:—

(1) Protection of live stock and cultivated plants from contagion and epidemics.

(2) Agricultural insurance. By extending the area of insurance, premiums would be greatly reduced, *e. g.*, drought in Argentine would not be likely to occur at the same time as in Russia. The whole crops of a country could only be insured if insurance were a State enterprise, and State enterprises were federated.

(3) Forestry. Protection of forests is only possible in many cases if it is international.

(4) Adulteration of agricultural products. International study of this subject and an international code are necessary.

(5) Immigration and emigration, and Labor Exchange.

(6) International organ to diffuse knowledge of production and a Central Institute of Meteorology are necessary.

(7) Co-operation.

(8) International organization against rings, monopolies, and speculative dealings is desirable.

The Conference arrived at an agreement,* a Convention was signed, and the International Institute of Agriculture came into existence with

---

* There was only one important difference of opinion. The proposal of the Italian Government was that the Institute should be a Union of States, and that it should be formed by delegates of the Governments of States. Austria-Hungary, supported by Germany, proposed that the Institute should be formed by delegates elected by Agricultural Associations, and that delegates of Governments should be allowed to attend the sittings, but should have no power to vote. The Italian proposal was accepted, and the Austrian rejected.

a most elaborate constitution* and imposing buildings in Rome. But the diplomatists and their Governments confined the field of its operations to very narrow limits. Article 9 of the Convention of 1905 limits its functions "within an international sphere" to the collection, study, and publication of statistical, technical, and economic information about agriculture, prices, wages, diseases, co-operation, insurance and credit, and to the power to "submit to the approval of the Governments, if there is occasion for it, measures for the protection of the common interests of farmers and for improvement of their conditions." The main work has, in fact, been the collection and diffusion of agricultural statistics and infor-

---

* The constitution is extraordinarily elaborate. Its organs consist of:—
  (1) *The General Assembly* of the delegates of States, which meets once a year.
  (2) *The Permanent Committee* consists of special delegates of the States resident in Rome, and really carries on the work of the Institute, acting as an Executive Committee of the General Assembly. It is subdivided into four Permanent Commissions.
  (3) *The Special Committee*, composed of the President and Vice-President of the Permanent Committee and the Presidents of the four Commissions.
  (4) *Commissions* nominated by the General Assembly. In these Commissions each nation has one vote.
  (5) *Permanent Commissions* appointed by the Special Committee.
  (6) *Special Commissions*.
  (7) *Four Bureaus*, which deal with the administration of the Institute.

The signatory States, which now number fifty-five, are divided into five groups; the contribution to the expenses of the Institute and the voting powers in the General Assembly and Permanent Committee vary according to the group to which the State belongs. States have the right to choose the group to which they will belong.

mation. This is carried out through the publication of three monthly Bulletins, and a Year Book, viz.: *The Bulletin of Agricultural and Commercial Statistics*, the *Monthly Bulletin of Economic and Social Intelligence*, the *Monthly Bulletin of Agricultural Intelligence and Plant Diseases*, and the *International Year Book of Agricultural Statistics*. Much of this information is potentially of great value, and could only be obtained and published rapidly through the kind of International Administration set up by the Institute. Thus, the first Bulletin every month issues broadcast over the world information relating to "the agricultural production of the entire world, the area sown, the state of crops, the forecasts and the harvests actually yielded, the import and export trade in the principal agricultural products, their price, and the amount of visible stocks." The regular and rapid publication of such accurate statistics obviously ought to have important effects upon the world's markets for food products, and the claim has been made, though it is not an easy one either to prove or to disprove, that the Institute, by its Monthly Bulletin, has already contributed to the checking of speculation in and the cornering of markets of food products.* An indirect effect of some importance is that these publications have led to improvement and greater uniformity in the

* The monthly circulation of these Bulletins is, I believe, about 6,000 copies. There can be no doubt that no other body could produce them, if only because the Governments of the whole world are under obligation to supply their statistics to the Institute, and to the Institute alone.

official agricultural statistics of some countries, *e. g.*, Russia.

It will be seen that the broader problems and the wider interests of the peoples of nearly all countries which were envisaged in Mr. Lubin's scheme have not been entrusted to the International Government of the Institute. The General Assembly and the Permanent Committee are occupied almost exclusively with questions of statistics and plant diseases. The causes of this narrowing of function have been the diplomatic theory of the independence of national Government, a jealousy of anything which appears to limit that independence, and an identification of the interests of certain narrow groups, such as shipowners, with national interests. Yet it is difficult to see how the interests of the producers and consumers of agricultural products in efficient production and in efficient and cheap distribution are less national interests than the interests of shipowners in high freights. The real interests of nations would seem to lie in the international organization of efficient agriculture over as wide a surface of the earth as possible, and in an international organization "against rings, monopolies, and speculative dealings." So that once again we find that the true national interests are international, and can only be adequately served by some form of International Government.

It should, however, be observed that the American Government shares the international attitude and hopes of its citizen and delegate, Mr. Lubin, and does not despair of widening the sphere of the Institute. In 1914 the Senate and House of Representatives passed a resolution instructing the United States' delegate to the Institute to present the following resolution to the Permanent Committee of the Institute in order that it might be submitted to the General Assembly which was to meet in 1917:

"L'Assemblée Générale charge l'Institut International d'Agriculture d'inviter les Gouvernements adhérents à prendre part à une Conférence internationale tendant à donner plus de stabilité aux prix des produits agricoles du monde entier.

"Cette Conférence sera composée de Délégués nommés par les Gouvernements adhérents à l'Institut, et devra considerer l'opportunité de formuler une Convention établissant une Commission Commerciale Internationale de la marine marchande et des frets maritimes, ayant des pouvoirs consultatifs et délibératifs, et pouvant également de sa propre initiative formuler des avis."

Before finally leaving the subject of the Institute of Agriculture, a small point deserves recording, in which the ardent internationalist may find some consolation. When the war broke out the official delegates of the belligerent States continued with the approval of their Governments to meet in and carry on the work of the Permanent Committee. Thus, for the first time, civilized States at war with one another maintained diplomatic relations through their official representatives on an international organ. It is a trifling point, but it at least shows that international relations are now so much a part of life that even war cannot entirely abolish them.

D.—*Morals and Crime*

The earliest function of the State was historically the control of morals and the prevention of crime, and a large part of its administrative activities are in most civilized countries still occupied with these functions. Before the nineteenth century, when international intercourse remained very limited, crime, with the exception of piracy, did not overstep national frontiers, and any competent National Administration would have been competent to deal with its own criminals. But national life has, as we have already seen, broken down in so many directions in the last century that no National Administration, however competent, could now cope even with its own criminals—to say nothing of international criminals—if it maintained its independence of and isolation from other Administrations. I propose to indicate only in their briefest outlines the directions in which the new conditions have shown that internationalism of administration is necessary.

In the eighteenth century the national frontier really meant a great deal to national life. To reach it and cross it was a slow and often difficult operation. If a crime were committed in France the French police had in nearly all cases only to think of arresting the criminals in France. But to-day it is probably easier to get out of France than it was in the eighteenth century to get out of Paris. In these circumstances no National Administration can deal adequately with its national crime unless it can pursue and arrest its national criminals who have left its jurisdiction. The enormous number of extradition treaties concluded in the last sixty years are the result of these new conditions; strictly speaking, they internationalize the law of extradition in the different countries of the world—and, therefore, belong to the next chapter—but the object of this internationalization of law is to internationalize administration where it is concerned with the arrest of criminals.

But modern society has also seen an immense growth in what may correctly be called international crime, and with international crime independent national administration is quite unable to cope. I propose to give two examples. The first is the slave trade. At the end of the Napoleonic Wars one of those curious waves of moral conviction which occasionally sweep over Anglo-Saxon communities descended upon the inhabitants of the United Kingdom. The whole country gave itself up to the Anti-Slavery agitation, and the British people, as opposed to their Ministers, insisted that the peace to be made at Vienna should have as its chief object, so far as they were concerned, the abolition of slavery from every corner of the world rather than the settlement of Europe or the aggrandizement of the British Empire. But it was realized at once that slavery and the slave trade are international crimes, which cannot possibly be put down by isolated national action, and require international action and administration. The famous clause inserted in the Treaty of Vienna recognizes the necessity of collective action. But it was many years before really effective international action was taken. At the Conference of Brussels in 1889–1890 an international Convention was signed by eighteen States which establishes an elaborate International Administration for the suppression of slavery in Africa. The enforcement of the provisions of the Convention is watched over by an international organ, Le Bureau international maritime de Zanzibar, upon which, according to Article 74, each Signatory Power has the right to be represented, and which meets monthly.* The second example is even more instructive from the point of view of internationalism. The White Slave Traffic is a trade which is organized internationally. The dealers in and exporters of women for the purposes of prostitution are in the different countries of the world in close touch with one another. The consequence is that even where legislation exists for putting down this traffic, the national administra-

* Closely connected with the suppression of slavery in Africa has been the question of the regulation of the sale of liquor and arms in that continent. In both cases international has had to take the place of national administration. The sale of liquor was regulated by Articles 90–95 of the Brussels Convention. The traffic in arms was finally subjected to international administration by a Convention signed by fourteen States at the Conférence chargée de reviser le Régime des Armes en Afrique, Brussels, 1908 and 1909. This Convention established International Bureaus at Aden and on the West Coast.

tion is quite unable by isolated action to suppress it. If an international gang in, say, Paris organizes the trade in Berlin, London, and Buenos Ayres, it is impossible for either the English, German, Argentine, or French police to secure the conviction of the principals without international action of some sort. Again, the offense itself is often international in the sense that it is constituted an offense by actions performed in more than one country. The offense is frequently one of procuring for a certain purpose, but while the procuring takes place in one country, the purpose can only be proved by what has subsequently happened to the victims of the procurers in another country. The necessity for some internationalization of administration was insisted upon first by International Associations of private individuals interested in the subject. This led to the holding of a diplomatic conference by fifteen States in 1902, and a further conference in 1910. The result has been an international agreement which has introduced some uniformity into the criminal laws of the different nations and uniformity and co-operation into the administration of those laws.

In this connection a curious incident deserves mention, for it shows how modern life tends to run along international lines. There are a considerable number of International Associations [*]

---

[*] *E. g.*, Association internationale pour la répression de la Traite des Blanches, which is composed of National Committees belonging to sixteen countries, Fédération Abolitioniste internationale, Union internationale des Amies de la Jeune Fille, Association Catholique des Œuvres de Protection de la Jeune Fille, etc.

which regularly hold International Congresses on the subject of the White Slave Traffic, and they have been instrumental in obtaining concerted Government action. Then between 1902 and 1910 came the diplomatic conferences and conventions, and also at intervals conferences of the police of different countries. Apparently the traffickers themselves became nervous at all this international activity, and they decided to hold an international congress to discuss what steps should be taken to counteract the preventive measures of the Associations and Administrations. Accordingly a secret international meeting was fixed for the night of November 9, 1913, in a night café in Warsaw in order to arrive at an international agreement as to the future conduct of the trade. The meeting was attended by eighty-nine representatives from all the different countries, and practically all the chief organizers of the trade were present. Unfortunately for these internationalists, the police got to hear of the meeting, surrounded the café, and arrested the whole congress. One of the men captured, called Silbermann, had been "wanted" for a long time, and had been, in the opinion of the police, one of the leading organizers of the traffic. Many of the traffickers had, however, to be released, as there was no evidence on which a definite charge could be preferred against them.*

It would be possible to give other examples in

* The facts are reported in *La Vie Internationale*, Vol. IV, 1913, No. 5, p. 432.

which national administration is inadequate under modern conditions for dealing with crime.* But enough has already been said, I think, to show that in the region of crime and criminal law and administration international interests are no less real, and international administration for their protection is no less necessary and feasible, than we have already found them to be in Communications, Industry and Commerce, and Public Health.

---

* Some of these examples have already been touched on above—*e. g.*, the protection of submarine cables is, from one point of view, a question of international police. The repression of the circulation of indecent literature has been subjected to international regulation by a Convention of 1910. The Commission pénitentiaire internationale also deserves mention. The Commission consists of Government delegates, and its objects and functions are the study of general measures for the prevention and repression of crime. It meets once every two years, and it arranges the programme of the Congrès pénitentiaires internationales, which meet every five years. The Commission has a Bureau at Berne, and publishes a Bulletin.

CHAPTER IV

COSMOPOLITAN LAW-MAKING

IF administration is the flower and fruit of the independent sovereign State, legislation may be compared to the vital principle which causes the flower to blossom and the fruit to grow. In a report of one of the Committees at a Pan-American Conference sovereignty is defined as consisting "explicitly in the right it (the State) always preserves of regulating by its laws such judicial acts as are consummated within its territory, and of trying these by its tribunals." Legislation is the Holy of Holies of the independent, sovereign State, and, therefore, of nationalism as opposed to internationalism. But we should not forget that the State is a form of human organization superimposed upon a complex material world of men and women, all with thoughts and feelings, desires, wants, and businesses of their own. If it does not fit into that material world, or if it does not reflect the thoughts and feelings of men and women, or if its form is incompatible with their aims and desires and modes of life, then one of two things must happen: either the form of organization must modify itself to suit its environment, or the environment—in this case,

PREVENTION OF WAR

human society—must modify itself in order to conform with the form of its own organization.

The organization of human beings to-day in independent, sovereign States with complete independence of legislation has, as I shall show in this chapter, already proved to be incompatible with modern society—by which I mean the sum of the every-day lives of the millions who follow their noses and their businesses and their desires through the 365 days of the year without ever thinking of such abstractions as sovereignty or the τὸ τί ἦν εἶναι of a State. This incompatibility shows itself principally in the inconveniences and impediments to which differences of laws in the different countries subject the development of international intercourse and social progress. This state of things has been met by that universal human expedient —compromise. We have in part capitulated to the tyranny of our national organizations, foregoing many wants in our every-day life, suffering innumerable inconveniences, putting off all kinds of repairs and improvements which the building of society urgently needs in order to preserve independence of national legislation; on the other hand, we have in several directions abandoned complete independence, and through new international organizations and international agreements instituted a system of unification of divergent national laws, a process of cosmopolitan law-making.

I propose in this chapter to consider in detail a few of these examples of cosmopolitan legislation, the importance of which seems to have escaped the attention of modern writers on Government, Political Science, and the relations of States. Before doing so, however, a few general remarks are necessary. This process of unifying the law over a wide stretch of territory under the jurisdiction of a number of independent States is a phenomenon which has only appeared in very recent times. It was practically unheard of before 1880. It is obviously a most important form of International Government, for it is international legislation in a very early stage. A study of those instances in which it has been attempted should throw much light upon the true relations of national interests to one another and to International Government. Finally, all through the study of this question I would urge the necessity of keeping these fundamental facts clearly before one's mind—namely, that all these tentative advances towards International Government are due to the natural impulses of the kind of life which men and women desire to live to-day. That kind of life is incompatible with the isolated independent State. That incompatibility will continue, and future generations will have to choose between two courses: either they will have to modify their conception of the national State in order to develop the kind of existence which they began to desire and to attain in the nineteenth century, or they will have to return to an earlier, poorer, more uncomfortable and—as I venture to think—less civilized kind of life in order to retain their conception of the independent national State.

A.—*International Maritime Legislation*

The first example of cosmopolitan legislation with which I propose to deal is the latest in point of time, but shows most clearly the different bearings of the international problem. The development of communications, as we have continually had to point out, made possible the development of international trade, which has revolutionized international relations generally. But the enormous system of industry and commerce of the modern world, consisting in the interchange of commodities, would have been quite impossible unless men had been able spontaneously to adapt the old and invent a new machinery of exchange and credit. In every civilized country the nineteenth century saw the gradual growth of an entirely new and vast body of commercial law and custom, and the growth and modification of this body of law and custom, which forms the machinery of both national and international credit and exchange, is still proceeding. In the working of this machinery certainty and uniformity are for commerce of the very first importance. As proof of this assertion it is only necessary to point out that if the laws and customs governing, say, Bills of Exchange were not firmly established with a considerable degree of uniformity in the different countries, the volume of the world's trade would shrink to very modest dimensions. The whole of that part of the machinery of international exchange which depends upon custom also exhibits a high degree of uniformity: the banker, the merchant, the shipper, the insurer are all continually trying to ignore or abolish, so far as their business is concerned, the national frontiers which separate their offices. But the independence and isolation of States have had the opposite effect upon that part of the machinery which depends upon commercial law. Commercial Law and laws which intimately affect industry and commerce vary enormously from country to country, and this not only impedes the growth of international trade by causing uncertainty, loss, and inconvenience, but it also impedes the development of a uniform machinery of exchange upon which the further evolution of international trade must depend.

To commercial men and commercial lawyers the inconveniences caused by this lack of uniformity became apparent very many years ago, and early in the latter half of the last century an attempt was made to remedy them. That attempt failed, and it is instructive to observe how it differed from the later attempt of the International Maritime Committee, which has already achieved a considerable amount of success. The persons who first took up the subject were jurists, and, conceiving that what was wanted was a uniform maritime law for the whole world, they proceeded to work out a complete commercial maritime code, and to present it for acceptance to all the nations of the world.* But they did not take the pre-

---

* *Vide* an article on "Le Droit de la Mer," in *La Vie Internationale*, Vol. III, 1913, No. 6.

caution to consult the persons most interested, the traders, shipowners, insurers, etc., and their code satisfied nobody. But the whole subject continued to demand attention, and in 1898 the International Maritime Committee came into existence.

The Maritime Committee is a remarkable example of a voluntary international association whose efforts have resulted in international legislation and government. The objects are defined in its statutes as:

(a) To further, by conferences, publications, and divers works, the unification of Maritime Law.
(b) To encourage the creation of national associations for the unification of Maritime Law.
(c) To maintain between these associations regular communication and united action.

The Committee itself is composed of delegates of national associations, and there are now seventeen national associations in existence, including all the chief maritime and commercial countries. The Committee entered upon its task with extreme caution. Its procedure is not to attempt to deal with Maritime Law as a whole, but to take it piecemeal. It first decides what part of the Maritime Law it proposes to study—for instance, Collisions or Salvage or Freight. It then circulates to the National Associations a detailed questionnaire. The replies are tabulated, and show at a glance the variations in the details and the principles of the existing systems of national laws. An attempt is then made to reconcile the differences and to find some principle which will be acceptable to the different associations. This is submitted to and discussed at a conference. If some agreement is arrived at a draft convention is prepared and discussed at a further conference or conferences. If the conferences result in the acceptance of the draft convention, the Committee then works to get it submitted to and accepted by a diplomatic conference and embodied in the law of the States of the world.

The Committee had been in existence only twelve years when it had its first complete success, the unification of an important part of the maritime law of the world. It began its operations by taking up the study of four departments of that law: (1) The law of Maritime Salvage, (2) the law of Collisions at Sea, (3) the law as to Maritime Mortgages and Privileged Liens, and (4) the law as to Limitation of Shipowners' Liability. In all these cases agreement between the National Associations was found possible, and draft conventions were submitted to, discussed at, and finally passed by the annual conferences. In 1905 the Belgian Government proposed to call a diplomatic conference to consider these projects: at first the British Government refused to take part, but eventually withdrew its refusal, and the conference met in October of that year, and again in 1909 and 1910. The result was that two conventions unifying the law of Salvage and Collisions were signed by nearly all the chief maritime countries of the world, and the Secretary of the Committee could justly claim with regard to them in 1913 that "more than three-quarters of the tonnage of the world is now regulated by uniform maritime law elaborated by the International Maritime Committee." The diplomatic conferences also examined the draft conventions on Maritime Mortgages and the Liability of Owners and referred them to a sub-committee for further study. Since 1910 the most important questions dealt with by the Maritime Committee have been an international agreement on Safety at Sea and a draft convention on the law of Freight.

Such is the bare history of this attempt at International Legislation: there are several points which merit attention. In the first place, the composition of the National Associations and of the conferences is of great importance, because success in unifying the law depends entirely upon the possibility of their arriving at agreement. The Associations are representative in the highest degree of legal opinion, and those groups in each country most affected by Maritime Law. The conferences are equally representative, and in their proceedings, therefore, the relation between national interests and International Government and agreement becomes peculiarly manifest. How representative of national interests—in the widest and narrowest senses in which the words can be used, even by the most ardent Nationalist—these conferences are can best be shown by considering who the British delegates to the Copenhagen Conference of the Maritime Committee were in 1913. There were first two eminent K.C.'s, experts in maritime and commercial law, Sir Reginald Acland and Mr. L. Batten. Then there was the President of Lloyd's, Sir E. Beauchamp, and the President of the Chamber of Shipping of the United Kingdom, Mr. C. W. Gordon. The London Chamber of Commerce was represented by Sir A. K. Rollit; the Liverpool Steamship Owners' Association by Sir Norman Hill; and the United Kingdom Mutual Steamship Assurance Association by Sir Walter Runciman, Mr. A. Serena, Mr. H. R. Miller, and Mr. J. F. Wilson; the Glasgow Ship Owners' Association by Mr. J. B. Murray; the London Steamship Owners' Mutual Insurance Association by Mr. K. L. Bilbrough; and the North of England Steamship Owners' Association by Mr. Temperley and Mr. W. J. Noble. Anyone who knows anything of the shipping world will probably agree that it would hardly be possible to get together a body of men more representative of British maritime interests, and that these gentlemen were not likely to sacrifice those interests to a sentimental and cranky internationalism.

The delegates of the other National Associations are in the same way the leading men in the shipping and commercial worlds of the different countries. Now, these national groups are trade rivals and competitors, so that on the nationalist hypothesis they represent the most vital and the most conflicting of all national interests. One may therefore reasonably argue that if International Government and agreement can flourish in such soil, it can flourish anywhere. Secondly, they are dealing with national laws, customs, and interests to which men ordinarily cling most tenaciously, because they form part of the business environment, "the way we do our business in this country," in which they have grown up and made their fortunes. As soon as these shipowners, etc., began to consider the draft conventions they found that there were fundamental differences in the national laws on an enormous number of points, answering to different national views of commercial relations and obligations and responsibility and conduct, and that no unification was possible unless everyone was prepared to give up something. It cannot, therefore, be argued that International Government and agreement was possible or easy in the Maritime Committee because the interests involved were unimportant or obviously the same. Yet, in practically every case, and on the most controversial subjects, when face to face in the Conferences, these trade rivals were able to come to an agreement.

The verbatim reports of the Conferences are of extraordinary interest to the student of International Government, as showing in concrete form the relation of national interests in the world of shipping, the motives making for International Government, and the methods of obtaining that government through agreement. I propose to examine in some detail some of the points discussed and decided, because they will not only furnish the proof of the statements in the preceding paragraphs, but they will, I believe, help to throw light upon the general question of the relation of national interests to International Government and of international interests to National Government.

It is desirable to say a few words first about the two Conventions which were at length embodied by the States themselves in the law of nations. The Conventions signed in 1910 established a uniform law of the sea for:

> (1) Indemnities due by reason of damage caused to ships, persons, or things by collision, no matter in what waters the collision takes place.
>
> (2) Conditions under which remuneration for assistance or salvage becomes due.

Now to take one point only, in the Law of Collision there was a profound difference of principle in apportioning liability between Anglo-American and Continental practice. Before any unification of law could be achieved, the Committee had to face the task of obtaining the assent of one or other party to the abandonment of their national principle. Several cases of similar divergence had to be dealt with in regard to these two departments of Maritime Law. They were all solved, and most of the solutions were, to quote the report of the Committee itself, "in conformity with Anglo-

American law, and those which differ therefrom are not due to mere theoretical speculation, but have stood the test of long years—in some cases centuries—of judiciary practice in important countries, where they have given satisfaction." Again, in the Convention on Collisions, the Committee had to decide the extremely important and controversial question as to which court should have jurisdiction in collision cases. And in order to show what delicate questions were raised by these Conventions, it may be mentioned that the German delegate proposed at one moment that the Convention on Collisions should include a clause doing away altogether with the responsibility of shipowners for the faults of the masters—a proposal which, if accepted, would have revolutionized the law and commercial practice of most nations.

What becomes clear from the discussions on these Conventions is that despite the strong tendency to identify national interests with existing individual national practices, customs, and laws, the international interests in a uniform international practice and law are far stronger. The truth is that the interests of shipowners or traders are far more international than national—the interests of a group of German shipowners and a group of English shipowners, or of a group of French traders and a group of Swedish traders, are far more nearly the same than are those of British shipowners and British workingmen. The group interests of shipowners and traders lie predominantly in abolishing everything which impedes the international intercourse of trade, and therefore everything impeding that intercourse which results from national systems of Government.* That is why, when they are gathered together in the Conferences of the Maritime Committee, they are prepared to sacrifice the national and traditional customs and laws of commerce in which they have grown up in order to gain the uniformity of international laws and customs. I propose to give one or two examples of questions discussed in the Conferences which will show this psychology at work, and will more clearly exhibit the causes of it.

In the two conventions already referred to British law may be said generally to have triumphed over Continental; my first example will show British law yielding to Continental. At the conference of 1913, when the draft International Freight Code was being considered, Articles 8 and 9 as drafted permitted the withdrawal of the shipper from the contract before the commencement of the voyage, on payment of half freight. This provision is contrary to British practice and law, though it is in accordance with the law and

---

* It is perhaps necessary to point out that the support of a policy of protection by some of these groups does not invalidate the statement. The shipowner or trader who supports such a policy hopes or imagines that he will be able to impede international commercial intercourse for his rivals without impeding it for himself. If he believed that protection harmed himself as much as his rival he would be a free-trader. Of course, even shipowners and traders are sometimes mistaken as to where their true interests lie, and as to what is the real effect of their actions.

practice of the Continent. It was most strenuously resisted by the British delegates and supported by the Continental. Eventually the British delegation asked that the question should be postponed until the following day in order to allow them time for consultation. The British shipowners had expressed their doubts as to whether such a provision did not imperil the interests of the shipowner in favor of the shipper. But next day Mr. Batten, on behalf of the British delegates, withdrew their opposition in the following words:—
"We were profoundly impressed, I may say, not only with the manner in which they (the arguments of the Continental delegates) were stated, but with the real substance of the argument which formed the real force of the statements that were made. We were profoundly impressed also with the statement—that this code, as drafted, not only represents the considered judgment of the majority of seafaring nations of the world, but is found to work without difficulty or inconvenience in the disputes which unfortunately arise in the Courts of the different countries in which this law is enforced."

My second case illustrates well the actual forces at work in the minds of shipping and commercial men which make for international regulation and international laws. The Conference considered the question of Safety at Sea, and passed the following resolution:—"The Conference is of opinion that an International Agreement on the safety of navigation would be usefully directed to the formation of general rules in matters of wireless telegraphy, water-tight compartments, life-boats and life-saving apparatus, and deck-loads. The Conference further recommends the establishment of an international permanent body of a technical and advisory character with a view (a) to centralize all documentary information regarding the safety of life at sea, and secure its communication and interchange; (b) to facilitate the development of reciprocity between the nations as to the laws and regulations relating to such objects; and (c) to prepare all necessary reforms and amendments to the International Regulations, and secure uniformity of application."

In the discussion it was generally agreed that excessive deck-loads are a serious danger. But any attempt at national regulation immediately raises difficulties. In the first place, the very fact that it is national will probably unfairly damage some purely "national interests," because you will be subjecting your own shipowners to restrictions which it is impossible to enforce to an equal extent on foreign shipowners. Moreover, national restrictions, even if enforced, can, in the case of shipping which is continually passing out of the national jurisdiction into the jurisdiction of foreign States and foreign ports, only be enforced in a partial and erratic manner. These defects are clearly shown in the attempt of the British Board of Trade to regulate the height of deck-loads. Sir Edward Beauchamp described the position very well to the Conference. "In England," he said, "we are in a very anomalous position. We passed the Merchant Shipping Act of 1906 under the auspices of the Board of Trade. A provision was made that no vessel, either British or foreign, should come into any English port during certain months of the year carrying deck-loads. But they were unable to proceed any further; they could not restrict the carriage of these cargoes by British vessels when they were going to a Continental port; and therefore I think that, if it should be considered that it is dangerous to carry these cargoes, it seems to me necessary that it should be the subject of international agreement." The result was unanimity in favor of international legislation. Sir Walter Runciman, for instance, said:— "The height and weight of deck-loads, in my opinion, should be internationally fixed and regulated. I say that the deck-loads are abnormally high at the present time, without any restriction whatever, coming to foreign Continental ports. What I am contending for is that if there is to be an alteration in the deck-loads—that is, if they are to be reduced in any measure, it ought to be international." And Mr. Noble expressed it thus:—"What we do say from the British point of view is this: that whatever has to be done should be done on an international basis, and that we should all be on the same footing."

These examples will show, I think, that Internationalism and International Government are no fantastic ideals to the minds of great shipowners and the great captains of commerce. For them international interests are just as, or even more, real and insistent than national. But before leaving this subject of maritime law I cannot resist the desire to deal with one more question which shows with great clearness how modern conditions of industry and commerce are forcing the organization of society into international rather than national lines. When the draft code on freight was discussed by the Conference the proposed Article 20 gave rise to prolonged debate. This article dealt with "through bills of lading." In modern commerce the machinery of distribution is highly complicated, and a commodity produced in one country and consumed in another may pass through many different hands, by rail and ship, between the producer and seller in the first country and the wholesale dealer and buyer in the second. That this trade is and can only be carried on through a highly developed system of credit is an elementary fact of economics. The machinery of distribution through its bills of lading, its bills of exchange, etc., which become negotiable instruments, itself supplies the machinery of credit. A through bill of lading explains itself, but when converted, as it is converted by acceptance by a bank, into a negotiable instrument, it is an instrument of credit which covers the transport of a commodity through two or more different and distinct transporting hands. The through bill of lading is a comparatively modern invention of the American business world. Its conveniences are obvious so far as international trade is concerned, but it is also open to grave abuse, especially when the legal rights and obligations which accrue under it vary from country to country and are not clearly defined. For instance, the producer in America is to consign to the dealer in England 100 bales of cotton. These bales are to be put on the railway, consigned to an American port, where they are transferred from the hands of the railway company into the hands and vessel of a shipowner by whom they are to be delivered into the hands of the dealer in England. The through bill of lading is signed by an agent of the railway company in some country station in America, is accepted by a bank, and becomes a negotiable instrument so that the security of the holder is 100 bales of cotton said to have been loaded on to the railway. The through bill of lading covers not only the transport by rail, but also by ship. Now, suppose when the ship arrives in England there are found to be not 100, but only 50 bales of cotton, what are to be the legal rights and obligations of the several parties? Against whom, for instance, is the holder to claim—against the railway company or the shipowner, or both? And, as Sir Norman Hill showed, very great difficulties and much litigation have already arisen over this system. The planter and the railway official who has to receive the cotton may be friends; they may go out fishing together at the time of delivery. Then, perhaps, the railway man signs the through bill of lading for 100 bales and only 50 bales are loaded on the railway. When the bill is handed over at the port to the master of the ship he finds that there are only 50 bales. Then he is told that the other 50 bales are coming on later and can be loaded into the next ship—a sort of occurrence which is by no means uncommon, as every shipowner knows. The master is faced with having to refuse the 50 bales—a course which may occasion great loss and inconvenience—or, if he accepts them, with making himself liable on the through bill of lading to the holder for 100 bales, of which 50 were perhaps never delivered to the railway at all. As Sir Norman Hill said: "Considerable frauds have been practised by through bills of lading. If banks are careless, they can be used to perpetrate the most serious frauds."

Yet the convenience of this system of through bills under modern conditions of transport is obvious. They are, in fact, a natural development of the machinery of credit and transport to meet the requirements of modern international trade. Only it is essential, if they are to be used without being abused, that all parties through whose hands they pass shall know what uniform legal obligations and rights result from them. Article 20 of the draft Convention discussed by the Conference attempted to lay down what these uniform legal rights and obligations should be. There were two alternative suggestions. Under the first, where goods are carried under a through bill of lading, no carrier would be liable except for loss or damage done to the goods whilst he is in charge of them, but the consignee would be at liberty to sue the last or through carrier for any loss or damage done to the goods. Under the second proposal, which came from the German delegates, the holder of a through bill of lading would have the right to claim delivery of the merchandise from the last carrier, and the latter might not allege as defense against him that the loss or damage had occurred during an anterior portion of the through carriage. At the Copenhagen conference there was considerable difference of opinion upon these two proposals, but there was no difference of opinion as to the necessity of some international legislation.

B.—*International Labor Legislation*

Labor legislation, in the modern sense of legislation for the protection of the worker against the evils of our factory and industrial system, is, of course, entirely a growth of the nineteenth century. The British Act of 1802 was the first attempt of the State to deal with the factory question, but for many years after that date the intervention or non-intervention of the State was the subject of embittered controversy. To-day in most of the countries of Europe men have outgrown that controversy. Practically everyone now admits that the industrial system which men have invented, if allowed to operate uncontrolled by any collective regulations, must end in disaster to the wage-earner. Labor legislation of this kind is essentially group interest legislation. The organization of industry in factories which has followed the invention of machinery, if unregulated by some force external to the two groups of employers and employed, leads inevitably to the sacrifice of the interests of the latter group to those of the former. In all this kind of labor legislation, from the first British Factory Act of 1819 to the last regulation issuing from the Home Office, or the Reichsamt des Innern, or the Ministère du Travail, the State is attempting to protect the group interests of the wage-earner against the group interests of the capitalist and employer.

It is possible, therefore, to assert dogmatically that to-day in all the countries of Europe the opinion is universal that industrial relations of employer to employed must, in the interests of the latter, be subjected to the control of national government, and must be the object of national legislation. But that in practice this control has been efficient or satisfactory very few people would assert. Everywhere millions of wage-earners live on the verge of or in extreme poverty, everywhere hours of labor are inordinately long and wages inordinately low, everywhere children are forced into the factories when they ought to be in schools, and everywhere conditions under which the men, the women, and the children work are such as to cause physical degeneration, the most horrible "occupational diseases," and premature death. The main causes of this failure and of these inconvenient facts that stare our civilization in the face are two. First, nationally the group interests of the employer are everywhere not only enormously stronger, but are considered to be more important than those of the employed.

That German or English capitalists and manufacturers should win or lose a "market" or a concession where they can perform the noble task of selling dear to and buying cheap from the naked and unsuspecting savage (and often eventually exterminate him by the rapid process of shooting or the slower process of cheap gin), that the German or English financier should have a fair chance of swelling his bank balance, are universally recognized to be matters of such vital national importance that in peace the respective Foreign Offices are always expending the last ounce of their brains upon them, and in many a war the nation has been ready with its proverbial shilling and drop of blood. These are considered to be such elementary facts that even the working classes of each country have been again and again deluded into identifying the group interests of the employers and financiers with national interests. It is still a paradox to talk of high wages and short hours and the non-employment of children as national interests: the interests of labor are still almost entirely outside the purview of Foreign Offices—where the diplomatic hall-porter knows many a financier by sight, but has never seen a trade union leader—and the first shilling and the first drop of blood have still to be spent in war on a national interest which is even remotely working class.

This identification of the group interests of the small, wealthy governing class with national interests has had a further effect. The regulation of industry by the State in the interests of the wage-earners is *primâ facie* against the interests of this small class. Therefore, whenever any practical proposal to regulate industry in that way has been made, it has always been opposed on the ground that it is contrary to vital national interests—and the argument is sound, provided that we admit the extremely doubtful assumption that the interests of the small national group are more national than the large national group. That this argument has continually been successfully used can best be shown by examples. Everyone knows that little more than half a century ago the State restriction of hours of labor of women and children was resisted by the altruistic employers in the interests of the women and children themselves. The day has, however (or had before July, 1914), gone by when it was possible to convince people that it was to the interest of the twelve-year-old son of a cotton spinner to work fourteen hours a day in a factory, and we no longer even believe that it is in the interest of a girl of the working class that her living body should gradually decompose from phosphorus poisoning contracted in making matches. It is admitted to-day that it is in the interests of both the child and the girl that the State should regulate industry in such a way that they should neither of them be able to obtain employment of that kind. But whenever a proposal is made for the State to make such kind of employment illegal, it is still resisted by the employing groups, and a different argument is used. "It may be," they say, "in the interests of young persons and children of the working classes to restrict their hours of labor; but if we in England do this and the Germans and Belgians do not do it, the most vital national interests will be jeopardized. If we are prevented by law from working our employees more than ten hours, while the German employer works his eleven or twelve hours, how can we compete with him? By a law like this you will ruin us, and you will destroy this national industry which is a vital national industry of the country." This kind of argument has been used by the employing groups against every proposal to apply State regulations to conditions of employment, and, indeed, against every attempt to protect the interests of employed against employer. It has been used by them to resist increases of wages, limitation of the hours of labor, limitation of the employment of children and young persons, restrictions on the employment of women, the regulation of minimum wages and the abolition of sweating by means of Wage Boards, the regulation of dangerous trades, and the prohibition of the use of materials which poison the men and women who have to handle them. It is used not in one country, but in every country: the German employer pleads that he cannot reduce his hours because the Belgian employer will not reduce his, the Belgian cannot reduce his because of the French employer, the French employer cannot reduce his because of the British employer, and the British cannot reduce his because of the German—and so we get the complete and noble circle of vital national interests of employers.*

Thus, here again, in another department of modern life, there emerges out of the complications of society an international interest which can only be served by international government and cosmopolitan legislation. If it is to the interest of every State to regulate the conditions of employment within its territory, but it is prevented from doing so unless all the other States do likewise, then clearly the solution ought to be found in unification of the Labor laws of the different countries through international agreements. Robert Owen, who during his life was

---

* It is only fair to the twentieth century employer to say that he is no less altruistic than his predecessor of the nineteenth. The employer to-day resists these reforms in the interest not of himself and his class, but of his work-people and of the nation. Just as the employer fifty years ago opposed the interference with the liberty of a child of twelve to work as long as he or she wanted to work because such interference was against the interests of the child, the working classes, and the nation, so the employer to-day argues that to limit the hours of labor or to raise wages, or to fix a minimum wage will be disastrous to the wage-earner and the nation. If hours are shortened or wages raised, we shall not be able to compete with the foreigner, our industry will perish, and the wage-earner will find himself without employment and without wages. Naturally, many of the workers themselves are terrified by these altruistic arguments. Unfortunately, or fortunately, in practice whenever regulations are made, or hours shortened, or wages raised, these terrible prophecies are not fulfilled. Export trade flourished even where wages have risen; short hours produce increased output and increased earnings; and the Trade Boards Act, which was going to ruin the Chain Trade and the sweated women who worked for   an hour, only seemed to benefit both (see on these points the Annual Report of the Chief Inspector of Factories and Workshops for the Year 1914, *passim*, and particularly p. 59, as regards hours and output, and as regards the Trade Boards Act).

certainly the most typical of cranks, but since his death has been numbered among the greatest of the prophets, was the first to perceive this international interest and the need of International Government, and in 1818 he "urged that the Congress of the Holy Alliance, in session at Aachen . . . should appoint a Commission to examine" how this need could be met. Owen, in nearly all his ideas, was at least fifty years before his time, and, though Daniel Legrand followed in his footsteps, it was not until the second half of the nineteenth century, and that movement towards internationalism which displayed itself in International Congresses and the formation of International Associations, that the importance of this idea of international labor legislation became widely recognized. Then, "Congresses of charitable bodies, Congresses concerned with questions of hygiene and of social reform, promoted the diffusion of the idea, associations of working men gave it support, Prince Bismarck recommended it for consideration, and the theologian Thiersch appealed to the German Emperor to take the initiative." By 1876 the idea had got as far as the Swiss Federal Council, which subsequently proposed to invite the Governments of Europe to a diplomatic Conference. It took another fourteen years for the Conference to materialize, and then, in 1890, it met in Berlin, under the auspices of the Emperor of Germany.*

---

* The facts and quotations in this paragraph are taken from an article by Ernst Francke on "International Labor Treaties," in the *Economic*

The official and diplomatic Conference of 1890, like so many others of the same kind, was able to agree on certain "principles," but did not agree to put these principles into practice. But the need for international legislation continued to exist and to grow more insistent in the minds of those who were concerned to alleviate something of the evils of industrialism in the different countries. At last there was formed in 1900 a voluntary international association, the International Association for Labor Legislation, the object of which is to do for Labor Laws what we have seen the International Maritime Committee doing for Maritime Commercial Law. Like that Committee, the Association is formed of national sections, which elect representatives to a central Committee, which has its seat and an International Labor Office at Basle, in Switzerland. There are now thirteen national sections. The Committee holds a general meeting every two years, and at these meetings the Governments of all the principal industrial countries are represented. The revenue of the association was in 1911 about 85,000 frs., of

---

Journal of June, 1909. The edict of the German Emperor, quoted by Herr Francke, shows the idea of those responsible for the Conference, and the facts which made international legislation necessary: "I am determined to lend my support to improving the conditions of work of German workmen as far as lies in my power, which is limited by the necessity of maintaining the international position of German industry and of securing its existence and that also of the working-classes. . . . . If the difficulties to be treated at the International Conference . . . . cannot be surmounted by an understanding between the countries anxious to command international markets, they may at least be minimized."

which 63,550 frs. came from subsidies from fourteen Governments.

The International Labor Association has, like the Maritime Committee, succeeded in obtaining the signature of a large number of States to two international treaties, the object and effect of which are to unify national laws. It is, therefore, another example of a voluntary association taking a direct part in the development of International Government and of cosmopolitan legislation. Its success has, however, been far less complete within its own sphere than that of the Maritime Committee within the sphere of Maritime Law, and I propose therefore to consider briefly the methods and constitution of the two associations and the interests involved, because it is these differences of methods, constitution, and interests which have caused the differences in achievement.

The constitution of the Labor Association differs materially from that of the Maritime Committee. The strength of the latter lay, as we saw, in its being so representative of the group interest most nearly affected by Maritime Law. Even the Foreign Office could hardly think that an agreement supported by the President of Lloyd's, the President of the London Chamber of Commerce, and all the principal Shipping Associations could be damaging to vital British commercial and shipping interests. The Committee is so important because it provides machinery for representation of these group interests in an international organ, and allows these group interests which run in international rather than national lines to operate.' The Labor Association can hardly be said to do the same. The group interests most nearly affected by Labor Laws are those of employers and employed. The lines in which they run are in reality also international rather than national. Many people may be disposed at first sight to deny this assertion; but it is clearly proved by the facts; first, that organized labor in the different countries and those international federations of organized labor, about which more will have to be said in a later chapter, are almost always in agreement as to what they desire in labor legislation, and, secondly, that the attitude of employers towards such legislation is the same in all countries. But the Association is not representative of these two groups in the same way as the Maritime Committee is representative of shipping and commercial groups. It would not be unfair to say that within the Association the impetus comes mainly from people who can be described as "social reformers," and secondly from Labor. The capitalist and employing interest is hardly represented at all. This can best be shown by a consideration of the membership of the British Section. It will be found that the individual members are almost all social reformers, while the affiliated societies consist of nearly thirty labor organizations, nearly ten societies of which the object is some kind of social reform, and only one association of employers. The result is that at a general meeting of the International Committee you do not find the great captains of industry present or the national federations of capitalists and employers represented, and the conferences are composed of the delegates of Governments, social reformers, representatives of organized labor, and a very few of the more enlightened employers.

I do not for one moment wish to imply that the International Association for Labor Legislation has not accomplished a great deal in its short existence, but it is of the highest importance to point out its relation as an international organism to an association like the International Maritime Committee, because the difference of their constitution has affected their achievements. The Labor Association, like the Maritime Committee, attempts through its national sections to draw up and obtain agreement to International Conventions which will unify Labor laws in the different countries, and thus fix, for instance, an international maximum working day for women, children, or young persons, or establish an international prohibition against the use industrially of dangerous substances and processes. But when the Association has succeeded in obtaining agreement in its own bosom, it is not nearly in so strong a position as the Maritime Committee in approaching the Foreign Offices and asking for the acceptance of its draft conventions by a diplomatic conference. It cannot claim that *all* the most important group interests involved are in agreement. The capitalist and employing interests and groups have not been represented, and are not in agreement; and those groups, as we have seen, have the greatest control over the different national governments, and have succeeded in inducing the popular belief that their interests are peculiarly national interests. This is the misfortune, not the fault, of the Labor Association: it would probably be quite impossible to get into one Association the two groups of employers and employed, and even if you did, you would not get them to agree upon Labor legislation. That is because we are here dealing with group interests which, unlike national interests, are really in conflict in modern society. The real cleavage here is between employer and employed, not between German employer and British employer, or between German worker and British worker. The vital interests follow, in fact, international, not national, lines. If the German and British employer can compete on an equality against one another when both are at liberty to work women ten hours a day, neither of them will be in a worse or a better position as against the other if British and German Labor laws reduce the legal day for women from ten hours to eight. International legal limitation of hours thus does not alter the relations between national groups, but it does very materially alter the relations between the international groups, Capital and Labor. That is why both the German and the British employer will be found to resist such limitation, and why neither enters the International Labor Association. The fact that the employers themselves base their resistance on national interests is not

PREVENTION OF WAR

relevant. It only shows how successfully they delude people into identifying the employers' interests with national interests. Belief in a fact is certainly a fact, but is no proof of the trueness of the belief. The belief that it was in the national interest to roast citizens alive who held certain religious opinions used to be a fact: we now recognize that such action was only in the interest of a small religious group. So some day it may be widely recognized that to overwork and underpay the majority of the workers of the nation, though it may be in the interest of a small international employing group, is not a national interest.

The preceding paragraph is not a digression. The necessity of applying International Government to labor legislation has been recognized, as we saw, even by a King of Prussia and German Emperor. The attempt to apply it in practice has met with serious difficulties. The important point is that the difficulties are due not to a conflict of national, but of class, interests. Yet, despite this and despite the overwhelming influence of the employing class in national government and Foreign Offices, the International Association for Labor Legislation has had a certain measure of success. The first subjects which it took up were the use of white phosphorus in the manufacture of matches and the employment of women at night. In both cases the Association worked out the basis of an international convention. The Swiss Government was then induced to propose a diplomatic conference. The Conference eventually met at Berne in 1905 and again in 1906, and two conventions were signed. These two conventions are worthy of brief study.

The first prohibits, with certain exceptions, night work for women. Article 2 lays down that the interval of repose at night shall be a minimum of eleven hours, and that within those eleven hours shall be included the period from 10 p.m. to 5 a.m. This very moderate regulation was not obtained without great difficulty, and the argument was freely used by the representatives of States "backward" in their Labor Laws that prohibition of night work would damage certain industries and national interests. However, this treaty was signed by thirteen States, including all the chief industrial countries of Europe. To meet the wishes of the "backward" States allowance of from two to ten years' grace was made for them to give effect to the terms of the treaty after adherence. When steps began to be taken in the national legislatures to put the treaty into operation, considerable opposition arose in some countries. In Spain, for instance, when a Bill was introduced in the Cortes in 1911, agitation against it began in the Catalonian cotton-spinning trade, and it was asserted that the trade would be ruined if night work of women was prohibited. Finally, however, the Act was passed, with the provision that it should not come into operation until 1914. It is interesting also to note that the Swedish Parliament at first refused to ratify the Convention for another reason, namely, because the women of that country objected to legislation discriminating between male and female labor. However, in this case, too, the opposition eventually gave way, and in 1909 a Bill for the prohibition of night work for women passed through both the Swedish Houses of Parliament. The unification of the law in all the signatory countries has, therefore, now been carried through.

The history of the white phosphorus convention is even more instructive from an international point of view. By the time that the conference met, an efficient substitute for this substance in the manufacture of matches had been discovered, and several States had legislation designed to prevent the use of white phosphorus. The convention proposed at the conference of 1905 prohibited the manufacture, import, or sale of matches made with this material in the territories of the signatory States. Great opposition was, however, raised by several States on the ground that if they signed it and Japan, an exporting country, which was not represented at the Conference, did not sign it, their own export trade would be subjected to unfair competition. Accordingly, the majority of the States made the signature by Japan a condition of their adherence, and the matter was left in this position at the close of the Conference. At the Conference of 1906 Japan was again unrepresented, and only seven * States signed the convention, while of these seven, as

* The seven States were Germany, Denmark, France, Italy, Holland, Luxemburg, and Switzerland.

Professor Reinsch points out,* "the prohibition was already in force in five . . . while in the sixth the industry was almost negligible." But the matter did not rest there: the Association worked through its national sections to obtain the adherence of other countries. The result has been that Spain, Great Britain, India, and the majority of the British Colonies and Possessions, Norway, and Belgium have since adhered, and other States have adopted legislation which conforms to the Convention.† This was achieved in part by a kind of international pressure which immediately resulted from the original international agreement. For instance, as Professor Reinsch remarks, Great Britain refused to sign the treaty on the grounds that her export trade would suffer by being subjected to restrictions not borne by competitors. "The effect of the treaty was, however, practically to exclude British matches from European markets," and so in 1908 an Act was passed prohibiting the manufacture, sale, and importation of white phosphorus matches, and Britain adhered to the Convention. The same sort of pressure is being brought to bear upon Japan, which still stands outside the treaty, for the closing of her markets in India and Australia will be a strong incentive to her to join. At any rate, it is remarkable that to-day Japan and Sweden are the only

* Public International Unions, p. 46.

† E. g., the United States, whose constitution prevents it from conforming by federal legislation to the Convention; but by an Act of 1912 she has placed a tax on the manufacture of white phosphorus matches, and has prohibited their exportation or importation.

two manufacturing countries which stand outside the Convention.

The Association also took up the questions of the hours of labor of women and young persons, and of the night work of boys. In 1913 these subjects were again submitted to a diplomatic conference at Berne by the Swiss Government. Bases of two Conventions were accepted, but the spirit in which the diplomatists acted can best be shown by quoting the opinion of one of the leading members of the Association, Miss Constance Smith: "The draft Conventions were far from admirable; their framers went so far in the spirit of compromise to meet the objections of the backward States that the provisions laid down, had they been accepted without modification, would have tended to depress rather than to raise the standard of international opinion on the questions to be affected by them."

It will be seen, therefore, that the complication of interests to be affected by cosmopolitan Labor Legislation is greater than that affected by cosmopolitan Maritime Legislation, and the success of the Association has been more difficult and less complete than that of the Maritime Committee. But it is relevant to the question of International Government and International Social Structure to note that the Association has deliberately worked with success towards the unification of Labor Laws by a method other than that of International Conventions. In an earlier chapter, I remarked that these voluntary International Associations, like the Labor Association, act as direct organs of International Government. They do this by forming international opinion and international agreement among their members, who themselves in many cases have great influence upon their own National Governments. This process has been most noticeable in the Labor Association, and constitutes it a real organ or organism of International Government. In the first place, the officials of all the chief industrial countries who administer the labor laws are represented at the biennial Conferences of the Association. The presence of these Government officials has two effects. It keeps before the eyes of the social reformer in the Association the practical difficulties which are immediately apparent in a scheme to an administrator: it prevents the work of the Association from becoming a Utopia of pious resolutions. But it also has a considerable effect upon the officials themselves. Through these meetings they are brought into touch with men, who, like themselves, are administering Labor Laws in nearly all the chief industrial countries of the world. They discuss the technique of Labor Legislation with fellow administrator experts and with unofficial experts and labor men. They learn of the experiments in State regulation, its successes and failures, throughout the world; in a word, their experience and their outlook are to some extent internationalized. In the modern State, the official who is high up in a Government office can influence legislation as well as administration. The effect of the internationalization of the outlook and experience of the official is clearly observable in the history of Labor Legislation and Administration in the several countries. There has been a notable tendency in recent years towards unification quite apart from the international conventions. It is merely a process of one State learning from the experience of another, and it frequently originates from the—sometimes unconsciously—internationalized official. But, in any case, the result is the same cosmopolitan legislation.

But this internationalization of the mind and aims and experience is not confined to the officials: it is even more observable in the members of the Association. And this helps to form an international rather than a national public opinion on Labor Legislation. And so in each different country we find the pioneers in this legislation working for the same objects. A very good example of this process is referred to by Miss Constance Smith. Minimum rates of wages have, as we saw, been resisted because of "international competition." For the last eight years State regulation of minimum wages has been discussed and studied by the Association. At first the differences in national conditions of industry and life produced the most decided differences of opinion among the representatives of the different sections, and in "1906 . . . a few daring delegates met in corners and whispered under their breath the words 'Wages Board.'" Yet, in 1912 "a two-day conference on the legal minimum wage preceded the meeting of the Association, and a whole sheaf of minimum wage bills introduced by private members into the Chambers of different countries was before the delegates, together with an official measure of the French Government." "To watch this change of attitude," writes Miss Smith, "was to see international thought in the making. . . . The remarkable advance towards definite action on the part of the State in relation to the establishment of minimum rates for home workers which took place between 1906 and 1913 could not have been achieved in so short a time but for the labors of certain voluntary associations, led by men of insight, candor, and indefatigable devotion."

C.—*Other Examples*

Several other examples of cosmopolitan legislation could be given. Some, of course, have already been dealt with in Chapter III, because the unification of administration which was the main object of international agreement could in some cases only be carried out by some unification of national laws. I propose, however, to deal very shortly with only two other examples.

The first is the question of international copyright. The question is particularly interesting because here we see International Government creeping into a department of life very different from those which we have hitherto been considering. The statesman of ancient Athens would have counted art and literature and music among the most vital of national interests to be protected and encouraged by the State; but no one in a modern State imagines that the artist or his art can affect or be affected by anything which could remotely resemble such national interests as those of prestige, diplomatists, finance, industry, and commerce. But here again human beings have proceeded to develop their lives with little heed to their own theories and beliefs as to the independence of States and the hierarchy of national interests. For instance, they read and they write books without reference to these theories and beliefs, and the change in the world's ways which we have noticed in so many directions during the last century extended to the reading and the writing of books. First there was the enormous increase in readers and writers, and literature became not only an art, but a profession which might be extremely lucrative. Then the literary and artistic product came within the orbit of national legislation. From the earliest times, for example, the Common Law of England had given to the author the exclusive right to his own writings, and as early as 1710 a Statute assured him the exclusive right of printing his works for twenty-one years. Until the nineteenth century, owing to the limited number of readers and writers and the lack of international intercourse, the problem of literary and artistic property necessarily remained a national one. But as soon as the number of a people who could and would read books began to be numbered by thousands instead of hundreds, and as soon as the material and immaterial barriers between nations began to break down and thousands of people in one country would take an interest in the thought and art and literature of other countries, the problem became an international one.

The problem, of course, consisted in the question of the property rights in works produced by foreigners and outside the national jurisdiction. Originally practically everywhere it was settled on purely national lines. The author, for instance, of a French book published in France had no property rights in it in the United States. But it is interesting to note that this extremely "Nationalist" solution did not safeguard even so insignificant a national interest as literature. For in a book compiled by the Secretary of the American Publishers' Copyright League in 1896 * we find the author complaining that the fact that the English author could not obtain copyright of his books in America was harming the American publisher, the American author, and the American reading public. The publishing of an English work was for the publisher merely a scramble to be first in the field. The American author was hit, because the publisher was not going to pay him a fair price for a book when he could get much the same kind of book from an English author and pay the Englishman nothing. The American reader gained nothing except cheap paper-covered reprints of English novels, because the American publisher could not

---

* *The Question of Copyright,* by Geo. Haven Putnam. 1896.

take the risk of publishing the better-class foreign works when he knew that if any of them began to be successful he would immediately be subjected to the competition of half-a-dozen other American publishers.

Thus it was that everywhere in the nineteenth century the necessity of some form of international copyright began to be realized. The problem was complicated by the variation in the different national copyright laws. The first movement for an international agreement and a unification of national laws came, as I remarked in a previous chapter, in 1878 from the International Association founded by Victor Hugo. From the earliest times there were on the subject two schools of thought, one in favor of complete unification of the laws of copyright, and the other in favor of assuring to the foreign author uniformity of rights. When in 1886, after several diplomatic conferences, an international treaty was signed and an international Union of States formed, it was the latter school which triumphed. The Union which establishes international copyright is now governed by the Convention of 1908, and is composed of fifteen States. The Convention results in a partial unification of the copyright laws of the several States, for it assures to foreign authors the protection, in every country within the Union, which the law of that country gives to its own authors. This has necessitated in many countries the codification and alteration of the national law, *e. g.*, as in the case of the British Acts of 1886 and 1911.

Certain States are not in this Union—for instance, Austria and the United States—but even they have found it necessary to conclude separate conventions giving a certain measure of reciprocity and to alter their national laws accordingly.* It is unnecessary to say more upon the forces making for this cosmopolitan legislation, and the relation of national interests to it, except in one particular. The United States is prevented from becoming a member of the Union by the retention of what is called the "manufacturing clause" in their Act. According to Section 15 of the Act of 1911, books for which protection is sought "shall be printed from type set within the limits of the United States." The best comment on this provision is that of Leon Poinsard, quoted by Professor Reinsch: "The United States, in fact, subordinates the primordial right of authors to the narrow interest of American printers and their employers." Here again, therefore, we see the interests of a single very small group identified with national interests—and the fact is worthy of note, because in a report of a Sub-Committee appointed by the British Government during the war to report on British trade after the war we read: "As regards copyright, the most important suggestion made to us was by the representatives of the printing trade to the effect that the United Kingdom Copyright Law should be brought into line with that of the United States; at present printed works to

---

* *E. g.*, the United States Copyright Acts of 1891 and 1911.

be copyrighted in both countries have to be produced in the United States for the purposes of copyright there, and consequently have to be manufactured in the United States, wholly or in part, even if for sale in this country." And the Sub-Committee recommends that the United Kingdom Copyright Law should be brought into line with that of the United States, apparently on the assumption that the only national interest involved in literature is the interest of printers, for the only evidence on the subject which they appear to have taken was that of the printers!

The question of industrial property, *i. e.*, trade-marks and patents, is in many respects similar to that of literary and artistic property, and a similar international problem has arisen. It has been solved partially in a similar way. In 1883 a convention was signed by eleven States establishing an International Union of Industrial Property with an International Bureau. This Union has effected a partial unification of patent and trade-mark laws, for it assures to the citizens of any State within the Union the advantages and protection in any other State which the latter accords by its laws to its own nationals. Professor Reinsch calls this an administrative arrangement, and in a sense, of course, it is, but it is also a partial unification of national laws, for the first effect of the convention is that every State has to treat the foreigner in the same way in its patent laws. As in so many other cases, this cosmopolitan legislation necessarily produces international administration, and the work of the International Bureau at Berne is a most interesting example of such administration. A certain number of the States in the Union, by a subsidiary agreement, have made the Bureau a true international registry of trade-marks, and a trade-mark registered there and in one of those States is protected in each of the others. It may be mentioned that, between 1893 and 1911, 11,684 trade-marks were registered at the International Registry, of which over 6,000 were French.

CHAPTER V

INTERNATIONAL SOCIETY AND INTERNATIONAL STANDARDS

SO far, in dealing with International Government, we have been examining cases in which State Government, represented either by Legislation or Administration, is concerned. It is true that government through voluntary associations of the individual citizens of several States is, as we have seen, frequently a most valuable instrument for establishing the internationalization of administration or the cosmopolitanization of law which the ever-increasing international interests of modern life require. I now, however, propose to pass altogether out of the regions of States, Powers, and Principalities into that of voluntary associations of individuals and groups of individuals of different States. I hope to show that in a large number of directions these associations have elaborated organs and systems of International Government, and that even a brief review of this novel social fabric will throw much light upon the future of international organization and its relation to national interests.

The essence of government is organized regulation of relations within a community. I have had already again and again to refer to the sudden, enormous increase of international relations during the nineteenth century in that largest of all human communities, the world. Wherever the relations within a community become many and complicated, the only alternative to anarchy is government, or the organized regulation of those relations; and in the civilized world government is, or at least should be, organized regulation of relations based upon agreement between individuals or groups of individuals. And State Government is everywhere in that world insufficient for the manifold relations of the manifold groups into which our society divides and subdivides itself. This is well recognized in individual States, where the development and working of voluntary associations, such as churches, trade unions, associations of employers, joint stock companies, clubs, etc., have been studied and traced. All these bodies are organs of government, and therefore combine with the State organs to regulate the relations of citizens. The whole problem of international government, and therefore of the prevention of war, consists in the elaboration of a similar organized regulation of international relations. In this chapter I shall examine the growth and possibilities of this kind of organization in international society, omitting State organization, which has already been dealt with, and certain industrial and commercial organizations, which will more conveniently be treated in a separate chapter.

The outstanding fact is that in every department of life society has become international; that is to say, the relations between individuals and groups in the different nations are many, and the human interests involved, the broad and the deep interests, are not conflicting, but the same from nation to nation. I propose to take various departments of life and to trace briefly the need and the beginnings of organized regulation of these international relations which belong to them.

The simplest and the most obvious of such departments is science. It is a commonplace that science is international, but what is not often realized is that though the interests of science are so obviously international, they cannot be adequately served without organized regulation; in other words, International Government. And already the application of International Government to science has gone very far, and has been eminently successful. In the first place, scientific progress has depended and must continue to depend upon the interchange of knowledge and discoveries of scientific workers, not in the small geographical areas called States, but over the whole world. A vast international organization has already grown up to meet this international need. There is hardly a branch of science for which there is not a voluntary international association, the object of which is, by publications and discussions in periodic congresses, to break down the barriers of national frontiers and language which impede the exchange of knowledge and the progress of science.

And in almost every case it is the leading men in all the different countries who are members of and take an active part in the proceedings of these associations. To attempt to show in detail how this has resulted in the rapid internationalization of the different branches of science would require many volumes: it would, in fact, necessitate the writing a complete history of science in the nineteenth century, from Mathematics and Psychical Research to Astronomy and Meteorology; it must, therefore, suffice to take a single example and show from it how this process has worked. To no part of science has this form of organization been more completely applied than to the medical sciences. For every subdivision of the art and science of medicine there is an international society, association, or congress. Here is a list of a few taken at random from the pages of the review *La Vie Internationale*:—Occupational Diseases, Medical Electrology and Radiology, Tuberculosis, Dentistry, Veterinary Surgery, Surgery, Psychology and Psychotherapy, Mouth and Teeth, Rhino-Laryngology, Thalasstherapie, Otology, Comparative Pathology, Physiology, Anatomy, Neurology and Psychiatry, Embryology. There have been two important results. In the first place, the complication of international structure has called for and produced some organization and regulation of its parts. Several of the international medical Congresses overlap, and the need of some centralizing and controlling body has become apparent. This need has to some extent been met by the formation of a Permanent International Commission of International Congresses of Medicine. Secondly, this international organization has had an enormous effect upon the science itself. Not only are the leading investigators in each country kept aware through the congresses and associations of what is being done elsewhere, but medical treatment right down the scale of investigator, specialist, and general practitioner is internationalized. One example alone will suffice. There can be no doubt, for instance, that the discussion of the Freudian theories and methods by the leading alienists at an international medical congress not only was of immense value in showing the weak and the strong points in the theory and methods, but for the first time brought accurate knowledge of the treatment devised by this Austrian physician to a large number of medical practitioners of other countries. The result has been an immediate increase in the use of Freudian methods, particularly in this country.

This kind of association is a rather primitive form of organization, the main object of which remains to spread scientific knowledge across the national frontiers. A second step has, however, been taken by certain associations to organize internationally scientific research and to subject it to a more elaborate International Government. Of such associations one of the most influential is the International Association of Academies, founded in 1899. It consists of all the great national scientific Academies—it now numbers 22 members—and its work may be best defined by its own statutes: "To prepare or initiate scientific works, and to facilitate scientific relations between countries." In other words, it aims at organizing scientific work internationally which cannot be adequately carried on on a national basis. For instance, one of the things which hampers scientific progress is the variation in national scientific standards. The need for the unification of standards in science is as pressing as the need of unification of commercial laws in commerce. And so we find that one of the first things that this International Association took up was the unification of a standard, *i. e.*, it appointed an international commission to consider the question of unification of standards of color. Again, it appointed an international commission on the calendar, and it passed a resolution asking Governments to adhere to the draft Convention elaborated by the Paris International Conference on Time of 1912, a convention which would result in the unification of national systems of time and the establishment of A Permanent Government International Commission on Time.* It is also a sign of the need for and the growth of a new international struc-

---

* It is significant that here we find the leading body of scientific men in the different countries demanding the State "internationalization" of Time as being in the interests of science, while the leading business men are demanding precisely the same thing as being in the interests of commerce. The fifth International Congress of Chambers of Commerce, in which nearly all the chief chambers of commerce of thirty different countries are represented, passed a resolution asking for a diplomatic conference to establish a fixed international calendar.

ture that one resolution of this Association recommends that it should be consulted by Governments before they take part in any new International Scientific Association. There can be no question, when one considers the status of the members of this Association, that its request is not unreasonable, and if it is complied with, we shall have in this International Association a supernational scientific body bearing the same relation to the community of States and international society as, for instance, the Royal Society bears within the national boundaries to the British Government and the British people.

There are some sciences in which progress is particularly slow and necessarily circumscribed unless it can be organized internationally, and it is in these that the most advanced forms of international organization can be observed. The most obvious example is Astronomy, for here international co-operation between observers and observatories is often a necessity, and therefore a unification of methods of work and observation has to be organized. It is therefore not surprising to find a large number of International Astronomical Associations. There is, first, the Central Bureau of Astronomical Telegrams, created at Kiel in 1882, which receives and transmits astronomic news from and to affiliated observatories. Then there is the International Union for Co-operation in Solar Research, founded in 1904, to which thirteen countries belong; it has seven international commissions for determining international standards of measurement, etc. There is an International Committee for the Execution of the Photographic Map of the Sky; all the great observatories are represented on the committee and are co-operating in the execution of the map: a portion of the sky is assigned to each observatory, uniform methods of work are determined by the committee, and the complete uniform map will be completed by 1925. Finally, there met in 1911 a Congrès internationale des Ephémérides astronomiques, at which were the directors of ten observatories and of Astronomical Almanacks of various countries. This congress passed resolutions of a highly technical and detailed nature, the result of which is to unify methods of work and observation.

The interests involved in science are obviously international. The international organization is primarily directed to forward those interests, but in so scientific an age as the present it necessarily has the indirect effect of internationalizing society, of breaking down peculiar national habits and customs. The importance of this operation cannot be exaggerated, because it is where nations represent different levels of "culture" and are yet in intimate and continual relationship, that the difficulties of applying government to their relations are most formidable. When one turns from science to other departments of life, one sees in the organization and government of voluntary associations even more clearly the beginnings of an organized process of internationalizing society and the growth of international social tissue which, if consciously developed and used, might perform the functions in the wider community of nations which are performed in the community of a nation by similar and older institutions.

We have already seen in the International Association for Labor Legislation how an association of this kind tends to internationalize the ideals and objects of those interested in a particular department of life. The whole vast accumulation of International Associations which are concerned with social reforms, or what are sometimes called on the Continent the Social Sciences, are everywhere producing the same effects. Thus, international educational associations and congresses are very numerous, and they unite in a single body the pure social reformer, the practical teacher, the expert, and the administrator. There can be no doubt that this organization has contributed to a unification of educational methods in Europe.

And if one turns to very different groups of associations one finds a similar process at work. Many of the professional associations have had the effect of internationalizing professional methods. The decisions of an international congress have, for instance, resulted in the internationalization of medical nomenclature, while the work of an international actuarial association has caused the adoption of British actuarial methods throughout the world.

In all these examples, it will be observed, the process is one of unification. Now, it is remarkable that Government in civilized communities tends more and more to concern itself with unifications. In national communities, for instance, the tendency has been to enlarge the area of uniformity of law, to unify customs regulations and taxes generally, education, trade union structure and regulations, industrial and financial and commercial organization. It is more than doubtful whether this passion for uniformity of government and organization and regulation produces the good results that human beings seem to expect of it, whether, in fact, diversity is not as desirable in certain departments of life as uniformity in others. It by no means follows that because uniformity of customs regulations in Northumberland and Cornwall is convenient, therefore precisely the same educational system will produce the best results in the primary schools of these two counties. However, to apply reason to practical affairs or to bring communal conduct into any kind of touch with general principles is so unpopular, and has so often been condemned by men of affairs, that this blind passion for uniformity will certainly continue to be a leading characteristic in the regulation of human society for many years to come. And this much can at least be said for it, that where society is as highly organized and as interdependent as it is in Europe, a certain degree of uniformity, obtained by organization and regulation, is a necessity in many departments of life.

One of the most remarkable forms of unification is what may be called organized standardization.

In every direction to-day we find uniform standards being set up almost always as the result of agreement obtained through large organizations. The ordinary human being has to live his life according to standards to a far greater degree than he is aware of. For instance, all industrial production is becoming daily more and more standardized; all the different parts of articles of common use, from bicycles to houses, are coming to be produced according to fixed standards arrived at by agreement between associations of producers or experts. But it is significant that in the last thirty years the tendency towards international standardization of this kind has become very marked, and despite the delicate questions of national pride and prejudice involved, little difficulty has been experienced in establishing international standards through international associations. I propose to give a few examples of this kind of International Government.

Of all standards the most important for human progress is the scientific standard. Science, and, through science, production and commerce, are hampered by the absence of accurately determined scientific standards or by their variation in different countries. We have already had to refer to the determination and establishment of some scientific standards, *e. g.*, of color. But the most noteworthy achievement in this direction is the work of the International Electro-technical Institute and the International Congresses of Electricians. The electrician is faced with two problems, one purely scientific, the other partly scientific and partly industrial.* In the first place, he requires scientific units to express, *e. g.*, resistances to electric current or the power of a machine. Hence arises the need for scientific standards, and the first problem of the scientist is to determine scientifically and accurately these standards and to get them adopted internationally. But even after this has been done a second problem remains. Electrical industry and engineering is hampered by the difference of language and usage in the description and specification of materials and machines in the different countries. Professor Thompson points out that dynamo means an entirely different kind of machine in Germany, France, and England. An international classification of electrical materials and machines thus becomes an international interest of electrical scientists and engineers. For a full history of how this has been and is being achieved the reader must refer to the article by Professor Thompson already quoted. The important points in that history may, however, be briefly summarized. In 1881 was held the first International Congress of Electricians, the delegates being appointed by Governments and scientific institutions. This Congress adopted international names for certain electric units, such as the ohm and volt, and appointed an international commission for determining the ohm. Gradually all the dif-

---

* *Vide Le But et L'Œuvre de la Commission Electrotechnique Internationale*, by Professor Sylvanus P. Thompson, in *La Vie Internationale*, V, 1914.

ferent units were named and determined internationally by means of congresses, commissions, and organized interchange of visits between representatives of the laboratories of different countries engaged upon the work of determination. Then Governmental conferences, such as that of 1908, met and adopted the definitions of units so determined. Finally, in this country, Orders in Council have given legislative force to the determinations of these international standards. But the most remarkable development of organization was the establishment of the Electro-technical Commission, the statutes of which were agreed to in 1906. This association, the constitution of which is extraordinarily elaborate, is composed of National Electro-technical Committees, of which in 1911 there were fifteen. The National Committees are appointed by Governments or technical societies. The Commission is engaged on the work of an international classification of machines and materials; in other words, it is helping to standardize the electrical machines and materials for the world.

The growth of industrial and commercial standardization has been in recent years no less remarkable than that of scientific standardization. There are two entirely distinct tendencies at work: first, that of producers to agree through associations to standardize the materials from which commodities are produced, in order to facilitate division of labor and large-scale production; second, there is a movement on the part of the consumer, the better-class commercial man, and the State to fix a minimum standard of quality, particularly for food commodities. But here again the interests involved are found to be international rather than narrowly national. International trade bulks so largely in the minds of the manufacturer and producer that the motives which impel him to accept industrial standards soon compel him to make those standards international. On the other hand, it is much easier to protect the consumer by a minimum standard of quality, if the same standard is fixed in all or most of the consuming and producing countries. The result of this process upon the lives of the ordinary man and woman is not often realized. Most people still believe that they live in the houses, eat the food, and consume commodities which they desire to live in, eat, and consume, and that the production of these commodities is influenced to a considerable extent by that desire. But it is becoming more and more true that we live in houses, eat food, and buy commodities, the materials, size, quality, etc., of which have all been fixed either by the State or by associations of producers and scientific industrial experts according to standards. And when this form of organization and government becomes, as it is becoming, international, it means that the commodities produced for the peoples of the several nations conform to a fixed type or standard.

It will only be necessary to end this chapter with a few examples of international organization designed to establish these kinds of international standards. Some of the most common are those which deal with international standards and methods of analysis. For instance, it is stated that nitrates, phosphates, and nearly all fertilizing materials are now analyzed according to international methods arrived at by international agreement. The International Petrol Commission, a powerful association, consisting of sixteen national sections, financed by their Governments or the industry or both, has undertaken the task of international unification of methods of analysis, and its decisions have been generally approved. Progress has also been made with international standardization of food analysis. As a result of the Congress of Applied Chemistry there was created in 1903 a permanent International Commission for the Unification of Methods of Analyzing Food Commodities. The members of the Commission belonged to twenty different countries, and it set itself the task of preparing a Code alimentaire internationale to be submitted to the Governments.*

---

* In 1910, an International Conference on this subject was held, to which seventeen States sent representatives. The Conference formulated a series of rules as to the methods of expressing analytical results. A proposal was also made that an International Office should be established to consider questions connected with the unification of analytical methods. The British aversion to international action was, as usual, displayed to this proposal, but the French Government was requested to formulate a scheme. A second Conference was held in 1912, to which the British Government sent no delegates. At this Conference a Convention was signed by seven States giving effect to the rules drawn up at the first Conference, and a second Convention dealing with the establishment of a permanent International Office was signed by five States, including France.

Another interesting association in another sphere is the International Association for the Testing of Materials, which was created in 1895. Its object is the unification of methods of testing materials, and it has three sections, dealing with (1) metals, (2) cements, stone, etc., (3) other products. It consists of administrations and affiliated societies belonging to fifteen different countries. Its influence may be gauged from the fact that its sixth congress in 1912 was attended by 800 persons, and twenty States sent official representatives.

Finally, two examples may be given to show the curious ramifications of this process of organized international standardization. A Congress Pomologique has established an international commission for unifying the nomenclature of apples. The International Association of Agriculture is standardizing international breeds of chickens. It deals with international exhibitions, trade, standards of breed, etc., and at the General Assembly of 1913 a resolution was passed that the standards of each country shall be submitted for approval of the Federation, and their ratification by the Federation shall make them obligatory for all other countries. In future, therefore, even our chickens will be internationalized.

CHAPTER VI

THE INTERNATIONALIZATION OF COMMERCE, INDUSTRY, AND LABOR

COMMERCE and industry provide the most remarkable paradox of nationalism. No national interests are represented as so vital as those of trade, and the internationalist is continually being confuted as a dreamer by the picture of the bitter, irreconcilable competition of international trade. And yet, in no department of life has International Government been more firmly or more widely established. We have seen already how often the complicated network of commercial and industrial relations between national groups has necessitated the establishment of international administration and legislation. In this chapter I shall show how often these groups themselves, apparently composed of trade rivals, have discovered that their interests coincide rather than conflict, and that co-operation and organized regulation of relations serve them better than competition.

This is so large a subject that I cannot pretend to do more than indicate in the roughest outline some of the more important tendencies. It is a truism, for instance, that capital is international, and a study of the international organization of finance would be of great interest to the student of International Government. Such a study would, however, require a volume to itself. When, however, we turn from finance to trade and industry we find two main tendencies—first, the formation of regular international associations of commercial groups, with regular organs of International Government, to protect the international interests of the national groups; secondly, the application to industry and trade of various forms of international regulation and agreement, the object of which always is to regulate international competition and to substitute for it some form of cooperation.

Of the first tendency I shall give only one example, and that an instructive one.* The Baltic and White Sea Conference, which was created in 1905, is an International Association of the type already described, with a central bureau and a regular organ of government, and an annual conference. It consists of the shipowners of eleven different countries interested in shipping in the North of Europe. It controls 905 ships of 1,764,-603 tons out of 1,816 ships of 2,988,635 tons interested in the trade, and only the smaller shipowners have remained outside. It originated from the realization of owners that competition had cut freights for wood from the Baltic to next to

---

* Other examples of great interest are the International Congress of Chambers of Commerce, to which reference has been made, the International Federation of Flax and Tow Spinners, the International Federation of Cotton Manufacturers and Spinners, and L'Association Internationale du Froid.

nothing. The object of the Association was to regulate competition and to fix a minimum freight tariff. It must be admitted that a rather similar attempt to regulate international competition during a period of contracting trade had failed. But the Baltic Conference was established during a time of expanding trade, and up to the war had undoubtedly succeeded in its objects. The members meet in annual conference, and by a majority vote fix a minimum rate binding upon the members. The formation of the Conference was certainly followed by a rise in freights.

The Baltic Conference succeeded through a regular organ of government in limiting international competition between capitalist groups and in fixing an international minimum rate. In other words, the shipowners discovered that their group interests were international rather than national, and could best be served by international regulation and government instead of by competition. The same phenomena are observable in every department of industry and commerce. Everywhere a most striking tendency in recent years has shown itself for the capitalist and employing groups in the different countries to merge more or less completely into international trusts or cartels, or to regulate international trade and competition by elaborate agreements between the groups. The extent to which this international capitalist system of government has developed is not generally realized, and, indeed, it is by no means easy, owing to the fact that the international agreements are usually carefully kept secret, to trace its ramifications. Its tendencies may, however, be indicated best by a few examples.

Perhaps the best known instance of internationalization in industry is that of the armament firms. The Japanese naval scandals and one or two other cases have revealed something of its ramifications, but perhaps the most remarkable evidence is afforded by the list of the "groups" included in the international association, the Union des Mines, which was founded for the purposes of "economic co-operation" in Morocco and other parts of Africa in 1907. The list was published in *L'Humanité* of March, 1911, and is quoted in *Ten Years of Secret Diplomacy*, by Mr. E. D. Morel. The association was composed of "French, German, British, Spanish, Italian, Austrian, Belgian, and Portuguese manufacturers, bankers, and even political personages." The utopianism of International Government and agreement is curiously shown by the inclusion within this association of the Cie. des Forges de Chatillon-Commentry et Neuves Maisons, in the French group; Krupps, the Metallurgische Gesellschaft, of Frankfurt, and the Nationalbank für Deutschland in the German, and Mr. Bonar Law, M.P., and the *Times*' correspondent at Tangier in the British.

Intimately connected with the internationalization of armament firms is the internationalization of the metal industries. Here we see the two tendencies—that of the formation of trusts and regulation by agreements between the different national groups—both at work. It is extremely difficult to obtain information as to the agreements, but much interesting information was given in a speech by a Deputy in the French Chamber in 1913. He maintained that almost all the metal and allied industries were being gradually internationalized in the sense that in each case the tendency is for all the supply for the whole world to be united in the hands of one international syndicate, or to be regulated by international agreements between small national groups. He alleged that this had already taken place in the case of iodide, bismuth, platinum, nickel, lead, zinc, potash, aluminum, and he gave facts to prove his statement. Most of his speech may be read in a number of *La Vie Internationale* for 1914 (Vol. V, No. 1, page 104), and I will only quote here the facts applying to one or two of the industries. In the case of platinum, for instance, we see a very good example of international regulation through the formation of a trust. Originally the supply was in the hands of two Russian, one German, one French, and several minor companies. It is now completely internationalized in one international trust. The same process has been taking place with zinc. On the other hand, with nickel, bismuth, and lead the process has been one of dividing up the markets of the world by agreement between national groups. Thus the supply of bismuth used to be concentrated in the hands of certain German and American firms; but subsequently, by agreement, these firms divided up the world between them into spheres. Nickel, so far as the European market was concerned, used to be controlled by Rothschilds, while American firms controlled the American market: subsequently the whole world market was divided up between the two groups in two spheres.

The most remarkable instance of International Government in the metal industries has occurred in connection with the manufacture of steel rails. Its history has been traced in some detail by Mr. H. W. Macrosty.* In 1883 the International Rail Syndicate was formed, composed of seventeen out of eighteen British firms, all the German firms except two, and Belgium. On the basis of the previous three years' trade, Britain was allotted 66 per cent. of the business, Germany 27 per cent., and Belgium 7 per cent. Orders were to be allotted to each country in the same proportion, while each retained its own domestic trade. "In each country the individual works were assessed according to their capacity, and orders were divided according to the ratio of the individual to the total capacity, adhesion to the rules being secured by a penalty." Prices immediately rose, and the pool continued in existence until 1886. Then it dissolved, and English and German manufacturers substituted an agreement "to respect its each other's territory." In 1904, however, a far more elaborate agreement was signed, this time between the British, Ger-

---

* *The Trust Movement in British Industry*, pages 63–66.

man, French, and Belgian manufacturers. "To each country its own territory was assigned, and the export trade was syndicated for three years on the basis of 1,300,000 tons annually," at a minimum price of £4 7s. a ton. Britain was allotted 53.50 per cent. of the export trade, Germany 28.83 per cent., Belgium 17.67 per cent., and France 4.8 per cent., 5.89 per cent., and 6.4 per cent. for the three years. In 1905 the American manufacturers came into the agreement.

An international organization of a different type, not uncommon on the Continent, also deserves notice. An international kartell of glass factories has been for some years in existence. In 1913 most of the adhering manufacturers formed what was called a Continental Commercial Union. The object was to unify the sale of glass in the markets of the world by centralizing commercial services of different factories. Instead of each factory having an agent in each market, the organization acted as a single agent for the sale of the product of all the factories. Thirteen factories joined: five Belgian, three German, three French, one Austrian, and one Dutch. The organization has at its head a Conseil d'Administration, which communicates through a general secretariat with the different services. It is divided into five departments: (1) Technical, with an engineer at its head, (2) accounts and statistics, (3) management of sales in the English market, (4) ditto French market, (5) ditto market of other countries.

These examples will serve to show the attitude of the capitalist and the manufacturer to the national interests of commerce and industry and to international agreement and government. If belief in social and political internationalism is the sign of the amiable crank, a belief in industrial and capitalist internationalism is the mark of a practical man of business. The great capitalists and captains of industry show by their actions that they are by no means convinced that the national interests of commerce and industry are best served by international competition. It is not perhaps a curious fact that where international government promotes the interests of the strong it is found to be reasonable and practical, but so often where it would promote the interests of the weak it is merely utopian. The trend of modern industry is, as everyone knows, towards combination. The capitalist has been faced with the question of whether that combination shall stop at the national frontiers. How he has answered the question and why his answer is what it is cannot be better shown than by a quotation from Mr. Macrosty, though he is speaking only of combination in this country:—"The weakness of every form of combination in the United Kingdom is due to the free admission of foreign competition. If that can be removed, their strength is enormously increased. . . . Apart from tariffs, this result may be attained in various ways. All the international interests may be gathered up into one British company, as in the case of Borax Consolidated, or the foreign interests may be partly extirpated by and partly brought into alliance with a British company, as in the case of J. and P. Coats, Limited. Prices and output may be regulated in common, as in the Nitrate Combination, or territory may be divided, as in the International Rail Syndicate. Or while reserving certain territories for individual exploitation there may be co-operation in the development of others, as in the alliance of the Imperial Tobacco Company with the American Tobacco Trust. In one way or another the world's trade in rails, tubes, nails, screws, sewing-thread, bleaching powder, borax, nitrates, and tobacco is to a greater or less degree brought under international control, while at least till lately, dynamite was so controlled, and repeated efforts have been made similarly to syndicate the whole steel industry."*

From the world of capital one turns naturally to the world of labor. Nowhere has the solidarity of international interests been more clearly recognized or more passionately and idealistically proclaimed than among the workers of the world. Yet at first sight the results of this recognition and the international working class organization are wont to provoke contempt or disappointment according to the difference of outlook and prejudice of the inquirer. Nevertheless, certain sides

---

* The International Agreements signed by American, British, and German capitalists, shipowners, and shipbuilders on the formation of the International Mercantile Marine Company or Atlantic Shipping Trust should also be mentioned.

of the international labor movement deserve more attention than is usually given to them. I propose here only to say a few words about that side of it, the international trade union movement, which ought in a sense to be the complement in organization of the kind of combination which we have seen to be so marked a characteristic of capital.

On paper the International Trade Union Movement is very strong. It has a twofold organization. There is first the International Federation of Trade Unions, which came into existence in 1901, under the name of the International Trade Union Secretariat. The organization is composed of National Federations affiliated to the International Federation. The National Federation in turn consists of individual trade unions which elect to affiliate to it. In 1912 nineteen countries, including all those in which the trade union movement is well developed, had national federations affiliated, and the number of members of affiliated unions was over 7,000,000. The total number of trade unionists in the world is estimated at 15,000,000. This form of combination is based solely upon the national unit: it seeks to unite in a national section all the trade unions of a country, and then to federate the national sections. The second form is based both upon the nationality and the occupation of the worker. In 1912 there were thirty-two international occupational federations of workers, of which the three largest were the International Metal Workers' Federation, with a membership of 1,100,000; the International

Federation of Transport Workers, with 880,000 members, and the International Union of Woodworkers, with about 400,000 members.

Such is the skeleton of the international organization of Labor. The question with which I am particularly concerned is the extent to which it has produced International Government, and has affected the national and international interests of Labor in its struggle with an internationalized capitalist system. The first thing to be noted is that the main International Federation of Trade Unions is of very recent growth, and that it still confines itself almost entirely to the collection of statistics and information: it is in the occupational federations that organization for the protection of the international interests of the workers must be sought.

There are three distinct ways in which international Labor interests affect the trade union movement. There is the organization of the movement itself, there are the conditions of employment with which the organization is concerned, and there are the methods—particularly strikes—by which the organized workers seek to obtain through these organizations particular conditions of employment. International relations have affected each of these three departments of trade union action and policy, and in each case the beginnings of international trade union government have resulted. For instance, the elementary question involved in organization is to get the individual worker into the union. The non-union, unorganized worker is the thin edge of the wedge by which again and again the employer breaks down the trade union standard, and employer and employed are well aware of this. The revolution in communications has seriously affected "the fluidity of Labor," and the introduction of the foreign worker, with different standards of life, is everywhere a practical problem for the unions. In these circumstances, it is of great importance, especially where trade union organization is highly developed, that the worker who leaves his own country to find work—temporarily or permanently—in another should immediately enter the local union of the latter, and should not be left to become the tool of the employer against trade union conditions. Nearly all the International Federations have, therefore, concerned themselves with this question. In many cases the system adopted provides that any member of a union affiliated to the Federation, if he goes abroad to work, can join the local affiliated union without paying an entrance fee.* This international organization of the trade union movement is of very recent growth, and there is no doubt that it will be greatly developed.

As to conditions of employment, it is extremely

---

* For instance, the rules of the International Federation of Woodworkers provide that members of every affiliated Union working abroad may be admitted to the national organization without entrance fee. They are entitled to benefits in proportion to the contributions paid by them to their home organization. Members must have foreign traveling certificates from their home Union, and are entitled to traveling money from the foreign Union.

interesting to note how the International Trade Union movement has been forced already to develop a system of International Government and regulation in order to safeguard national standards. The industrial systems of the different countries are so interdependent that the conditions of employment in one are continually being influenced by those in another. The employer uses this fact as a weapon against the worker's organization. The result is that the organized worker finds that without international organization he cannot safeguard his conditions. The secretariats of international occupational federations have, therefore, in many cases been forced to become organs for establishing something like an international trade union standard. Examples taken from the work of one federation will show the direction in which this development is proceeding.

The Secretariat of the International Metal Workers' Federation is continually preventing the undercutting of conditions in one country by firms in another, and also the employment of foreign workers by firms which do not conform to the trade union requirements. Thus in 1911 the British Section was asked by the silver-workers of Birmingham whether a certain firm in Brussels was a "fair firm," as they were seeking workmen in England. The information was immediately obtained from the Belgian section and forwarded to Birmingham. In 1913 the men of Kugellagerfabrik, Rheinland, A.G., in Germany, complained that Hoffman Manufacturing Co., Chelmsford,

England, were selling solid ball-bearings 10 per cent. cheaper than they could produce, and that the cause was one of wages. The list of wages in the two firms was obtained by the Federation and interchanged, and the result was a successful strike in Chelmsford.

These examples will prove that international trade union organization is already by no means without effect. But it is natural that these manifestations of it have been overlooked, and attention concentrated upon its application to the strike. All the occupational federations and the general federation itself have concerned themselves with the possibility of organizing international support for national strikes. It is true that these efforts on the whole have not had very much result, and the reason is obvious. The unions which are affiliated to the International Federations cannot afford to pay substantial subscriptions. The Federations are, therefore, financially weak, and support for a strike out of their funds is impossible. In consequence, nearly all of them have a rule that in cases of important strikes the International Secretariat shall appeal for funds to the National Sections. The method of obtaining funds is left to the National Section.* Anyone who knows the extreme difficulty of raising money in nearly all

---

* The rules of some federations authorize special levies—*e. g.*, the Secretary of the International Federation of Lithographers can authorize a levy for international support of from 2 to 25 pf. a week, the total maximum support not to exceed 5,000 marks. In 1913 the Metal Workers' Federation passed a resolution authorizing special levies of 1d. per member per week for six weeks.

working-class movements will not be surprised that under these circumstances international financial support for strikes is rarely possible on any considerable scale.*

Bakounin, the father of Anarchism, saw in the international organization of strike funds the strongest weapon for destroying capitalist society. He preached this doctrine nearly fifty years ago, long before the modern international organization of the trade union movement had begun. To-day it is clear that the financial position of the local union and of the individual worker makes the application of International Government to strike funds a matter of peculiar difficulty. That, however, has not and should not blind trade unionists to the fact that their local and national struggles against their employers involve the international interests of labor, and that there are other ways in which international trade union organization is necessary for the protection of those interests. The international labor market is continually being used by employers as a method of obtaining strike-breakers or of under-cutting union rates. Two methods of trade union organization have been adopted by Labor to counteract this action of the

---

* In certain cases international appeals have brought in considerable sums. Thus, in the great Swedish General Strike of 1909, which is said to have cost the workers 39 million crowns, an international appeal was made for support through International Federations to the trade unions, and no less than 2 million crowns was levied and subscribed. Of this over a million crowns came from Germany. The financial position of the International Federations is shown by the fact that the largest, the Metalworkers, had a revenue for the three years ending 1910 of under 50,000 fr. a year.

capitalists, and both admit of considerable elaboration and extension.

In the first place, the International Secretariat of National Trade Union Centers publishes an International News Letter, which continually contains notices of strikes and warnings to foreign workers to keep away from places where such strikes are proceeding. Thus the letter of December 24, 1913, begins with a heading, "Copenhagen Closed for Dockers," gives an account of the dockers' dispute in progress there, and warns all dockers "to keep away from Copenhagen."*
Secondly, the occupational Federations themselves perform a similar function of keeping the international ring for Labor. For instance, in 1913 the engineers on a certain vessel in Newcastle struck. The employers then sent on the vessel to Rotterdam to be completed there. The Secretary of the British section of the International Metal Workers' Federation was informed, and he immediately communicated the facts to the Fed-

---

* A very interesting example of the international organization of Capital, producing an international counter-move on the part of Labor, occurs in the same letter. International "Free Labor" Agencies have made their appearance in recent years: they undertake to supply gangs of foreign workers at fixed rates of pay—which, curiously enough, are more often than not lower than Union rates. The *International News Letter* publishes a "circular" of one of these agencies with which Russia and East Europe had been flooded. The circular announces that: "The General Agency, 'The Transatlantic,' in London has been commissioned to place 1,500 men in the following works:—'The Dominion Steel Corporation' and 'Dominion Coal Co., Ltd.,' in Glace Bay, and the 'Dominion Iron and Steel Co., Ltd.,' in Sydney and in Canada." Then follows a detailed list of men required, and the rates of pay. The *News Letter* issues a warning that all the rates of pay and hours are lower than the local Union rates.

eral Office at Stuttgart. The Federal Office informed the Union at Rotterdam, and the Union officers sought out the vessel, and called out the men at work on her.

CHAPTER VII

SOME CONCLUSIONS

I HAVE tried in the preceding chapters to trace the strands of interests, government, and organization which are international in the network of relations which we vaguely describe as the community of nations. The recording of facts, whether boring or interesting, is, in my opinion, not an end in itself, but only a means towards some new vision or new understanding of that inextricable error, the world. I propose, therefore, to turn back to Chapter I, and to consider briefly whether the mass of facts which I have reviewed since then can give us such a new vision or understanding of the problem there stated, the relation of national to international interests and the relation of both to International Government. And it will be convenient to deal first with the general problem of International Government, and afterwards with the special problem of such government as a means of preventing war.

If anyone who has succeeded in reading the preceding chapters will attempt to rise above the individual facts and envisage them as a whole he will, I believe, get a vision of the world somewhat different from that which we are accustomed to get when looking at it across our national frontiers. We are accustomed to regard the world as neatly divided into compartments called States or nations. The legislative, administrative, and judicial divisions into States appear to trace a clear-cut line; in many places differences of language serve to deepen and differences of customs, food, clothing, and ideals to broaden that line. School books, statesmen, diplomatists, lawyers, journalists, politicians agree in representing this line as an impassable chasm, and the most "advanced" writers consider the State or nation as eternally the ultimate unit of communal organization. Hence the rigid theory of the independence and sovereignty of States; hence the idea that internationalism and patriotism are incompatible; hence the fanatical worship of the State, the nation, or the country.* But this vision of a world divided into isolated compartments is not a true reflection of facts as they exist in a large portion of the earth to-day. A modern State, in so far as it represents a community of individuals, is not an isolated independent unit, containing within itself all that it requires for its life and their lives.† It is in perpetual and intimate and intricate re-

---

* It may be noted that many Englishmen who condemn the fanatical worship of the State in some foreign countries seem to be unaware that they themselves worship it in the same way, but under another name—*i. e.*, my country.

† As I write this, by a curious coincidence, I find in a book just published, *European International Relations*, by J. Murray Macdonald, M.P., words which admirably describe this conscious or unconscious attitude of mind which has been so disastrously prevalent in Europe. "Hitherto," he writes, "each of them (the nations of Europe) has been too ready to assume that its freedom and independence rested on its own isolated power

lationship with other States; it cannot carry on the work of internal government, legislative or administrative, which modern conditions of life require, without continual co-operation and permanent organs of International Government; complete independence to-day is merely a legal fiction, and if we are to make it a fact we shall have to destroy the international form of society which grew up in the last century and revert to the national isolation of a former age. So much for the State. As for the individuals who compose it, we have seen that there is no department of life in which their most vital interests and relations are not international and have not become so insistent as to bring into existence a whole network of International Government and organs of government. Here again you must either sweep away these international relations of trade, labor, science, literature, social reform, etc., or you must continue to develop their organized regulation through International Government.

Now it is clear that so far as the development of internationalized inter-State government, or an international authority in the sense in which it was used in the first part of this book, is concerned, the question of independence and sovereignty is of the first importance. In Part I the legislative power

---

of maintaining its life against the others; and its relations have been too largely regulated by this assumption. Each has assumed that it had within itself all the means necessary to a completely self-sufficing life; or that if it had not it had an inherent right, without regard to other nations or their interests, to adopt such measures as might seem to it expedient to secure these means."

PREVENTION OF WAR

of the Conference or Council was limited to questions which did not affect the independence of the Sovereign State in the strictly legal sense, and this was done because, as I pointed out then and still believe, no nation would at this precise moment of time consent to enter such an authority under any other conditions. But though the sane man who finds himself in a world of madmen may be wise to act like a lunatic, there is no call upon him to think like one; and even if other good Europeans compel us for the moment to act as if we thought we were independent—and every Sovereign State suspended like Mohammed's coffin in a special international vacuum of its own—that is no reason why we should actually think this so if it is not. And the whole of the first part of this book no less than the second proved that the great stumbling-block to the growth of international inter-State government is the theory and passion for independence.

"Ah, 'passion' for independence," the critic will say; "so you have at last mentioned that which no theory and no reason can touch, and which explodes into the air all this nonsense about international authorities and government and associations for breeding international chickens. Patriotism and nationalism are instinctive passions of the human race, and there's an end of it." But the critic has, I believe, fallen into a very common politico-philosophical error. It is extremely common for people, when anyone proves that something in the world or society is wrong and might with advantage be altered, to think that all further thought, argument, or action is rendered useless by their pointing out that unfortunately all this is due to an unreasoning instinct or passion in the human race. This view implies the obviously false assumption that instincts are incapable of control, of being deflected from bad objects to good, by reason and a consciousness of truth and facts. The unreasoning instinct and passion of the majority of the human race to boil one another alive because of differences of religious opinion was certainly not abolished by an act of God, and few people would be ready to assert that its partial suppression to-day is not in some degree due to the protests and arguments of a minority, who remarked that the desire to satisfy this instinct was partly caused by a mistaken view as to facts and as to the efficacy of the process of boiling heretics.

Certainly the passion for independence exists, and a consciousness of nationality and patriotism exists, and anyone who writes about the future of international society and affects to ignore them must be very blind or very stupid. But their existence does not imply that in their present form they are either admirable or will continue so to exist for all eternity. I do not assert that the theory of and passion for independence and national interests as they are taught to-day will disappear off the face of the earth any more than I assert that men will cease to hold other false theories or to pervert other good instincts to bad uses. But I do assert that the legal, political, and diplomatic theories of the independence and sovereignty of States are illogical and the result of confused and timid thinking, and that the passion, directed and controlled only by false theory, is destructive of the best things in society which mankind has so slowly and so laboriously acquired.

The problem of independence is not peculiar to International Government; it appears in every kind of government. It is part of that old, stale, unsolved "paradox of self-government." In every community, from that of a sewing-club to that of nations, human beings still have to learn how to combine liberty with government: the effects of their failure to learn the lesson differ according to the size and ferocity of the communities: in the sewing-club they may be negligible, among nations they destroy the progress and imperil the very existence of man as a species. For you have only to look at men and women with complete detachment for a moment—a very difficult thing to do —to see that they still remain animals standing on their hind legs—and no animal, though it does stand on its hind legs and wear trousers, will be able to maintain itself indefinitely in the struggle for existence if it persists in destroying itself with high explosives.

The problem of independence and government everywhere is to allow people to manage their own affairs without infringing the power and desire of other people to manage their own affairs. In the international community the desire to manage one's own affairs in national communities and States, the desire for independence, the ties and passions of nationality, will, of course, continue to exist. That they can be among the noblest of human feelings and instincts and productive of great good no sane man will deny. But I claim that in the previous chapters there will be found evidence that they are not incompatible with a highly organized system of International Government, and that they do not require for their existence the independence of government which the lawyer and the diplomatist pretend is essential to the independent, sovereign State.

In the nineteenth century, in certain parts of the world, we seemed to be slowly working out a rational system of human government. The chief characteristic of such a system was that the existence of very large communities was recognized, that the existence of smaller communities of every variety and kind within the larger was recognized, that communities and parts of communities were to be left to manage for themselves matters which only affected themselves; but that, where the relations of communities or parts of a community were many and intricate, organization and organs of government should be provided for joint regulation. Whenever an attempt is made to put this ideal—for it remains nothing more than an ideal —into practice, whether in the British Empire or a federation of trade unions, difficulties will occur, and in theory any intelligent person could fill a large volume with criticisms and objections; yet there is ample evidence that in practice, with a very moderate amount of good will and good sense, a workable system of society and government can or could be erected on this principle. And the great merit of such a system is that it consciously recognizes that where the units of a community are through their infinite relations dependent upon one another and not independent, an organized regulation of those relations, reflecting that interdependence, must be provided.

This, too, is the first lesson which the preceding chapters teach. The varied growths of international inter-State Government and of organs of International Government show how this organization can be developed for the community of nations. In no case can it be argued that the entry of a nation into one of these unions, even where such entry involved the limitation of its administrative independence, has in any way injuriously affected its real and desirable independence or national interests. If this were once generally admitted, if the fact were seen that a nation still remains a national unit, an undimmed center for the passion of patriotism, even though it does enter with other nations into such organs of government, an immense field for development would be immediately opened. The enormous benefit which would result from such International Government may be realized from the sardonic thought that its establishment would imply the recognition by statesmen and Foreign Offices that the aim and end of foreign policy and offices should be international co-operation.

The second point to be noticed is a problem common to many, if not all, departments of Government. Throughout this book, whenever the effect of the establishment of International Government was considered upon interests, it became at once clear that all kinds of different group interests are affected in different ways. Now in a great many directions it is becoming clear that one of the problems most in need of solution by society is the relationship of Government to group interests. In the vast majority of cases the organization of Government follows the geographical group. In the State, in national and municipal government, an immense importance is usually given in organization to geographical groupings. In the House of Commons, for instance, representation is only given to geographical group interests. Prior to the nineteenth century, it is probable that a man's interests on the whole coincided with those of the geographical group to which he belonged, because of the primitive nature of communications and the comparatively simple organization of society. But this is no longer true of the world to-day. A man's chief interests are no longer determined by the place he lives in, and group interests, instead of following geographical lines, follow those of capital, labor, professions, etc. But government and organization of government have not kept pace with this change of social organization, and in the House of Commons, for instance, representation is based on geography instead of the vital group interests. The inconvenience and injustice of this are shown by the growing practice by which Ministers, when any important measure is proposed, go to the organized associations which do represent group interests and try to explain to, cajole, or bargain with them. And this is done, as Members of Parliament often complain, behind the backs of the Houses of Parliament. The reason is that members no longer, except in a few agricultural districts, represent any real group interests, while the House of Lords represents predominantly the group interest of landowners. Hence, to a great extent, the breakdown of representative political government. It is essential, if the organization of government is to work fairly and smoothly, that it shall provide for the due representation of group interests.

This is not a digression, for it has an important bearing upon International Government and its relation to national and other interests. Over and over again, when we analyze what are called national interests, we find that they are really the interests, not of the national, but of a much smaller group. A nation or State is from one and a most important point of view only a geographical expression, a community of persons living within a certain geographical area. In the modern world interests of individuals are less and less determined by geography, and this has necessarily had an immense effect upon national interests. This is the explanation of the appearance in the last century of so many international group interests binding together groups of persons in the different nations. The international association is the spontaneous growth to meet the needs of those international groups, just as the trade union is a spontaneous growth to meet the needs of a national group.

From these considerations two conclusions may be suggested. All arguments against International Government based on assertions that it would endanger vital national interests should be regarded with the greatest suspicion. The most vital interests of human beings are hardly ever national, almost always international. The interests which most nearly affect a man's life are those of the international group—*e. g.*, labor or capital, to which he belongs, not of his national group. Unfortunately, while the capitalist denies this by his words and accepts it by his deeds, the workingman has accepted it in word and denies it by his deeds. Nine times out of ten in foreign politics, national interests, if analyzed, resolve themselves into either the interests of a tiny class in one nation as opposed to a tiny class in another nation, or, as the interests of the ruling or capitalist class in a nation as opposed to those of the unpropertied, powerless, or working class. Take, for instance, the question of Morocco between Germany and France, which very nearly provoked a European war. In whatever way that question had been finally settled, it could not possibly have affected the lives or property, the happiness or unhappiness, the mentality or morality, of 999 out of every thousand Frenchmen and Germans. It could only have affected the purses of a small number of French and German capitalists, and, of course, that prestige of France and Germany which appears to be rather an unanalyzable concept than a tangible interest. The application of International Government and organized regulation to such questions would undoubtedly seriously affect the interests of these tiny but powerful groups—which is the reason why it is so strenuously resisted. Or, again, International Government as in the case of Labor legislation, which promoted the true interests of the masses which make up the different nations, would in each nation strengthen their position in the bitter struggle which they are compelled to wage against the exploitation of capital. This is well understood by the capitalist and industrial interests which oppose International Government, not because it will undermine their position against the foreigner, but because it will undermine their power over their fellow citizens.

The second conclusion is only a development of the first. Purely national government makes no provision for the representation of vital group interests, and therefore makes it so easy for the ruling and powerful classes to delude whole nations by specious appeals to patriotism and vague references to vital national interests. A sane and practical internationalism implies the regulation of the relations of national groups through organs of government. I have had to say much in these pages against a narrow nationalism, against the deification of geography and the worship of fictitious national interests; but I have never implied that the nation and sentiments of patriotism and nationality have not their place in the organization and society of the future. All I have tried to do is to examine the facts and to see things in their right proportions. The nation will remain the unit of international organization, the center of the sentiments of patriotism and nationality, and the outward and visible sign that men bound together by bonds of birth, blood, or geography desire, as far as possible, to manage their own affairs in their own way. But there is no reason in the world why an international organization which is based upon the nation as a unit should not be combined with an organization which provides for the representation of group interests which are not national. In the international association we have already the skeleton of a social structure and organization through which these group interests might operate. A little development, a closer association between the various organs of International Government, if accompanied by the loss of some widely held human illusions and delusions, might open a new page in the history of society.

It may be of interest, even at the risk of appearing Utopian, to consider for a moment in what directions such a development might be practically possible. Undoubtedly the most hopeful road of development would lie along the path of those novel forms of international association to which I have already referred in describing L'Association Internationale pour la Lutte contre le Chômage. In such an organ of government we find both forms of representation, the vertical or national and geographical and the horizontal or international, provided for. The horizontal group interests of, say, Labor and Capital, are there combined in one body with the vertical groups of national and even municipal interests. For while the great organizations of capital and labor are members of the association, they themselves are organized in national sections, and geography and nationality are again provided for by the presence of representatives of States, Towns, and Municipalities. The result is that the organization of government and the organs of government follow strictly the complication of group interests in the world of facts.

Let us turn for a moment from this association, in order if possible to edge away from that terrible precipice of Utopianism, to a question of International Government which has actually arisen in the world of practical men. It will be remembered that in dealing with the International Institute of Agriculture we saw that the American Senate and House of Representatives seriously proposed the formation of an International Commission to deal with the question of freights. The opposition to this proposal comes from group interests, because international control of freights is precisely one of those questions which intimately affect a whole mass of group interests. In the White Sea Conference we, in fact, saw an international organization which united in one body one of these groups, the Shipping group, to control freights in the interests of that group. But the modern ideal of government is not to regulate affairs in the interests of one small group, but to establish and maintain a balance between various group interests, and this was the kind of control which the Americans contemplated in the case of freights.

It is clear, therefore, that the American idea could never be efficiently realized unless International Government were applied to the freight question through an organization which allowed the different group interests to be adequately represented. And there is no reason (except the undue power of certain group interests) why this should not be done to-morrow through an International Commission or Commissions established on the lines of the Association contre le Chômage. Many different forms might be suggested for the details of such a development, but it is worth while briefly to consider some of them. The Commission would have to be established through an International Conference, at which the representatives of States would attend in the usual way. The Commission itself would probably in the first instance be merely deliberative with the power of recommending proposals for adoption by an International Conference, but eventually it might, within prescribed limits, be given power to pronounce binding decisions or even administrative powers, as in the case of the Sugar Commission and the International Unions. There are, broadly, two forms upon which the Commission itself might be organized. It might in the first place be constituted of official representatives of national sections, each nation having the right to a fixed number of representatives and a fixed number of votes. In that case the different nations would be left to organize their national sections or sub-commissions in their own way, just as we find is the case with the International Maritime Committee and the International Electrotechnical Institute. But in the national section the different group interests, as well as the State, would have the right of representation. Thus we should have, for instance, a British International Freight Sub-Commission upon which were represented the shipping interests through the Shipping Associations, the railway interests through the Railway Companies, the consumers through the Co-operative Movement, Labor through the Trade Unions, and so on, while the State would also have its representatives. The decisions of this body would determine the action of the British representatives upon the International Commission itself. On the other hand, it might be possible to constitute the International Commission by giving direct representation upon it to the group interests in the different countries. In that case, following more closely the form of the Association contre le Chômage, the different interests in this country, the Shipping Associations, the Trade Unions, the Co-operative Movement, etc., would have the right to send representatives with the State representatives to the Commission.

This is only one way and in one direction that the tissue of International Government, examined in these chapters, might be utilized and developed. I am well aware that it will appear to many merely as a piece of revolutionary Utopianism. Perhaps, after all, the road to many good things, unattainable to-day, lies only through revolutions and Utopias. And if anyone prefers a tamer suggestion, here is one, namely, that nothing more than a closer co-operation between the Foreign Offices and Administrations of Europe with such Associations as the International Federations of Trade Unions, the International Labor Legislation Association, or the International Co-operative Alliance, would be itself in the nature of such a revolution and Utopia.

It remains to consider whether this inquiry throws any light upon the special problem of International Government as a means of preventing war. There have been many occasions in these pages upon which I have ventured to suggest that the experiments in International Government and organization throw light upon this problem. The whole question of national interests and the effect upon them of organized regulation in international organs of government is one which the pacifist and his opposite alike ought to face. One of my objects in these pages is to contribute something to the study of that question. And one may, I think, hazard certain other conclusions, lame though they

PREVENTION OF WAR 361

may appear. The questions which have in the past caused wars and which at first sight to many people will seem to be utterly different from those which come before the international organs which we have been considering are of a political nature. In Part I of this book the proposal was made that they should be submitted to a conference or council. The chief objections made to such a proposal by practical men are two—first, that the national interests involved in these questions are so vital that a nation cannot submit them to a conference; secondly, that by doing so a State would abrogate its independence.

The first objection involves a judgment upon a mass of extremely complicated facts. There are, I believe, in the preceding chapters a large number of facts which go to show that that judgment is mistaken. We have seen many cases in which exactly the same argument has been used to deter this and other countries from entering into unions for International Government. In those cases an analysis of the alleged vital national interests always showed that they were the interests of a minute section of the nation, and that the interests of the majority were promoted rather than sacrificed by International Government. Moreover, when nations have entered these unions the sacrifice of the vital national interests, so invariably prophesied, has never followed. Even in international affairs the people who perpetually are crying "wolf" may be justly regarded with suspicion. And the obvious plea that these questions of a political nature affect more vital national interests than those dealt with in these pages will not hold water. The people who would raise this plea are precisely those who would argue that the interests of trade and markets are for a nation some of the most vital. Yet again and again we have seen these interests subjected to International Government without any of these terrible results, and the great industrial rivals in the different nations discovering that their interests are promoted better by international agreements and co-operation than by competition. After all, the causes of wars do not differ very much to-day from those enumerated by Gulliver to the Houyhnhnms: "Sometimes the ambition of princes, who never think they have land or people enough to govern; sometimes the corruption of ministers, who engage their masters in a war, in order to stifle the clamor of the subjects against their evil administration. Difference in opinion hath cost many millions of lives; for instance, whether flesh be bread, or bread flesh. . . . Sometimes the quarrel between two princes is to decide which of them shall dispossess a third of his dominions, where neither of them have any right. Sometimes one prince quarreleth with another for fear the other should quarrel with him. Sometimes a war is entered upon because the enemy is too strong, and sometimes because he is too weak. Sometimes our neighbors want the things which we have, or have the things which we want; and we both fight till they take ours or give us theirs." And the horse, it will be remembered, remarked that this enumeration "does, indeed, discover most admirably the effects of that reason you pretend to; however, it is happy that the shame is greater than the danger . . . for your mouths lying flat with your faces, you can hardly bite each other to any purpose, unless by consent." Unfortunately, in this supposition, as we are proving to-day, the horse was incorrect.

Finally and fittingly we come back once more to the question of independence, that elusive key to the baffling riddles of human government. If war is to be prevented, States must submit to some international control and government in their political and administrative relations. Here to the eye of the ordinary man the independence of the State must be more jealously guarded than in any other relations. And in one sense this is correct. In considering the constitution of an International Authority as a practical problem of to-day, we found that it was necessary to define those questions upon which States could agree to be bound by the decision of an organ of International Government. Those questions were defined by excluding any which would affect the independence or territorial integrity of a State. For, as was pointed out, without this limitation the diplomatist, the lawyer, and every ordinary and practical man would argue, the very existence of a State might be voted away in the organ of International Government. What, for instance, would prevent an international council from deciding that Serbia should lose its independence to Austria, or Belgium to Germany, or Finland to Russia, that the British Empire should grant complete independence to Ireland or the German Empire to Poland?

If States agreed to the establishment only of this modicum of International Government under an International Authority, an enormous step would be taken towards the abolition of war. But that should not blind us to the facts which I have tried to investigate. To make a legal or a patriotic fetish of independence is to turn away from the clear path of human progress and to make periodic disasters certain. A modern State can only preserve its complete political independence either by cutting itself off from the rest of the world or by maintaining a mass of unregulated international relations which, sooner or later, must involve it in a deadlock which can only be ended by war. Is there, then, any way out of this dilemma, of which one horn is the necessity of preserving the power of a nation to control its own affairs, and the other is the necessity, where society has become international, for international regulation and government?

This is, of course, once more the "paradox of self-government," for which there is probably no cut-and-dried solution; but some hesitating contributions towards its unravelling may be suggested. The dilemma is more horny on paper than in practice. The idea that because States agreed to submit questions and disputes involving independence to the decision of an organ of International Government, attempts would immediately be made to destroy the national existence of some and to interfere in the internal affairs of others, is contradicted by the whole history of human government, makes no allowance for the practical difficulty of such action, and is, therefore, certainly illusory. In the first place, there is a skeleton in every national cupboard, and every nation would know that if it insisted upon pulling out its neighbor's, its neighbor would retort in the same way. Secondly, in the large number of instances of International Government and regulation which I have described in detail, there is no sign of any attempt, except in one case, to misuse the machinery in this way, although they have furnished obvious opportunities of undermining "national interests." The reason is that the logic of international co-operation is too strong even for diplomatists, if you once get them to meet round a table. In the third place, there is the iron law of facts to which human beings, for all their folly and blindness, inevitably bow. Wherever you have government, facts limit both the use and the misuse to which it may be put, and men unconsciously conform to those limits. One fact which imposes a limit upon the misuse of government is the will of the people to whom the system of government applies. If the nations of Europe, with their old-established traditions and systems of self-government, were in the next hundred years to establish an International Authority, even with far wider powers than those sketched in the first part of this book, it would be quite impossible in the council of such an authority to destroy the independent existence of a State like Serbia, to say nothing of the British Empire. To destroy the independent existence of Serbia you must first break the will of the Serbian people to maintain it, and you cannot do that by any resolution in a council chamber. The representatives in the council chamber know this, and, consciously and unconsciously, mould their actions and decisions accordingly. Theoretically, I admit, the organized force of government might be put in operation to break the will and to destroy the independence of Serbia. But the history of the world shows that where organized government exists between communities possessing a large measure of self-government attempts to suppress or destroy that self-government are far rarer than where there is no tie except that of unregulated violence or war. The real independence of communities, and especially national communities, is endangered by excessive or deficient centralization of government; in other words, where there is no local self-government or only local self-government. In the past national communities and States have vacillated between complete independence and complete dependence, and the second condition has continually been the result of the first. For when two completely independent communities engage in a dispute, each relies upon violence and war as the ultimate arbiter, and through war the will of the one is imposed absolutely upon the will of the other. The world is full of communities which have lost their souls, and they have lost them through war or by conquest. For so long as there is nothing between absolute independence and absolute dependence, the world must be divided between communities which oppress and communities which are oppressed.

In the British Empire and other loosely federated States, we see the beginnings of another system of government, and one to which International Government would necessarily approximate.* During the last fifty years the real independence of Australia has been far more safe from other communities in the British Empire than has that of Belgium or even France from communities which lay on the other side of their frontiers. Australia, too, has served as the center of the Australian's patriotism no less adequately than Belgium has served as the center of the Belgian's patriotism. Yet Belgium and Serbia to-day, and Poland yesterday, are and were independent sovereign States, while Australia has never enjoyed that mysterious and intangible privilege. Could any fact display more clearly the irony with which history visits the follies of men?

---

* International Government would necessarily begin by States, communities with almost complete and long-established systems of local self-government, entering into a loose union, in which international questions, affecting independence, would be submitted for decision to the International Authority. The line between dependence and independence would not be clearly defined. It is noticeable that in the Colonies of the British Empire—where, one may claim with justice, the problem of the relationship between national communities has been more nearly solved than anywhere else—the line between dependence and independence is in practice also left undefined.

PART III

ARTICLES SUGGESTED FOR ADOPTION BY AN INTERNATIONAL CONFERENCE AT THE TERMINATION OF THE PRESENT WAR

By The International Agreements Committee of the Fabian Research Department

I

INTRODUCTION

THE object of the Committee has been limited and practical. It has sought only to formulate, as a basis for international discussion and in the light of history and experience—especially as elucidated by the Memorandum by Mr. L. S. Woolf (which now forms Part I of the present volume)—the heads of an international agreement by which future wars may be as far as possible prevented. There is at least a hope that, as a result of the existing terrible experience, a war-weary world may presently be willing to construct some new international machinery which can be brought into play to prevent the nations from again being stampeded into Armageddon.

The first difficulty will be to get the Governments, either of the eight Great Powers or of the forty lesser States—all of them necessarily wary and suspicious—to agree to the creation of any such international machinery. It is therefore essential, if we are to be practical, to limit our proposals to that for which there is at least some reason to expect consent. What is suggested is, accordingly, no merging of independent national units into a "world-State," though to this Utopia future ages may well come. No impairment of sovereignty and no sacrifice of independence are proposed. Each State even remains quite free to go to war, in the last resort, if the dispute in which it is engaged proves intractable. Moreover, national disarmament—to which at this moment no State will even dream of taking the smallest step —is left to come about of itself, just as the individual carrying of arms falls silently into desuetude as and when fears of aggression die down before the rule of the law.

The new world that we have to face at the conclusion of the war will, perforce, start from the ruins of the old. All that will be immediately practicable can be presented as only a more systematic development of the rapidly multiplying Arbitration Treaties of the present century, and the conclusions of the two Conventions at The Hague. Only on some such lines, it is suggested, can we reasonably hope, at this juncture, to get the Governments of the world to come into the proposed agreement.

The alternative to war is law. What we have to do is to find some way of deciding differences between States, and of securing the same acquiescence in the decision as is now shown by individual citizens in a legal judgment. This involves the establishment of a Supernational Authority, which is the essence of our proposals.

What is suggested is, first, the establishment of an International High Court, to which the nations shall agree to submit, not all their possible differences and disputes, but only such as are, by their very nature, "legal" or "justiciable." Experience warrants the belief that the decisions of such a judicial tribunal, *confined to the issues which the litigant States had submitted to it*, would normally be accepted by them. Provision is made, however, for a series of "sanctions other than war," principally economic and social in character, by which all the constituent States could bring pressure to bear on any State not obeying a decision of the Court.

Alongside the International High Court, but without authority over it, there should be an International Council, composed of representatives of such of the forty or fifty independent sovereign States of the world as may choose voluntarily to take part. It is proposed that this International Council should be differently regulated and organized according (1) as it acts as a World Legislature for codifying and amending international law, and for dealing with questions interesting only America or Europe respectively; or (2) is invoked by any constituent State to mediate in any dispute not of a nature to be submitted to the International High Court. It is not suggested that the enactments or the decisions of the International Council should, except to a very limited extent, be binding on States unwilling to ratify or acquiesce in them. Subject to the provisions made to prevent the proceedings being brought to naught by a tiny and unimportant minority, on matters of secondary importance, it is suggested that the International Council must content itself, at any rate at the outset, with that "greatest common measure" which commands general assent.

Provision is made for an International Secretariat and an International Official Gazette, in which all treaties or agreements will be immediately published, no others being recognized or regarded as enforceable.

In view of the fact that no fewer than twenty-one out of the forty to fifty independent sovereign States of the world are in America, the suggestion is made that there should be separate Councils for Europe and America respectively, with suitable provision in each case for the safeguarding of the interests of other States. Moreover, as the position of the eight Great Powers (Austria-Hungary, the British Empire, France, Germany, Italy, Japan, Russia, and the United States), which govern among them three-fourths of all the population of the world and control nine-tenths of its armaments, differs so greatly from that of the other two-score States, provision is made both for their meeting in separate Councils and for ratification of all proceedings by the Council of the Great Powers. It is nowhere suggested that any one of the eight Great Powers can—except by its own express ratification—be made subject to any enactment or decision of the International Council that it may deem to impair its independence or its territorial integrity, or to require any alteration of its internal laws.

It follows, accordingly, that each State retains the right to go to war if, after due delay, it chooses to do so.

What the several States are asked to bind themselves to are (*a*) to submit all disputes of the "legal" or "justiciable" kind (but no others) to the decision of the International High Court, unless some special tribunal is preferred and agreed to; (*b*) to lay before the International Council, for enquiry, mediation, and eventual report, all disputes not "justiciable" by the International High Court or other tribunal; (*c*) in no case to proceed to any warlike operation, or commit any act of aggression, until twelve months after the dispute had been submitted to one or the other body; (*d*) to put in operation, if and when required, the sanctions (other than war) decreed by the International High Court; and, possibly the most essential of all these proposals, (*e*) *to make common cause, even to the extent of war, against any constituent State which violates this fundamental agreement.*

It remains to be said only that the adoption of this plan of preventing war—the establishment of the proposed Supernational Authority—is not dependent on, and need not wait for, the adhesion of all the independent sovereign States of the world.

II

THE ARTICLES

THE signatory States, desirous of preventing any future outbreak of war, improving international relations, arriving by agreement at an authoritative codification of international law and facilitating the development of such joint action as is exemplified by the International Postal Union, hereby agree and consent to the following Articles.

The Establishment of a Supernational Authority

1. There shall be established as soon as possible within the period of one year from the date hereof (*a*) an International High Court for the decision of justiciable issues between independent Sovereign States; (*b*) an International Council with the double function of securing, by common agreement, such international legislation as may be practicable, and of promoting the settlement of non-justiciable issues between independent Sovereign States; and (*c*) an International Secretariat.

The Constituent States

2. The independent Sovereign States to be admitted as Constituent States, and hereinafter so described, shall be:

(*a*) The belligerents in the present war;
(*b*) The United States of America;
(*c*) Such other independent Sovereign States as have been represented at either of the Peace Conferences at The Hague, and as shall apply for admission within six months from the date of these Articles; and
(*d*) Such other independent Sovereign States as may hereafter be admitted by the International Council.

NOTE TO ARTICLE 2

The forty-four States represented at one or other of the Hague Conferences were (i.) the eight Great Powers—viz., Austria-Hungary, the British Empire, France, Germany, Italy, Japan, Russia, and the United States; (ii.) the following fifteen other States of Europe—viz., Belgium, Bulgaria, Denmark, Greece, Holland, Luxemburg, Montenegro, Norway, Portugal, Roumania, Serbia, Spain, Sweden, Switzerland, Turkey; (iii.) the following eighteen other States of America—viz., Argentina, Bolivia, Brazil, Chile, Colombia, Cuba, Dominican Republic, Ecuador, Guatemala, Haiti, Mexico, Nicaragua, Panama, Paraguay, Peru, Salvador, Uruguay, Venezuela (these, together with the United States, and also Costa Rica and Honduras, constitute the twenty-one members of the Pan-American Union); (iv.) the following three other States—viz., China, Persia, Siam. Thus the only existing independent sovereign States which could conceivably be brought in—and some of these may well be deemed not independent in respect of foreign relations—are the American States of Costa Rica and Honduras (which were invited to the 1907 Hague Conference, and actually appointed delegates, who did not attend); the African States of Morocco, Liberia and Abyssinia; the Asiatic States of Afghanistan, Thibet and Nepaul; and the European State of Albania (besides Andorra, Lichtenstein, Monaco and San Marino, which have populations of less than 20,000).

It may be suggested that admission should be refused to any State (i.) which does not, in fact, enter regularly into foreign relations with more than one other State; or (ii.) of which the foreign relations are under the control of another State; or (iii.) of which the population is less than 100,000. The adoption of these rules would probably exclude all but two or three of the above-mentioned outstanding States.

Covenant Against Aggression

3. It is a fundamental principle of these Articles that the Constituent States severally disclaim all desire or intention of aggression on any other independent Sovereign State or States, and that they agree and bind themselves, under all circumstances, and without any evasion or qualification whatever, never to pursue, beyond the stage of courteous representation, any claim or complaint that any of them may have against any other Constituent State, without first submitting such claim or complaint, either to the International High Court for adjudication and decision, or to the International Council for examination and report, with a view to arriving at a settlement acceptable to both parties.

Covenant Against War Except as a Final Resource

4. The Constituent States expressly bind themselves severally under no circumstances to address to any Constituent State an ultimatum, or a threat of military or naval operations in the nature of war, or of any act of aggression; and under no

circumstances to declare war, or order mobilization or begin military or naval operations of the nature of war, or violate the territory or attack the ships of another State, otherwise than by way of repelling and defeating a forcible attack actually made by military or naval force, until the matter in dispute has been submitted as aforesaid to the International High Court or to the International Council, and until after the expiration of one year from the date of such submission.

On the other hand, no Constituent State shall, after submission of the matter at issue to the International Council and after the expiration of the specified time, be precluded from taking any action, even to the point of going to war, in defense of its own honor or interests, as regards any issues which are not justiciable within the definition laid down by these Articles, and which affect either its independent sovereignty or its territorial integrity, or require any change in its internal laws, and with regard to which no settlement acceptable to itself has been arrived at.

The International Council

5. The International Council shall be a continuously existing deliberative and legislative body composed of representatives of the Constituent States, to be appointed in such manner, for such periods and under such conditions as may in each case from time to time be determined by the several States.

Each of the eight Great Powers—viz., Austria-Hungary, the British Empire, France, Germany, Italy, Japan, Russia, and the United States of America—may appoint five representatives. Each of the other Constituent States may appoint two representatives.

Different Sittings of the Council

6. The International Council shall sit either as a Council of all the Constituent States, hereinafter called the Council sitting as a whole, or as the Council of the eight Great Powers, or as the Council of the States other than the eight Great Powers, or as the Council for America, or as the Council for Europe, each such sitting being restricted to the representatives of the States thus indicated.

There shall stand referred to the Council of the eight Great Powers any question arising between any two or more of such Powers, and also any other question in which any of such Powers formally claims to be concerned, and requests to have so referred.

There shall also stand referred to the Council of the eight Great Powers, for consideration and ratification, or for reference back in order that they may be reconsidered, the proceedings of the Council for America, the Council for Europe, and the Council of the States other than the eight Great Powers.

There shall stand referred to the Council for Europe any question arising between two or more independent Sovereign States of Europe, and not directly affecting any independent Sovereign State not represented in that Council, provided that none of the independent Sovereign States not so represented formally claims to be concerned in such question, and provided that none of the eight Great Powers formally claims to have it referred to the Council of the eight Great Powers or to the Council sitting as a whole.

There shall stand referred to the Council for America any question arising between two or more independent Sovereign States of America, not directly affecting any independent Sovereign State not represented in that Council, provided that none of the independent Sovereign States not so represented formally claims to be concerned in such question, and provided that none of the eight Great Powers formally claims to have it referred to the Council of the eight Great Powers or to the Council sitting as a whole.

There shall stand referred to the Council for the States other than the eight Great Powers any question between two or more of such States, not directly affecting any of the eight Great Powers and which none of the eight Great Powers formally claims to have referred to the Council sitting as a whole.

The Council shall sit as a whole for—

(*a*) General legislation and any question not standing referred to the Council of the eight Great Powers, the Council of the States other than the eight Great Powers, the Council for Europe or the Council for America respectively;

(*b*) The appointment and all questions relating to the conditions of office, functions and powers of the International Secretariat, and of the President and other officers of the International Council;

(*c*) The settlement of Standing Orders, and all questions relating to procedure and verification of powers;

(*d*) The financial affairs of the International Council and International High Court, the allocation of the cost among the Constituent States, and the issue of precepts upon the several Constituent States for the shares due from them;

(*e*) The admission of independent Sovereign States as Constituent States; and

(*f*) Any proposal to alter any of these Articles, and the making of such an alteration.

NOTE TO ARTICLE 6.

The suggested complex organization of the International Council is required in order: (*a*) To prevent the Council being swamped, when it is dealing with matters not affecting Central and South America, by the representatives of the twenty independent Sovereign States of that part of the world; and (*b*) to maintain unimpaired the practical hegemony and the responsibility for preventing a serious war which have, in fact, devolved upon the eight Great Powers, whose adhesion to these Articles is essential to their full efficacy.

The Council for America would consist exclusively of the representatives of the twenty-one independent Sovereign States of the American Continent now associated in the

Pan-American Union. Other States having dependencies on or near that Continent (viz., the British Empire in respect of the Canadian Dominion, Newfoundland, the British West Indian Islands, British Honduras, British Guiana, and the Falkland Islands; France in respect of St. Pierre and Miquelon, Guadeloupe, Martinique and French Guiana; Holland in respect of Surinam and Curaçao; and Denmark in respect of Greenland, St. Croix, St. Thomas and St. John) would be safeguarded by the power to require the transfer of any question to the Council of the eight Great Powers or to the Council sitting as a whole.

Membership of the Council and Voting

7. All the Constituent States shall have equal rights to participation in the deliberations of the International Council. Any Constituent State may submit to the International Council sitting as a whole any proposal for any alteration of International Law, or for making an enactment of new law; and also (subject to the provisions of these Articles with regard to the submission of justiciable issues to the International High Court) may bring before the Council any question, dispute or difference arising between it and any other Constituent State.

When the International Council is sitting as the Council of the eight Great Powers or as the Council of the States other than the eight Great Powers each of the States represented therein shall have one vote only.

When the International Council is sitting as a whole or as the Council for Europe or as the Council for America, the number of votes to be given on behalf of each State shall be as follows:—

[*The scale of voting strength will require to be prescribed in the treaty.*]

Note to Article 7

The question of the relative voting power in the International Council of the forty or fifty independent Sovereign States is one of the greatest difficulty. At the Hague Conference the smaller States successfully maintained the right of all the States, even the smallest, to equality of voting power. On the other hand, the eight Great Powers, which are probably administering three-fourths of the total population of the world, disposing of seven-eighths of its governmental revenues, and controlling nine-tenths of its armed forces, will certainly not submit to be outvoted by nine of the smallest States of America or Europe.

One suggested scale of relative voting power has the unique merit of having been actually agreed to at the Hague Conference in 1907 in the form of the relative participation of the Judges of the several States in the proposed International Prize Court. Devised for such a purpose, it somewhat overvalues certain States having exceptionally large maritime interests (such as Norway), and undervalues some having small maritime interests (such as Serbia). Other minor adjustments might now have to be made.

As agreed to by the Hague Conference, the relative position of the States works out into the following scale of votes:

Austria-Hungary, the British Empire, France, Germany, Italy, Japan, Russia, the United States of America	20 votes each
Spain	12 votes each
The Netherlands	9 votes each

Belgium, Denmark, Greece, Norway, Portugal, Sweden, China, Roumania, Turkey....	6 votes each
Argentina, Brazil, Chile, Mexico............	4 votes each
Switzerland, Bulgaria, Persia...............	3 votes each
Colombia, Peru, Uruguay, Venezuela, Serbia, Siam...................................	2 votes each
The other Constituent States...............	1 vote each

(These may include Bolivia, Costa Rica, Cuba, Dominican Republic, Ecuador, Guatemala, Haiti, Honduras, Luxemburg, Montenegro, Nicaragua, Panama, Salvador, etc.)

As regards the Council for America, it may be urged that the existing Pan-American Union has equal voting. On the other hand, the United States is not likely to allow such a Council to become an effective legislature if, with four-fifths of the population, it has only one-twenty-first of the voting power. The United States may, indeed, insist, in this Council, on an even larger relative voting power than was conceded for the Prize Court.

A possible compromise between the two views is suggested in Article 7—the principle of equality prevailing in the Council of the eight Great Powers and the Council of the States other than the eight Great Powers, whilst in the Councils for Europe and America and in the Council sitting as a whole the adoption of a scale of voting power is proposed.

It may, however, be deemed by the eight Great Powers a sufficient safeguard of their influence that any one of them can require any question to be transferred to the Council of the eight Great Powers, and that any decision of the other Councils is required to be submitted to this Council for ratification. It may be observed that, if this view is taken, and if the forty smaller States insist on equality of voting power in the Council sitting as a whole, the result would inevitably be detrimental to its influence as a legislature; and the tendency would be for it to be superseded, in all but unimportant and ceremonial matters, by the Council of the eight Great Powers.

Legislation Subject to Ratification

8. It shall be within the competence of the International Council to codify and declare the International Law existing between the several independent Sovereign States of the world; and any such codifying enactment, when and in so far as ratified by the Constituent States, shall be applied and enforced by the International High Court.

It shall also be within the competence of the International Council from time to time, by specific enactment, to amend International Law, whether or not this has been codified; and any such enactment when and in so far as ratified by the several Constituent States shall be applied and enforced by the International High Court.

Whenever any Constituent State notifies its refusal to ratify as a whole any enactment made by the International Council, it shall at the same time notify its ratification of such part or parts of such enactment as it will consent to be bound by; and the International Council shall thereupon re-enact the parts so ratified by all the Constituent States, and declare such enactment to have been so ratified, and such enactment shall thereupon be applied and enforced by the International High Court.

When any enactment of the International Council making any new general rule of law has been ratified wholly or in part by any two or more Constituent States, but not by all the Constituent States, it shall, so far as ratified, be deemed to be binding on the ratifying State or States, but only in respect of the relations of such State or States with any other ratifying State or States; and it shall be applied and enforced accordingly by the International High Court.

(*Query add: these additional Articles.*)

Legislation on Matters of Secondary Importance by Overwhelming Majorities

8A. *When any enactment of the International Council does not affect the independent sovereignty or the territorial integrity and does not require any change in the internal laws of any Constituent State, and has been passed by a three-fourths majority of the votes given by the representatives present and voting at the Council sitting as a whole (query add: provided that such majority includes all the eight Great Powers), it shall, irrespective of ratification by the several Constituent States, and notwithstanding objection by one or more of them, be deemed to have become law and to be binding on all the Constituent States, and shall be applied and enforced by the International High Court.*

The International High Court shall alone decide whether any enactment of the International Council affects the independent sovereignty or the territorial integrity, or requires any change in the internal laws of any Constituent State; and every enactment of the Council shall be presumed not to affect the independent sovereignty or the territorial integrity, or to require any change in the internal laws of any Con-

stituent State until the International High Court has decided to the contrary.

Facultative enforcement by overwhelming majority of legislation carried by overwhelming majorities even if of primary importance, and not ratified by a small minority of the minor States.

8B. *When any enactment of the International Council sitting as a whole has not received a three-fourths majority of the votes given by the representatives present and voting, or when such enactment has received such a majority but affects the independent sovereignty or the territorial integrity, or requires any change in the internal laws of any Constituent State, and when such enactment has not been ratified by all the several Constituent States, it shall nevertheless be within the competence of the International Council sitting as a whole, by a three-fourths majority of the votes given by the representatives present and voting (query add: provided that such majority includes all the eight Great Powers), to refer to the International High Court for decision the question of whether any Constituent State has, by any positive act changing the* status quo, *committed what would have been a contravention of the said enactment if it had been effectively made law by the Council and applied by the Court. If the decision of the Court should be that such contravention by positive act changing the* status quo *has taken place, it shall be within the competence of the Council sitting as a whole, but only by such special majority as aforesaid, to invite the Constituent State committing such contravention to make repara-*

tion or pay compensation; and the Council may, if it thinks fit, by the same special majority as aforesaid, require any or all of the Constituent States to enforce its decision in the same way as if it were a decision of the High Court by any sanction other than that of military or naval operations in the nature of war.

NOTE TO ARTICLES 8, 8A AND 8B

The legislative powers proposed for the International Council have to be limited, at the outset, because none of the independent Sovereign States of the world, large or small, would at present undertake, in advance, to be bound by the legislation enacted by such a Council. It would be a great gain to get any International Legislation, even if subject to ratification by each State. Even when every clause not ratified had been thrown out, the volume of such legislation—all the more authoritative because it had been specifically assented to—would steadily increase.

It is tentatively suggested that agreement might possibly be obtained to two carefully-safeguarded extensions of legislative capacity. On matters of secondary importance all the Constituent States might conceivably agree to be bound by an overwhelming majority, and thus avoid the inconvenience that might be caused by a single State, perhaps out of sheer obstinacy or misapprehension, refusing to ratify.

Moreover, even when the subject matter is of more than secondary importance, the Constituent States might be willing so far to bind themselves to respect the repeated decision of an overwhelming majority as to allow that overwhelming majority, if it thought fit, to restrain, by means stopping short of war, any recalcitrant State from flouting such a repeated decision of the States of the world *by any positive act which changes the "status quo."*

It may be that the eight Great Powers would consent to

either or both these extensions of the legislative authority of the International Council if the overwhelming majority required had always to include all the eight Great Powers themselves.

Non-Justiciable Issues

9. When any question, difference or dispute arising between two or more Constituent States is not justiciable as defined in these Articles, and is not promptly brought to an amicable settlement, and is of such a character that it might ultimately endanger friendly relations between such States, it shall be the duty of each party to the matter at issue, irrespective of any action taken or not taken by any other party, to submit the question, difference or dispute to the International Council with a view to a satisfactory settlement being arrived at. The Council may itself invite the parties to lay any such question, difference or dispute before the Council, or the Council may itself take any such matter at issue into its own consideration.

The Constituent States hereby severally agree and bind themselves under no circumstances to address to any other Constituent State an ultimatum or anything in the nature of a threat of forcible reprisals or naval or military operations, or actually to commence hostilities against such State, or to violate its territory, or to attack its ships, otherwise than by way of repelling and defeating a forcible attack actually made by naval or military force, before a matter in dispute, if not of a justiciable character as defined in these Articles, has been submitted to or taken into consideration by the International Council as aforesaid for investigation, modification and report, and during a period of one year from the date of such submission or consideration.

The International Council may appoint a Permanent Board of Conciliators for dealing with all such questions, differences or disputes as they arise, and may constitute the Board either on the nomination of the several Constituent States or otherwise, in such manner, upon such conditions and for such term or terms as the Council may decide.

When any question, difference or dispute, not of a justiciable character as defined in these Articles, is submitted to or taken into consideration by the International Council as aforesaid, the Council shall, with the least possible delay, take action, either (1) by referring the matter at issue to the Permanent Board of Conciliators, or (2) by appointing a Special Committee, whether exclusively of the Council or otherwise, to enquire into the matter and report, or (3) by appointing a Commission of Enquiry to investigate the matter and report, or (4) by itself taking the matter into consideration.

The Constituent States hereby agree and bind themselves, whether or not they are parties to any such matter at issue, to give all possible facilities to the International Council, to the Permanent Board of Conciliators, to any Committee or Commission of Enquiry appointed by either of them, and to any duly accredited officer of any of these bodies, for the successful discharge of their duties.

When any matter at issue is referred to the Board of Conciliation, or to a Special Committee, or to a Commission of Enquiry, such Board, Committee or Commission shall, if at any time during its proceedings it succeeds in bringing about an agreement between the parties upon the matter at issue, immediately report such agreement to the International Council; but, if no such agreement be reached, such Board, Committee or Commission shall, so soon as it has finished its enquiries, and in any case within six months, make a report to the International Council, stating the facts of the case and making any recommendations for a decision that are deemed expedient.

When a report is made to the International Council by any such Board, Committee or Commission that an agreement has been arrived at between the parties, the Council shall embody such agreement, with a recital of its terms, in a resolution of the Council.

When any other report is made to the Council by any such Board, Committee or Commission, or when the Council itself has taken the matter at issue into consideration, the Council shall, after taking all the facts into consideration, and within a period of three months, come to a decision on the subject, and shall embody such decision in a resolution of the Council. Such resolution shall, if necessary, be arrived at by voting, and shall be published, together with any report on the subject, in the *Official Gazette*.

A resolution of the Council embodying a decision settling a matter at issue between Constituent States shall be obligatory and binding on all the Constituent States, including all the parties to the matter at issue, if either it is passed unanimously by all the members of the Council present and voting; or (*query add: if it is passed with no other dissentient present and voting than the representatives of one only of the States which have been parties in the case*), or where the proposed enactment does not affect the independent sovereignty or the territorial integrity, nor require any change in the internal laws of any State, and where such enactment shall have been assented to by a three-fourths majority of the votes given by the representatives present and voting (*query add: and such majority includes all the eight Great Powers*).

NOTE TO ARTICLE 9

This provides, as regards non-justiciable issues, for (i.) a year's delay in all disputes, and for their coming before the International Council; (ii.) the utmost possible scope for investigation, consideration and mediation, and the greatest possible opportunity for ultimate agreement between the parties; (iii.) where no voluntary agreement is come to, the obligatory settlement of the dispute by the International Council (*a*) if the Council is absolutely unanimous; (*b*) if it is unanimous except for one of the parties to the case; and (*c*) where the Council's decision affects neither the independence nor the territorial integrity, nor requires any change in the internal laws of any Constituent State, and if the enactment is carried by a three-fourths majority (or by such a majority including all the eight Great Powers). (The tentatively suggested articles 16a and 16b should be considered along with this article.)

Beyond that point, as regards intractable disputes of a non-justiciable character, there seems at present no chance of getting the States to agree in advance to be bound by any Supernational Authority.

The International Secretariat

10. There shall be an International Secretariat, with an office permanently open for business, with such a staff as the International Council may from time to time determine.

It shall be the duty of the International Secretariat to make all necessary communications on behalf of the International Council to States or individuals; to place before the President to bring before the Council any matter of which it should have cognizance; to organize and conduct any enquiries or investigations ordered by the Council; to maintain an accurate record of the proceedings of the Council; to make authentic translations of the resolutions and enactments of the Council, the report of the proceedings, and other documents, and to communicate them officially to all the Constituent States; and to publish for sale an *Official Gazette* and such other works as the Council may from time to time direct.

Subject to any regulations that may be made by the International Council, the International Secretariat shall take charge of and be responsible for (*a*) the funds belonging to or in the custody of the International Council and the International High

Court; (b) the collection of all receipts due to either of them; and (c) the making of all authorized payments.

The International High Court

11. The International High Court shall be a permanent judicial tribunal, consisting of fifteen Judges, to be appointed as hereinafter provided. Subject to these Articles it shall, by a majority of Judges sitting and voting, control its own proceedings, determine its sessions and place of meeting, settle its own procedure, and appoint its own officers. It may, if thought fit, elect one of its members to be President of the Court for such term and with such functions as it may decide. Its members shall receive an annual stipend of   , whilst if a President is elected he shall receive an additional sum of
The Court shall hear and decide with absolute independence the issues brought before it in conformity with these Articles; and shall in each case pronounce, by a majority of votes, a single judgment of the Court as a whole, which shall be expressed in separate reasoned statements by each of the Judges sitting and acting in the case. The sessions of the Court shall be held, if so ordered, notwithstanding the existence of a vacancy or of vacancies among the Judges; and the proceedings of the Court shall be valid, and the decision of a majority of the Judges sitting and acting shall be of full force, notwithstanding the existence of any

vacancy or vacancies or of the absence of any Judge or Judges.

(*Query add: In any case at issue between Constituent States the Judge or Judges nominated by one or more of such States shall (unless all the litigant States otherwise agree) take no part in the case.*)

The Judges of the Court

12. The Judges of the International High Court shall be appointed for a term of five (*query: seven*) years by the International Council sitting as a whole, in accordance with the following scheme. Each of the Constituent States shall be formally invited to nominate one candidate, who need not necessarily be a citizen or a resident of the State by which he is nominated. The eight candidates severally nominated by the eight Great Powers shall thereupon be appointed. The remaining seven Judges shall be appointed after selection by exhaustive ballot from among the candidates nominated by the Constituent States other than the eight Great Powers. On the occurrence of a vacancy among the Judges nominated by the eight Great Powers, the State which had nominated the Judge whose seat has become vacant shall be invited to nominate his successor, and the candidate so nominated shall thereupon be appointed. On the occurrence of a vacancy among the other Judges, each of the Constituent States other than the eight Great Powers shall be invited to nominate a candidate to fill the vacancy; and

the International Council sitting as a whole shall, by exhaustive ballot, choose from among the candidates so nominated the person to be appointed.

(*Query add: but so that at no time shall more than one (or two) of the Judges be the nominees of any one State.*)

A Judge of the International High Court shall not be liable to any legal proceedings in any tribunal in any State, and shall not be subjected to any disciplinary action by any Government, in respect of anything said or done by him in his capacity as Judge; and shall not during his tenure of office be deprived of any part of the emoluments or privileges of his office. A Judge of the International High Court may be removed from office by a resolution of the International Council sitting as a whole, carried by a three-fourths majority.

The Court Open only to State Governments

13. The International High Court shall deal only with justiciable questions, as defined in these Articles, at issue between the national Governments of independent Sovereign States, and shall not entertain any application from or on behalf of an individual person, or any group or organization of persons, or any company, or any subordinate administration, or any State not independent and Sovereign. The International High Court may, if it thinks fit (*query: with the consent of all the parties*), deal with a suit brought by a Constituent

State against an independent Sovereign State which is not a Constituent State; or with a suit between two or more such States.

Justiciable Issues

14. The justiciable questions with which the International High Court shall be competent to deal shall be exclusively those falling within one or other of the following classes, viz.:—

(*a*) Any question of fact which, if established, would be a cause of action within the competence of the Court;

(*b*) Any question as to the interpretation or application of any international treaty or agreement duly registered as provided in these Articles, or of International Law, or of any enactment of the International Council; together with any alleged breach or contravention thereof;

(*c*) Any question as to the responsibility or blame attaching to any independent Sovereign State for any of the acts, negligences or defaults of its national or local Government officers, agents or representatives, occasioning loss or damage to a State other than their own, whether to any of the citizens, companies or subordinate administrations of such State, or to its national Government; and as to the reparation to be made, and the compensation to be paid, for such loss or damage;

(*d*) Any question as to the title, by agreement, prescription, or occupation, to the sovereignty of any place or district;

(e) Any question as to the demarcation of any part of any national boundary;

(f) Any question as to the reparation to be made, or the amount of compensation to be paid, in cases in which the principle of indemnity has been recognized or admitted by all the parties;

(g) Any question as to the recovery of contract debts claimed from the Government of an independent Sovereign State by the Government of another independent Sovereign State, as being due to any of its citizens, companies or subordinate administrations, or to itself;

(h) Any question which may be submitted to the Court by express agreement between all the parties to the case.

(*Query add:* (i) *Any question not falling within any of the classes above enumerated, which may be referred to the Court by the International Council by a majority of votes* (*or by a three-fourths majority, or by a three-fourths majority including all the eight Great Powers*).)

The question of whether or not an issue is justiciable within the meaning of these Articles shall be determined solely by the International High Court, which may determine such a question whether or not formal objection is taken by any of the litigants.

If any State, being a party to any action in the International High Court, objects that any point at issue is not a justiciable question as herein defined, the objection shall be considered by the

Court; and the Court shall, whether or not the objecting State enters an appearance, or argues the matter, pronounce upon the objection, and either set it aside or declare it well founded.

It shall be within the competence of the International High Court, with regard to any justiciable question in respect of which it may be invoked by one or more of the parties, summarily to enjoin any State, whether or not a party to the case, to refrain from taking any specified positive action or to discontinue any specified positive action already begun, or to cause to be discontinued any specified positive action begun by any person, company or subordinate administration within or belonging to such State, which in the judgment of the Court is designed or intended, or may reasonably be expected to change the *status quo* with regard to the question at issue before the Court, or seriously to injure any of the parties to the case. Any such injunction of the International High Court shall be binding, and shall be enforceable, in the same way as a judgment of the Court, in the manner hereinafter described.

Immediate Publicity for all Treaties, Existing and Future

15. No treaty or agreement between two or more independent Sovereign States shall be deemed to confer any right to invoke the International High Court, or shall be treated as valid, or be in any way recognized by the International Council

or the International High Court, or shall be held to confer any rights, to impose any obligations, or to change the status or legal rights of any person, company, subordinate administration, district or State, unless a duly authenticated copy of such Treaty or Agreement has been deposited by one or all of the States that are parties to it, in the Registry of the International High Court, within twelve months from the date of these Articles, in accordance with any rules that may from time to time be made by the Court for this purpose; or in the case of a Treaty or Agreement hereafter made, within three months from the date of such Treaty or Agreement.

It shall be the duty of the officer in charge of the Registry immediately after deposit to allow the duly accredited representative of any Constituent State to inspect and copy any Treaty or Agreement so deposited; and promptly to communicate a copy to the International Secretariat for publication in the *Official Gazette*.

Note to Article 15

It may perhaps be left to the rules as to registration, to be made by the International High Court, to provide for securing that the Treaties or Agreements presented for registration by one of the parties thereto shall be duly authenticated copies and translations, and accepted as correct by the other party or parties, in such a way as to prevent any question subsequently arising as to the validity of the bilateral obligation purporting to be created.

Undertaking to Submit all Justiciable Questions to the International High Court

16. The Constituent States severally undertake and agree to submit to the International High Court for trial and judgment every question, difference or dispute coming within the definition of a justiciable question as laid down by these Articles that may arise between themselves and any other independent Sovereign State or States; and at all times to abstain, in respect of such questions, from anything in the nature of an ultimatum; from any threat to take unfriendly or aggressive action of any kind with a view to redressing the alleged grievance or punishing the alleged wrongdoing; and from any general mobilization, or any violation of the territory of any other State or attack on the ships of such State or other military or naval operations, or other action leading or likely to lead to war.

(*Query: insert these two additional Articles.*)

Provision for Abrogation of Obsolete Treaties

16A. *Provided that any Constituent State may at any time, whether before or after any question, dispute or difference has arisen on the subject with one or more other States, claim to have it declared that any Treaty or Agreement to which it is a party has become obsolete, wholly or in part, by reason of the subsequent execution of another Treaty or Agreement by which the earlier Treaty or Agreement has been substantially abrogated, or by reason of one or other independent Sovereign State concerned in such Treaty or Agreement having ceased to exist as such, or by reason of such a change of circumstances that the very object and purpose for which all the parties made the Treaty or Agreement can no longer be attained. When such a claim is made by either of the parties to a question, dispute or difference, either party may, instead of submitting the question, dispute or difference as a justiciable issue to the International High Court, in the alternative bring before the International Council sitting as a whole its claim to have the Treaty or Agreement declared to be obsolete, wholly or in part; and shall at the same time submit the question, dispute or difference as a non-justiciable issue to the International Council sitting as a whole.*

The Council shall promptly take into consideration any claim by a Constituent State to have any Treaty or Agreement declared obsolete, whether or not any question, dispute or difference has arisen in connection with the subject, and shall take such steps as it may deem fit to ascertain the facts of the case, and may on any of the grounds aforesaid decide by resolution (query: passed by a three-fourths majority, or a three-fourths majority including all the eight Great Powers), that the said Treaty or Agreement is wholly or in part obsolete and ought to be abrogated, and in that case the said Treaty or Agreement shall be deemed to have been abrogated to such extent and from such date, and subject to such conditions as may be specified in the resolution of the Council.

If the Council passes such a resolution as afore-

said, and if any question, dispute or difference has been submitted to the Council in connection with the subject, the Council shall thereupon promptly deal with the question, dispute or difference as a non-justiciable issue in conformity with these Articles.

Note to Article 16a

It seems as if some such proviso as is here tentatively suggested were required, if all existing Treaties and Agreements are to be registered and made the basis for potential legal proceedings before the International High Court. It has not always been customary in Treaties specifically to repeal or abrogate the provisions of former treaties; and there is hardly ever any limit set to their endurance. There is no saying what weird cases might not be founded on the various clauses of the Treaty of Westphalia (1648) or on those of the Treaty of Utrecht (1713), or on one or other of the tens of thousands of uncancelled documents, all solemnly signed and sealed, and professedly part of the "public law" of Europe, that might be fished up out of the *Chancelleries* of Europe for registration and potential enforcement in the International High Court. To enable disputes as to Treaties to be decided by a judicial tribunal is the very first object of all proposals of this nature. Yet a vast number of the existing Treaties are, in fact, wholly obsolete. Provision ought to be made somehow for deciding, otherwise than by their repudiation by one party, which of them must be declared to have become null and void; and it is suggested that this is a matter for decision, case by case, by the International Council representing the States of the world. An alternative course—which might, however, so choke the machinery as to prevent the Supernational Authority even getting under way —would be to provide for some impartial scrutiny and consideration of all Treaties and Agreements when they are presented for registration, in order to admit to registration only those deemed to be still in full force.

Provision for Cases in which International Law is Vague, Uncertain, or Incomplete

16B. *Provided also that when any question, dispute or difference has arisen between two or more Constituent States, and such question, dispute or difference may be deemed to be a justiciable issue as defined in these Articles, any of the parties to such issue may, before it has been submitted to the International High Court, take exception to its being so submitted, on the ground that the International Law applicable to such issue is so vague, or so uncertain, or so incomplete as to render the strict application thereof to the issue in question impracticable or inequitable. The Constituent State taking such exception shall thereupon immediately submit the question, dispute or difference to the International Council instead of to the International High Court, and shall request the Council in the first place to consider and decide whether the exception is justly taken.*

If the Council decides by resolution passed by a three-fourths majority (Query add: including all the eight Great Powers) that the exception is justly taken, no proceedings shall be taken on the issue in the International High Court. The Council shall thereupon promptly decide by resolution either to formulate new and additional principles of International Law applicable to the issue, which (Query add: if enacted by a three-fourths majority, or by a three-fourths majority including all the eight Great Powers) shall be referred to the International High Court with instructions to decide the question, dispute or difference in accordance therewith; or the Council shall, in the alternative, promptly deal with the question, dispute or difference as a non-justiciable issue in conformity with these Articles.

NOTE TO ARTICLE 16B

It seems necessary to provide also for cases which, although apparently justiciable issues because there exists a certain amount of International Law dealing with the subject, could not equitably or properly be decided by the International High Court upon such law, owing to the vagueness, the uncertainty, or the incompleteness thereof. It is, therefore, tentatively suggested that it might be allowed to a Constituent State to take exception to a reference to the Court, and to submit the issue to the International Council on this ground, asking at the same time for a decision of the Council upon the exception. The Council could then, by an overwhelming majority, decide whether the exception is well taken. In that case the Council would then have to decide either to lay down new or additional principles of International Law applicable to the question, and remit the question with such new or additional principles to the High Court for trial as a justiciable issue. In the alternative, if it does not by such an overwhelming majority decide to enact new International Law, the Council shall deal with the question as a non-justiciable issue.

Enforcement of the Decrees of the Court

17. When in any case upon which judgment is given by the International High Court, the Court finds that any of the parties to the case has, by act, negligence, or default, committed any breach of

international obligation, whether arising by Treaty or Agreement, or by International Law, or by enactment of the International Council in accordance with these Articles, the Court may simply declare that one or other litigant State is in default, and leave such State voluntarily to make reparation; or the Court may, in the alternative, itself direct reparation to be made or compensation to be paid for such wrong, and may assess damages or compensation, and may, either by way of addition to damages or compensation, or as an alternative, impose a pecuniary fine upon the State declared in default, hereinafter called the recalcitrant State; and may require compliance with its decree within a specified time under penalty of a pecuniary fine, and may prescribe the application of any such damages, compensation, or fine.

In the event of non-compliance with any decision or decree or injunction of the International High Court, or of non-payment of the damages, compensation, or fine within the time specified for such payment, the Court may decree execution, and may call upon the Constituent States, or upon some or any of them, to put in operation, after duly published notice, for such period and under such conditions as may be arranged, any or all of the following sanctions—viz.:

(*a*) To lay an embargo on any or all ships within the jurisdiction of such Constituent State or States registered as belonging to the recalcitrant State;

(*b*) To prohibit any lending of capital or other moneys to the citizens, companies, or subordinate administrations of the recalcitrant State, or to its national Government;

(*c*) To prohibit the issue or dealing in or quotation on the Stock Exchange or in the press of any new loans, debentures, shares, notes or securities of any kind by any of the citizens, companies or subordinate administrations of the recalcitrant State, or of its national Government;

(*d*) To prohibit all postal, telegraphic, telephonic and wireless communication with the recalcitrant State;

(*e*) To prohibit the payment of any debts due to the citizens, companies or subordinate administrations of the recalcitrant State, or to its national Government; and, if thought fit, to direct that payment of such debts shall be made only to one or other of the Constituent Governments, which shall give a good and legally valid discharge for the same, and shall account for the net proceeds thereof to the International High Court;

(*f*) To prohibit all imports, or certain specified imports, coming from the recalcitrant State, or originating within it;

(*g*) To prohibit all exports, or certain specified exports consigned directly to the recalcitrant State, or destined for it;

(*h*) To prohibit all passenger traffic (other than the exit of foreigners), whether by ship, railway, canal or road, to or from the recalcitrant State;

(*i*) To prohibit the entrance into any port of the Constituent States of any of the ships registered as belonging to the recalcitrant State, except so far as may be necessary for any of them to seek safety, in which case such ship or ships shall be interned;

(*j*) To declare and enforce a decree of complete non-intercourse with the recalcitrant State, including all the above-mentioned measures of partial non-intercourse;

(*k*) To levy a special export duty on all goods destined for the recalcitrant State, accounting for the net proceeds to the International High Court;

(*l*) To furnish a contingent of war-ships to maintain a combined blockade of one or more of the ports, or of the whole coastline of the recalcitrant State.

The International High Court shall arrange for all the expenses incurred in putting in force the above sanctions, including any compensation for loss thereby incurred by any citizens, companies, subordinate administrations or national Governments of any of the Constituent States other than the recalcitrant State, to be raised by a levy on all the Constituent States in such proportions as may be decided by the International Council; and for the eventual recovery of the total sum by way of additional penalty from the recalcitrant State.

When on any decree or decision or injunction of the International High Court execution is ordered, or when any sanction or other measure ordered by the Court is directed to be put in operation against any Constituent State, it shall be an offense against the comity of nations for the State against which such decree, decision, injunction or execution has been pronounced or ordered, or against which any sanction or other measure is directed to be enforced, to declare war, or to take any naval or military action, or to violate the territory or attack the ships of any other State or to commit any other act of aggression against any or all of the States so acting under the order of the Court; and all the other Constituent States shall be bound, and do hereby pledge themselves, to make common cause with the State or States so attacked, and to use naval and military force to protect such State or States, and to enforce the orders of the International High Court, by any warlike operations that may for the purpose be deemed necessary.

III

APPENDIX—A SELECT BIBLIOGRAPHY

The projects for preventing war by some form of International social tissue—from *Le Nouveau Cynée* of Emeric Cruce, in 1623, down to the latest "pacifist" pamphlet—are literally innumerable. A convenient work is *International Tribunals: a Collection of various schemes which have been propounded, and of instances in the Nineteenth Century*, by W. Evans Derby, 927 pp. (4th edition, Dent, 1904). *The Peace Year Book* (286 pp., annual, the National Peace Council, 167 St. Stephen's House, Westminster, price 1s.) affords much information and gives a list of treaties.

For the Hague Conference of 1907 the most convenient source is not the three enormous volumes of proceedings officially published by the Dutch Government, but the British Blue Book, Cd. 4175, of July, 1908, which gives the Final Act and all the Conventions; or else the volume called *International Documents: Conventions and Declarations of a Law-making Kind*, by E. A. Whittuck (2 parts, 1908–9, Longmans), which gives also the conclusions of the Hague Conference of 1899. Descriptive accounts, embodying the results, are *The Two Hague Conferences*, by William I. Hull, 516 pp. (Quin, Boston, 1908); *The Hague Peace Conferences and other International Conferences concerning the Laws and Usages of War*, by A. Pearce Higgins, 632 pp. (Cambridge University Press, 1909); *The Hague Peace Conferences of 1899 and 1907*, by J. B. Scott, 2 vols. (1909, Baltimore).

For arrangements for the control of foreign policy by the Legislature, reference may be made to the British Blue Book, Cd. 6102, of 1912, on "The Treatment of International

Questions by Parliaments in European Countries, the U.S.A. and Japan."

Other works that may be mentioned are *The Arbiter in Council*, by F. W. Hirst, 567 pp. (1906, Macmillan); *Pax Britannica*, by H. S. Perris (1913, Sidgwick & Jackson, 5s.); *The Modern Law of Nations and the Prevention of War*, by Sir Frederick Pollock (a short chapter in Vol. 12 of *The Cambridge Modern History*); *Problems of International Practice and Diplomacy*, by Sir Thomas Barclay (1907, Sweet & Maxwell); *Armaments and Arbitration*, by A. T. Mahan (1912); *A Handbook of Public International Law*, by T. J. Lawrence (1913, 8th edition, Macmillan).